GREGORY

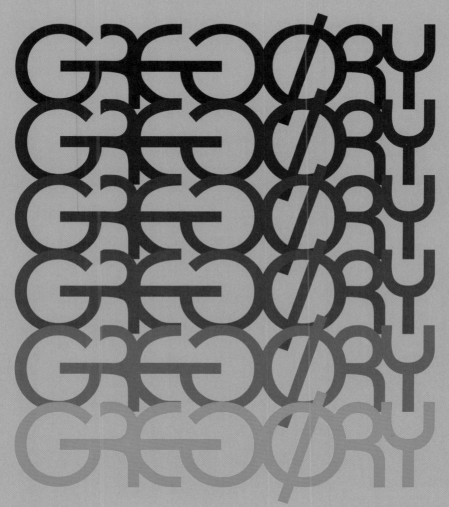

OPERATION MANUAL

```
var GREGORY_SUICIDE = {
        story: "Eric Grissom",
        art: "William Perkins",
        colors: {
                colorist: "William Perkins",
                post_process_colors: "Eric Grissom"
        },
        letters: "Eric Grissom",
        cover: {
                art: "William Perkins",
                design: [
                        "Eric Grissom",
                        "Casey Grissom"
                ]
        }
};
```

GREGØRY SUICIDE

ERIC GRISSOM + WILLIAM PERKINS

DARK HORSE BOOKS

RUN PROGRAM

PRESIDENT AND PUBLISHER
MIKE RICHARDSON

EDITOR
RANDY STRADLEY

ASSISTANT EDITORS
HANNAH MEANS-SHANNON
KEVIN BURKHALTER

BOOK DESIGN
ERIC GRISSOM

DIGITAL ART TECHNICIANS
ADAM PRUETT,
CONLEY SMITH,
and **MELISSA MARTIN**

Neil Hankerson Executive Vice President • Tom Weddle Chief Financial Officer • Randy Stradley Vice President of Publishing Matt Parkinson Vice President of Marketing • David Scroggy Vice President of Product Development • Dale LaFountain Vice President of Information Technology • Cara Niece Vice President of Production and Scheduling • Nick McWhorter Vice President of Media Licensing • Mark Bernardi Vice President of Book Trade and Digital Sales • Ken Lizzi General Counsel • Dave Marshall Editor in Chief • Davey Estrada Editorial Director • Scott Allie Executive Senior Editor • Chris Warner Senior Books Editor Cary Grazzini Director of Specialty Projects • Lia Ribacchi Art Director • Vanessa Todd Director of Print Purchasing • Matt Dryer Director of Digital Art and Prepress • Michael Gombos Director of International Publishing and Licensing

Published by **Dark Horse Books**
A division of Dark Horse Comics, Inc.
10956 SE Main Street, Milwaukie, OR 97222
DarkHorse.com

First edition: November 2017
ISBN 978-1-50670-226-1

10 9 8 7 6 5 4 3 2 1
Printed in China

To find a comics shop in your area, visit comicshoplocator.com

International Licensing: 503-905-2377

Library of Congress Cataloging-in-Publication Data

Names: Grissom, Eric, author. | Perkins, Will, artist.
Title: Gregory suicide / written by Eric Grissom ; art by Will Perkins IV.
Description: First edition. | Milwaukie, OR : Dark Horse Books, 2017.
Identifiers: LCCN 2017033708 | ISBN 9781506702261 (hardback)
Subjects: LCSH: Graphic novels. | BISAC: COMICS & GRAPHIC NOVELS / Science Fiction. | COMICS & GRAPHIC NOVELS / Fantasy. | COMICS & GRAPHIC NOVELS / General.
Classification: LCC PN6727.G7546 G74 2017 | DDC 741.5/973–dc23
LC record available at https://lccn.loc.gov/2017033708

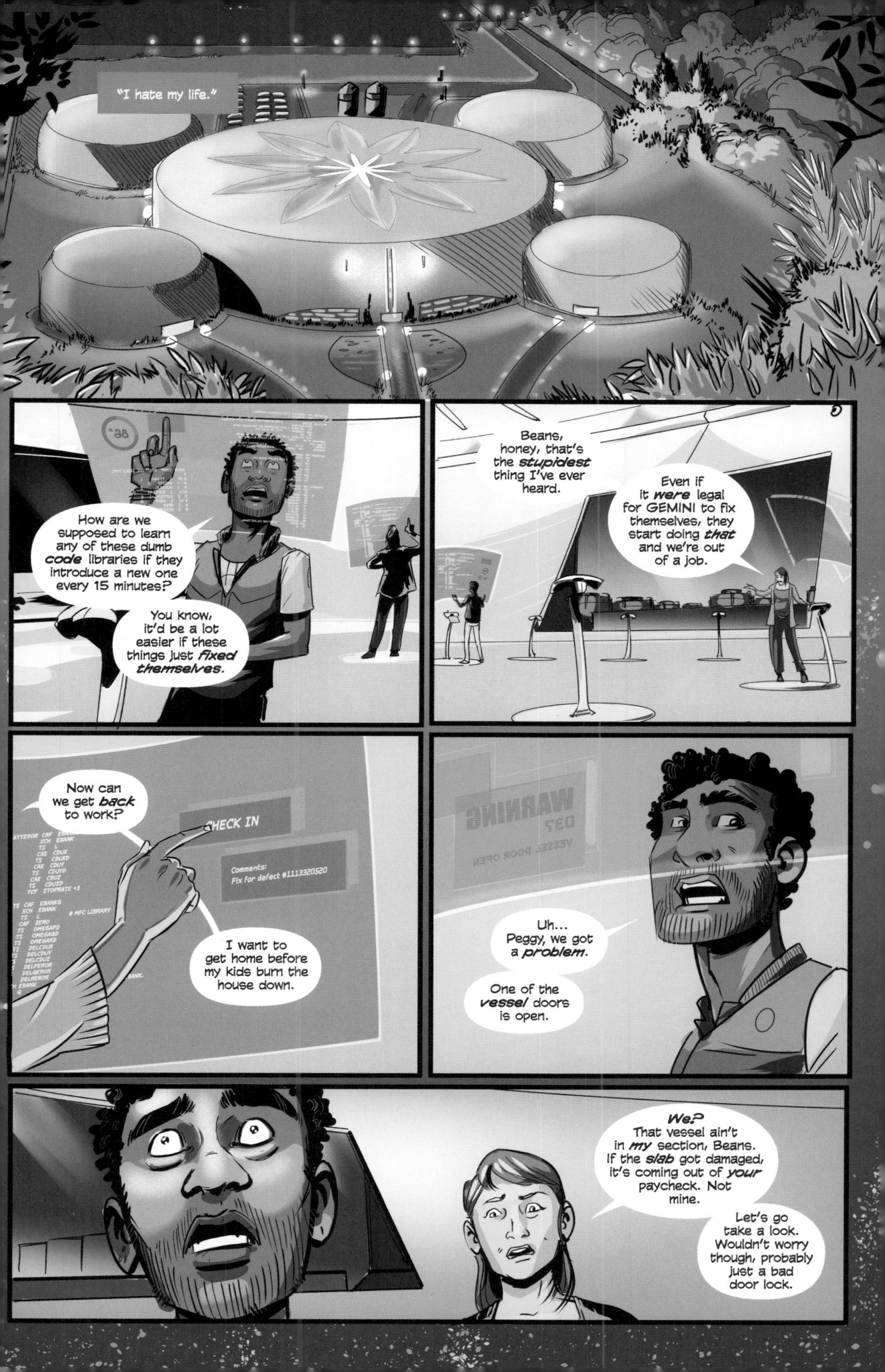
"I hate my life."
How are we supposed to learn any of these dumb code libraries if they introduce a new one every 15 minutes?
You know, it'd be a lot easier if these things just fixed themselves.
Beans, honey, that's the stupidest thing I've ever heard.
Even if it were legal for GEMINI to fix themselves, they start doing that and we're out of a job.
Now can we get back to work?
CHECK IN
Comments:
Fix for defect #1113320520
I want to get home before my kids burn the house down.
WARNING
037
VESSEL DOOR OPEN
Uh... Peggy, we got a problem.
One of the vessel doors is open.
We?
That vessel ain't in my section, Beans. If the slab got damaged, it's coming out of your paycheck. Not mine.
Let's go take a look. Wouldn't worry though, probably just a bad door lock.

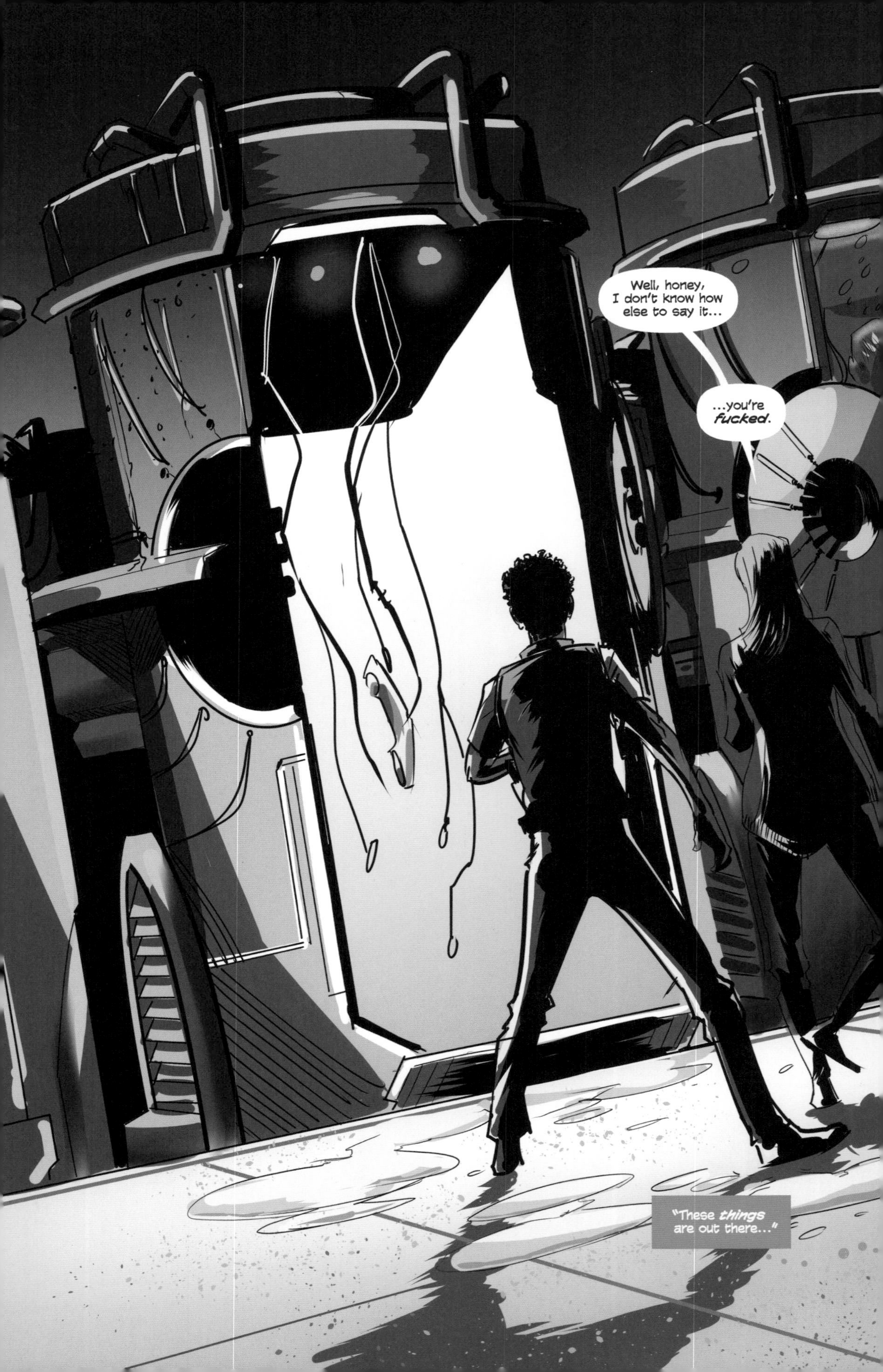
Well, honey, I don't know how else to say it...
...you're *fucked*.
"These *things* are out there..."

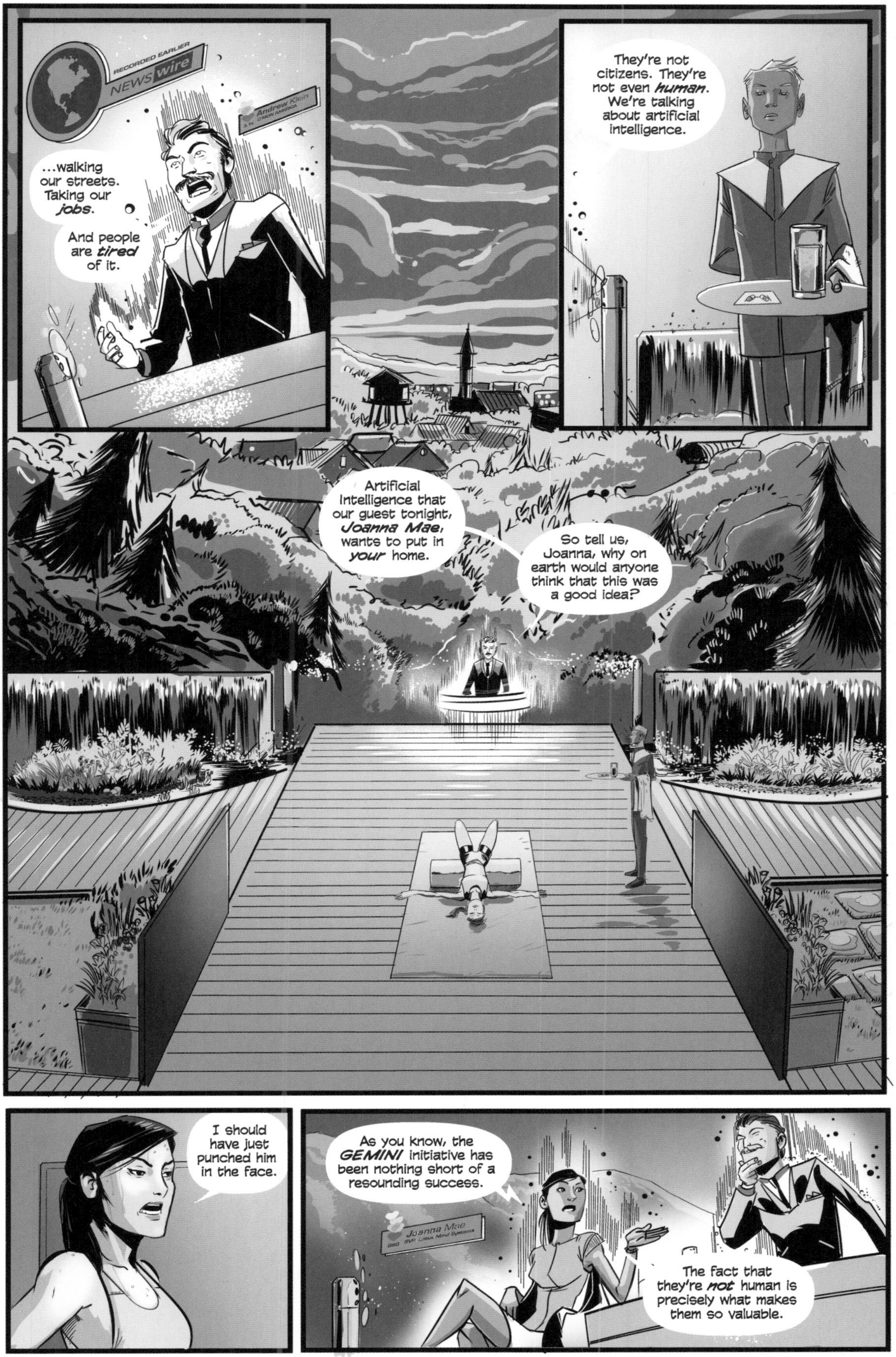
RECORDED EARLIER
NEWS wire
Andrew Klein
...walking our streets. Taking our *jobs*.
And people are *tired* of it.
They're not citizens. They're not even *human*. We're talking about artificial intelligence.
Artificial Intelligence that our guest tonight, *Joanna Mae*, wants to put in *your* home.
So tell us, Joanna, why on earth would anyone think that this was a good idea?
I should have just punched him in the face.
As you know, the *GEMINI* initiative has been nothing short of a resounding success.
Joanna Mae
The fact that they're *not* human is precisely what makes them so valuable.

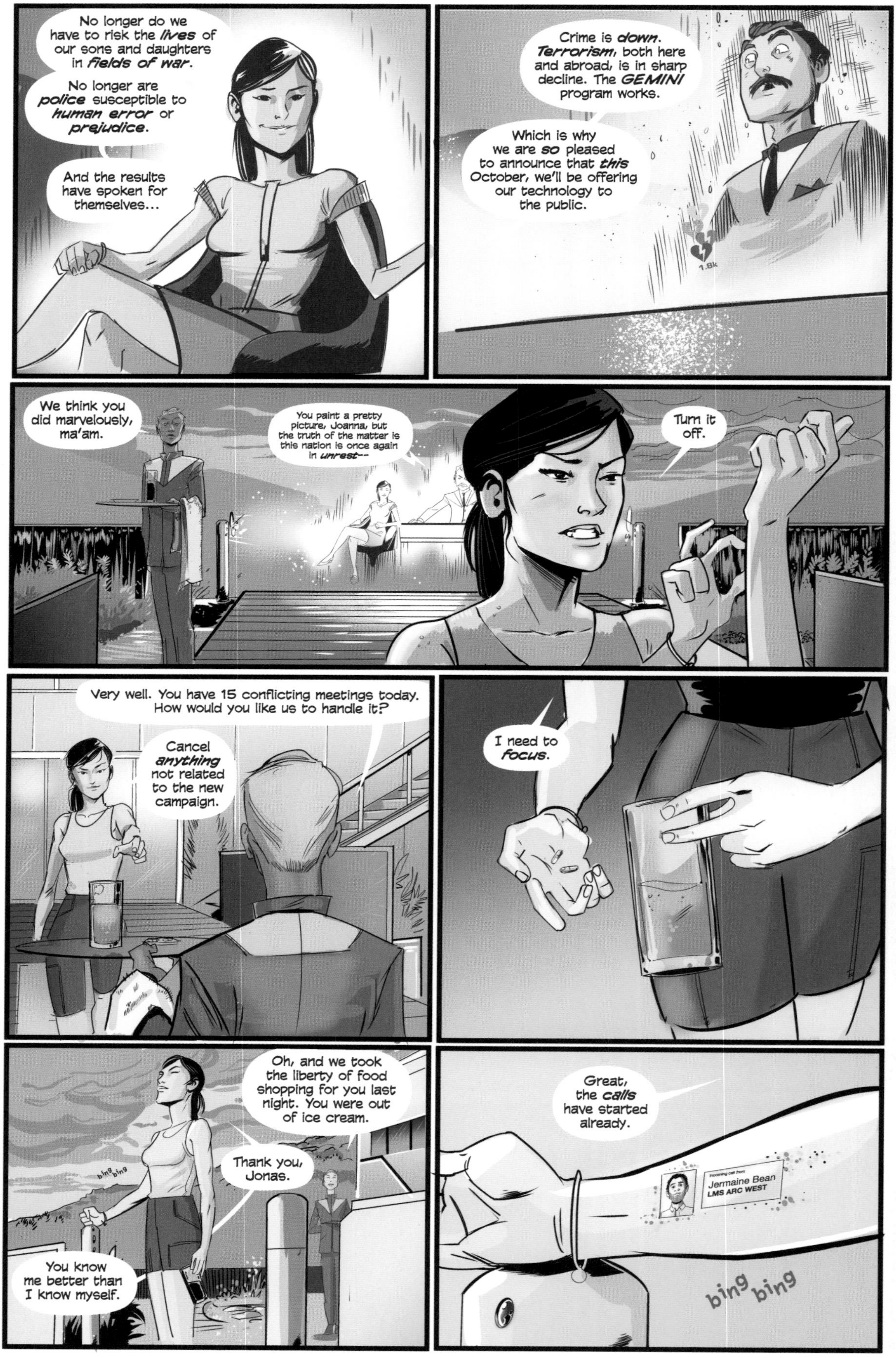
No longer do we have to risk the *lives* of our sons and daughters in *fields of war*.
No longer are *police* susceptible to *human error* or *prejudice*.
And the results have spoken for themselves...
Crime is *down*. *Terrorism*, both here and abroad, is in sharp decline. The *GEMINI* program works.
Which is why we are *so* pleased to announce that *this* October, we'll be offering our technology to the public.
1.8k
We think you did marvelously, ma'am.
You paint a pretty picture, Joanna, but the truth of the matter is this nation is once again in *unrest*--
Turn it off.
Very well. You have 15 conflicting meetings today. How would you like us to handle it?
Cancel *anything* not related to the new campaign.
I need to *focus*.
Oh, and we took the liberty of food shopping for you last night. You were out of ice cream.
Thank you, Jonas.
bing bing
You know me better than I know myself.
Great, the *calls* have started already.
Incoming call from
Jermaine Bean
LMS ARC WEST
bing bing

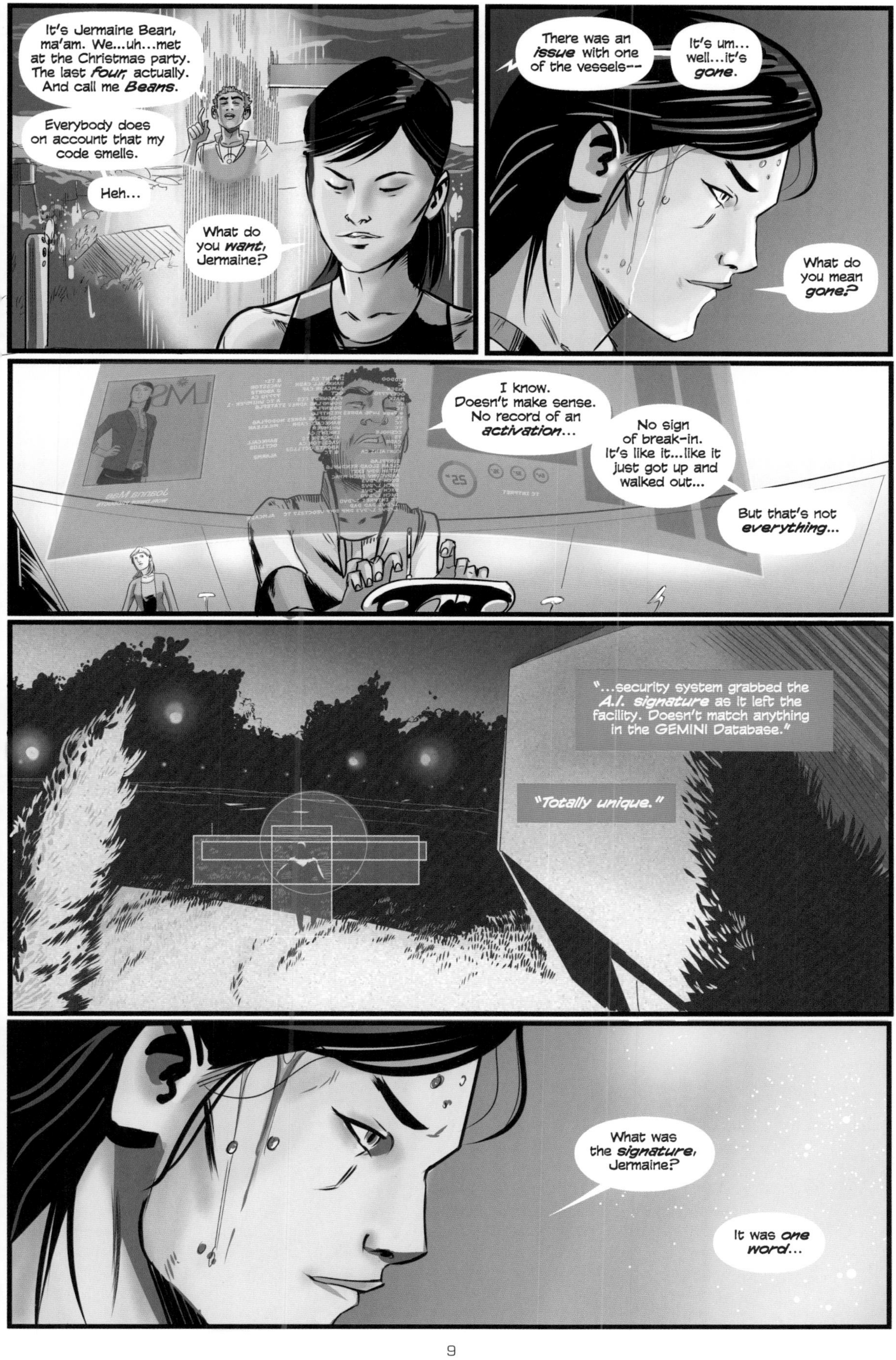
It's Jermaine Bean, ma'am. We...uh...met at the Christmas party. The last *four,* actually. And call me *Beans*.
Everybody does on account that my code smells.
Heh...
What do you *want,* Jermaine?
There was an *issue* with one of the vessels--
It's um... well...it's *gone*.
What do you mean *gone?*
I know. Doesn't make sense. No record of an *activation*...
No sign of break-in. It's like it...like it just got up and walked out...
But that's not *everything*...
"...security system grabbed the *A.I. signature* as it left the facility. Doesn't match anything in the GEMINI Database."
"Totally unique."
What was the *signature,* Jermaine?
It was *one word*...

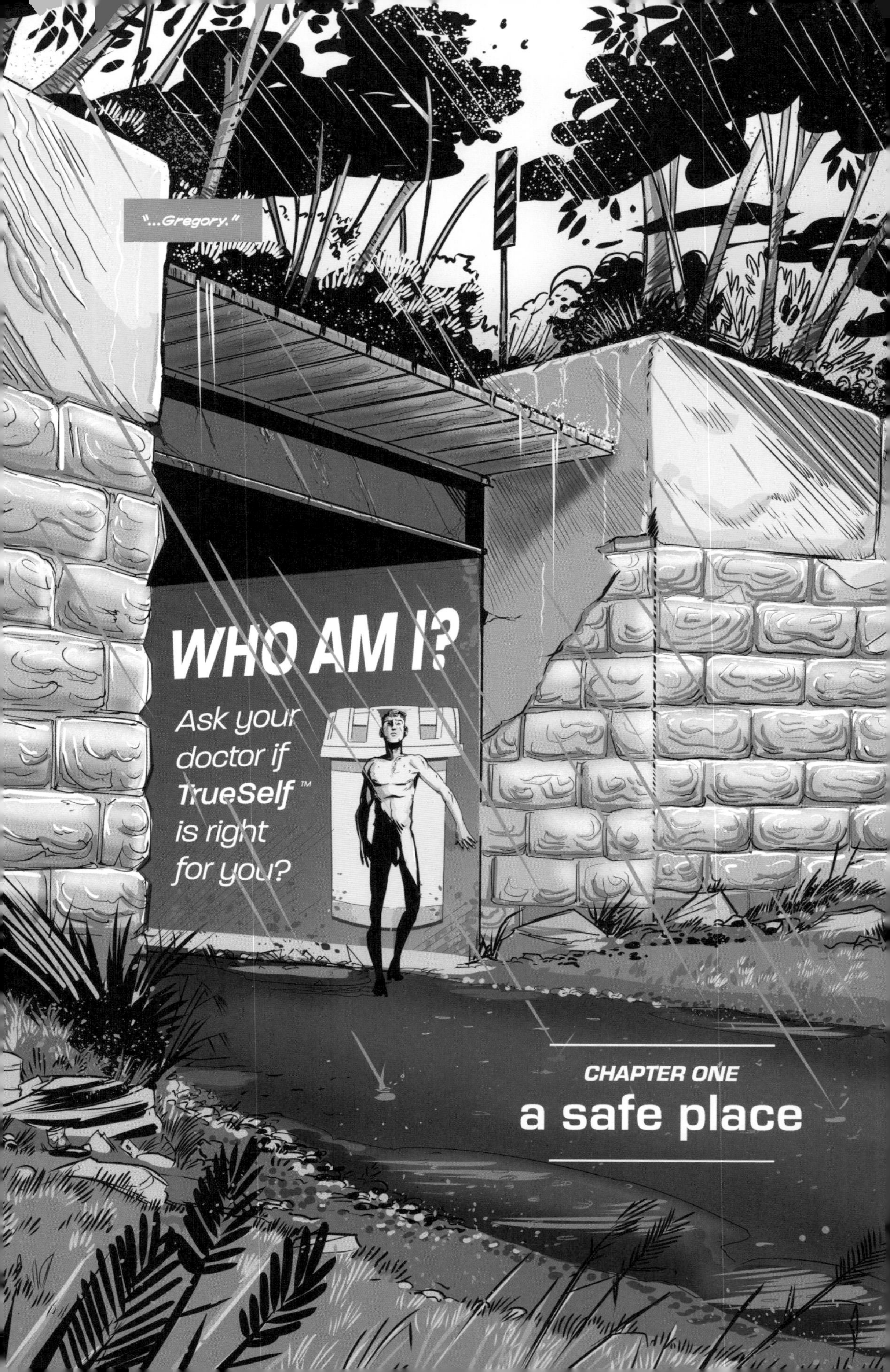
"...Gregory."
WHO AM I?
Ask your doctor if TrueSelf™ is right for you?
CHAPTER ONE
a safe place

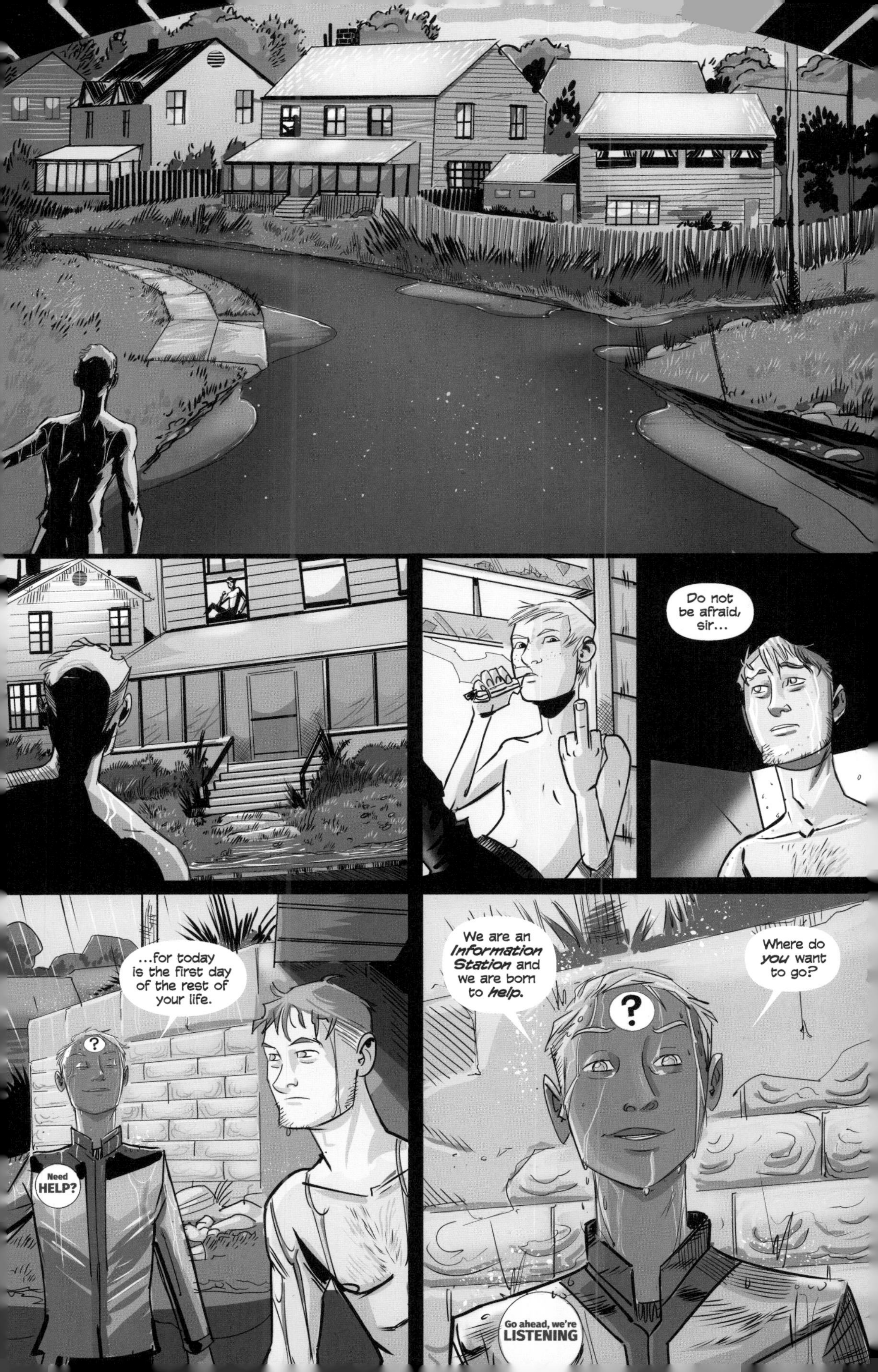
Do not be afraid, sir...
...for today is the first day of the rest of your life.
Need HELP?
We are an *Information Station* and we are born to ***help.***
Where do ***you*** want to go?
Go ahead, we're LISTENING

GREGORY
01

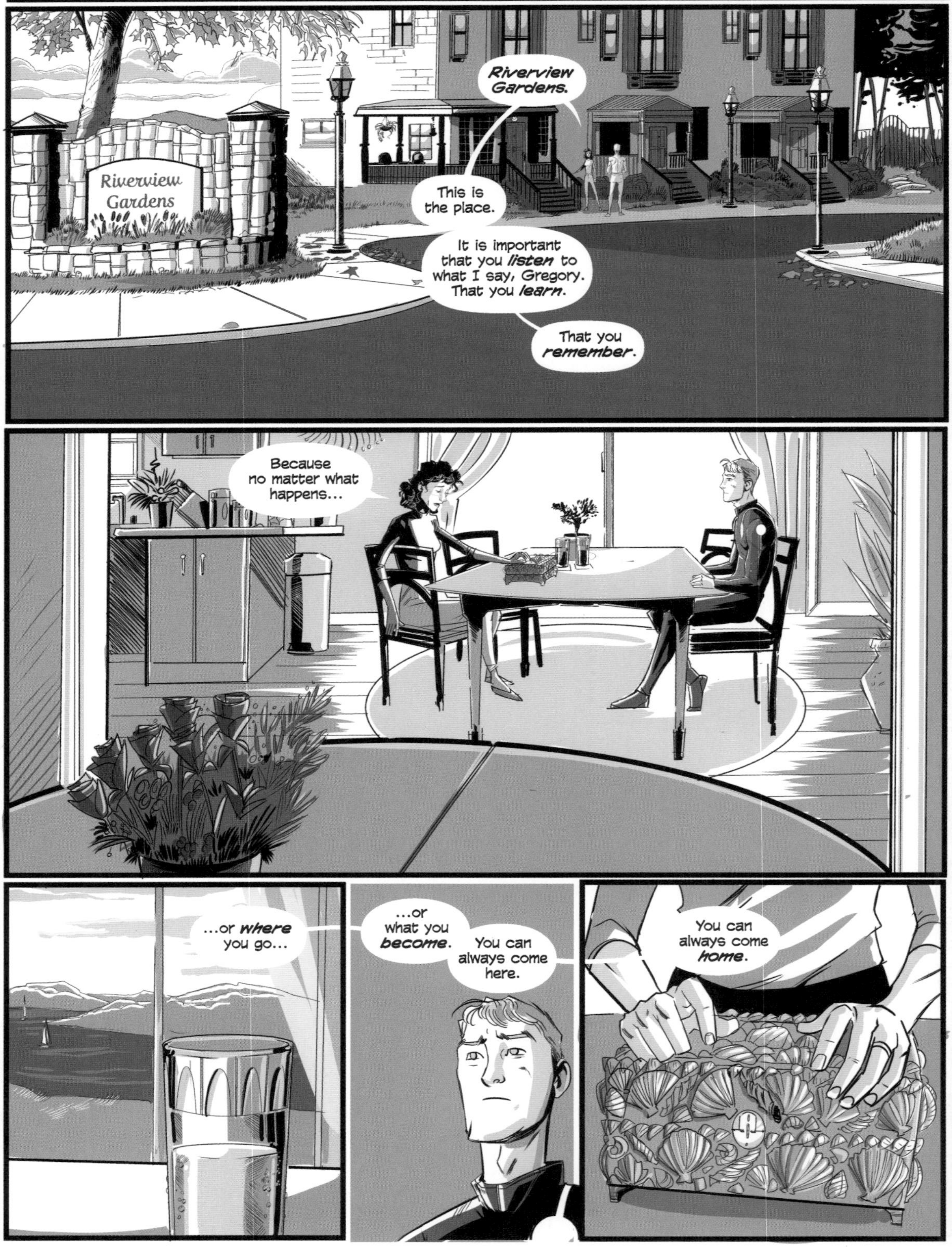

Riverview Gardens
Riverview Gardens.
This is the place.
It is important that you *listen* to what I say, Gregory. That you *learn*.
That you *remember*.
Because no matter what happens...
...or *where* you go...
...or what you *become*.
You can always come here.
You can always come *home*.

You're being given an *opportunity* unlike anything the world has ever known. You're becoming *history*, Gregory.

Embrace it.

If you look for me and I am gone, what do you do?

I come *here*.

That's right, Gregory...

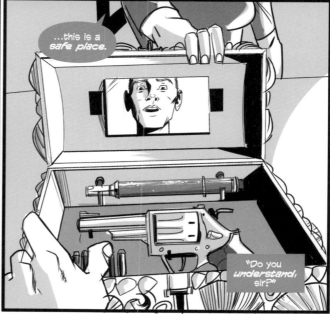

...this is a *safe place*.

"Do you *understand*, sir?"

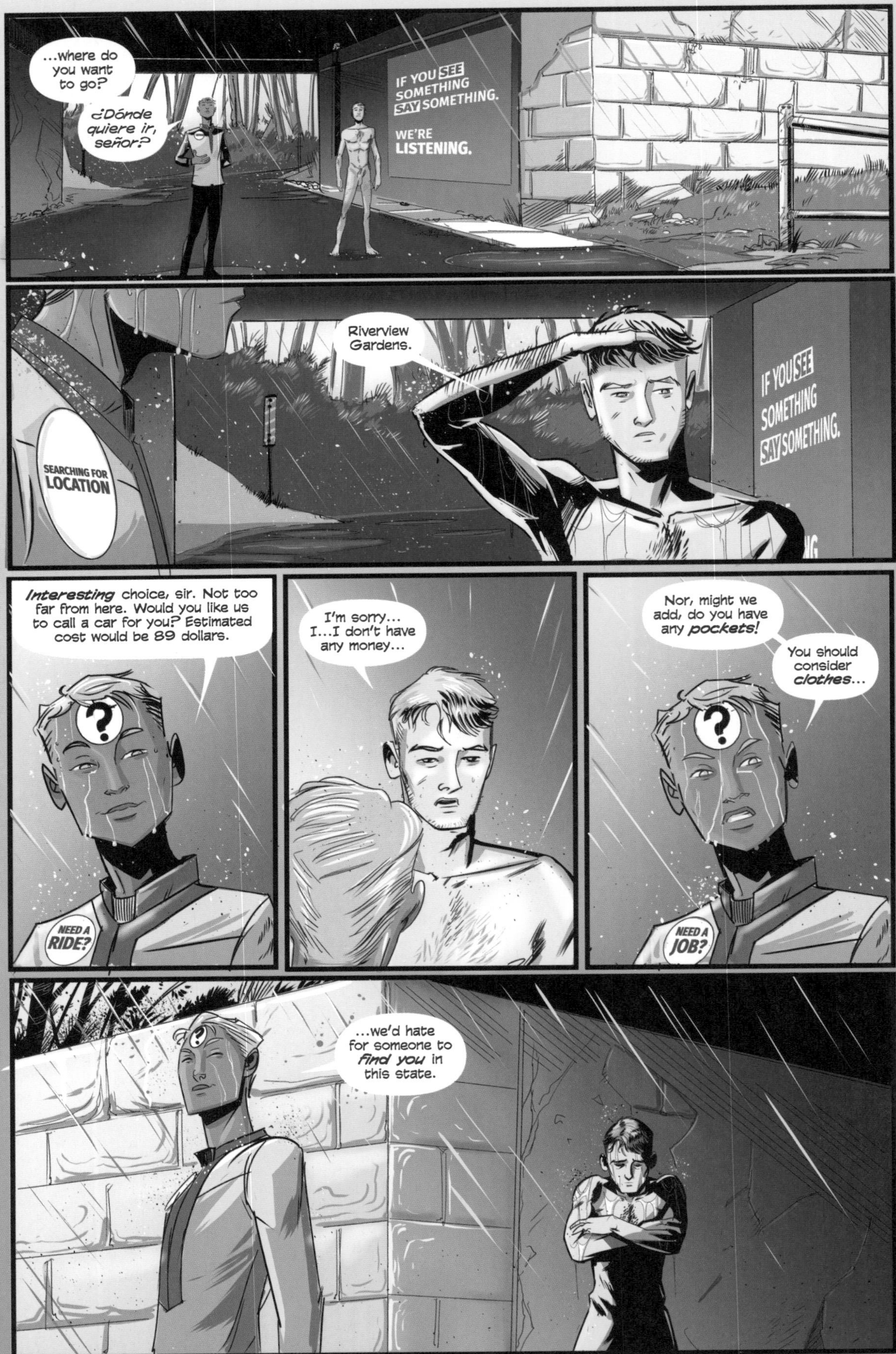
...where do you want to go?
¿Dónde quiere ir, señor?
IF YOU SEE SOMETHING SAY SOMETHING.
WE'RE LISTENING.
Riverview Gardens.
SEARCHING FOR LOCATION
IF YOU SEE SOMETHING SAY SOMETHING.
Interesting choice, sir. Not too far from here. Would you like us to call a car for you? Estimated cost would be 89 dollars.
NEED A RIDE?
I'm sorry... I...I don't have any money...
Nor, might we add, do you have any *pockets!*
You should consider *clothes*...
NEED A JOB?
...we'd hate for someone to *find you* in this state.

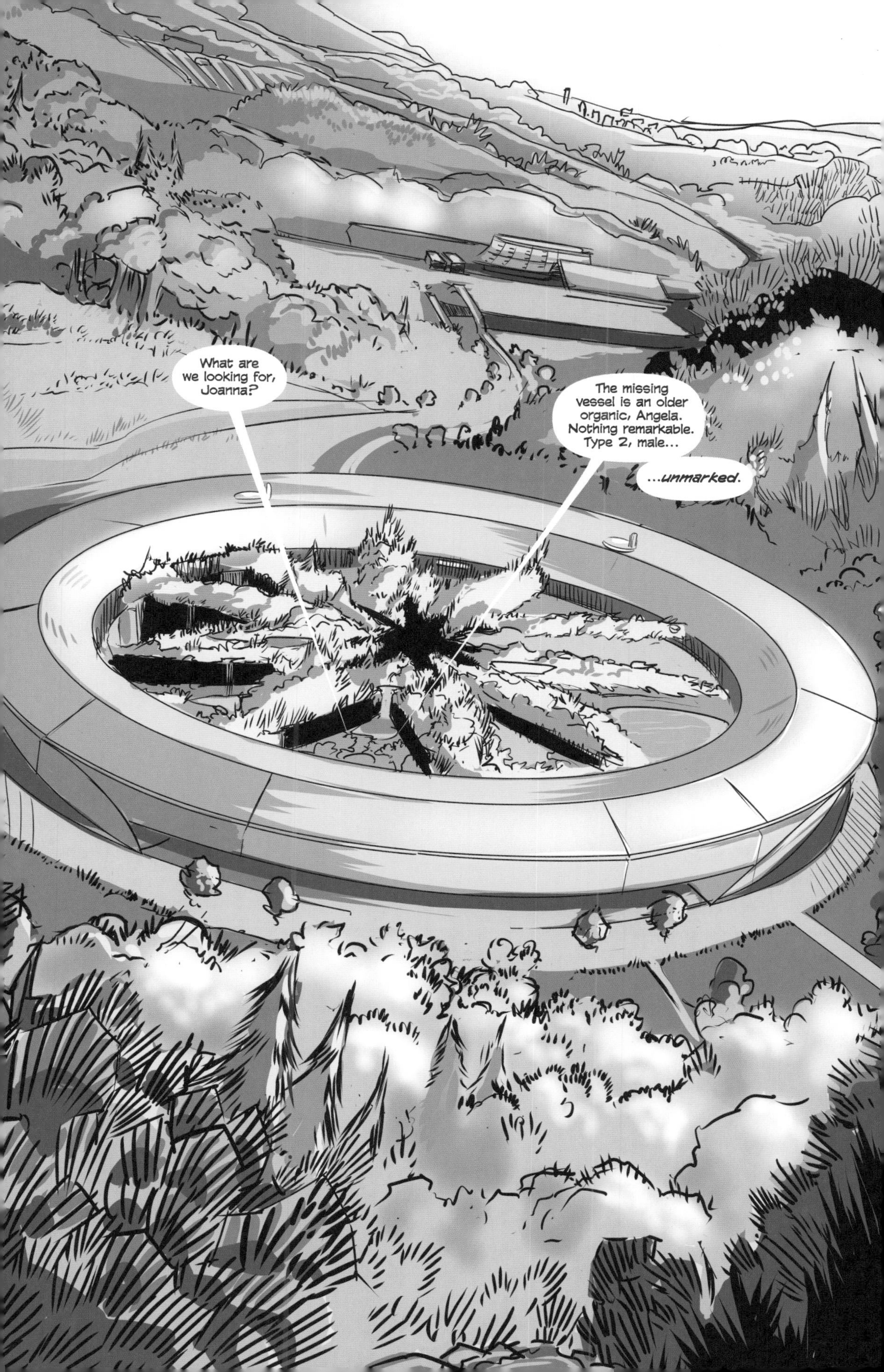
What are we looking for, Joanna?
The missing vessel is an older organic, Angela. Nothing remarkable. Type 2, male...
...unmarked.

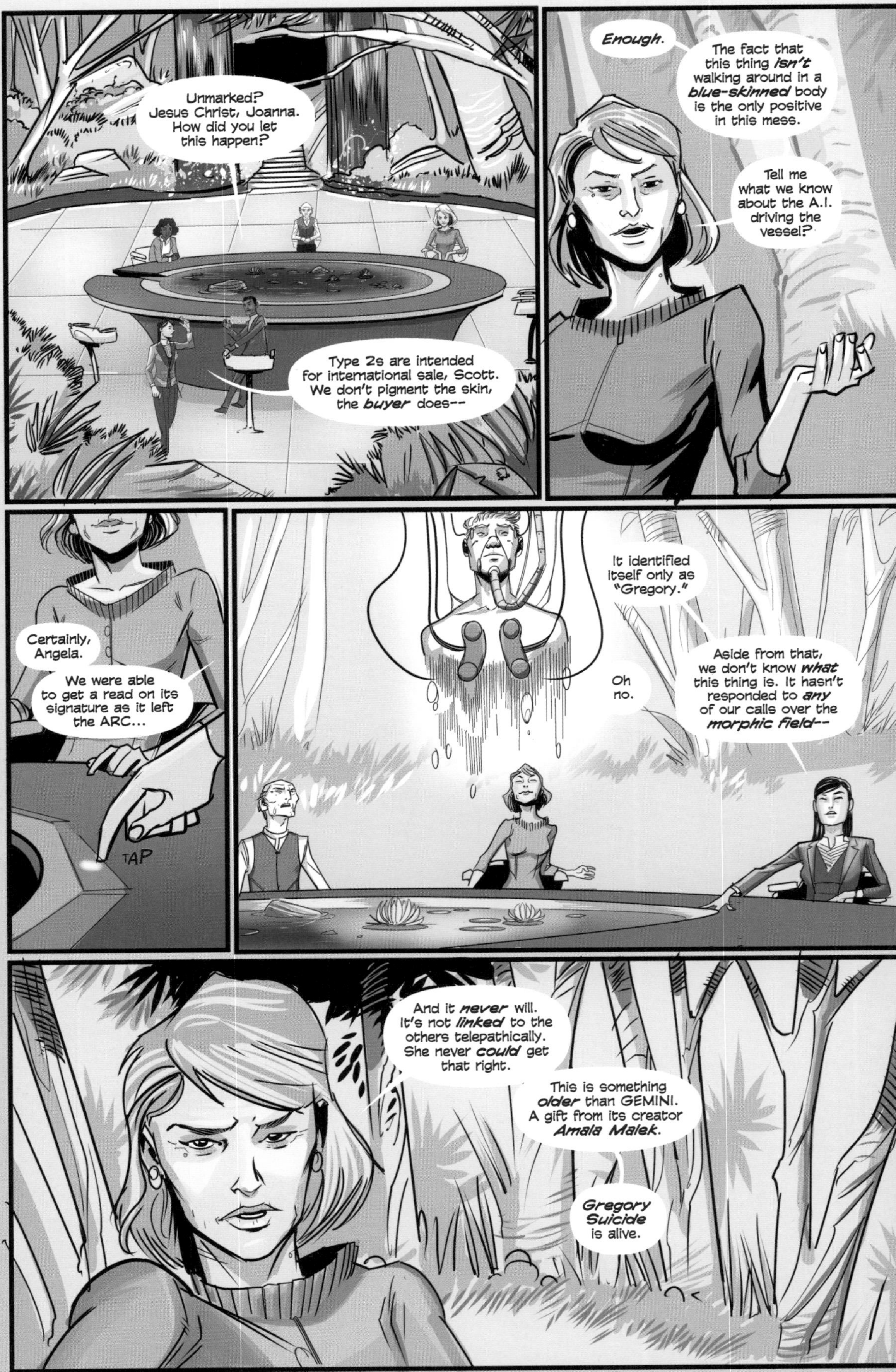
Unmarked? Jesus Christ, Joanna. How did you let this happen?
Type 2s are intended for international sale, Scott. We don't pigment the skin, the *buyer* does--
Enough.
The fact that this thing *isn't* walking around in a *blue-skinned* body is the only positive in this mess.
Tell me what we know about the A.I. driving the vessel?
Certainly, Angela.
We were able to get a read on its signature as it left the ARC...
TAP
It identified itself only as "Gregory."
Aside from that, we don't know *what* this thing is. It hasn't responded to *any* of our calls over the *morphic field*--
Oh no.
And it *never* will. It's not *linked* to the others telepathically. She never *could* get that right.
This is something *older* than GEMINI. A gift from its creator *Amala Malek*.
Gregory Suicide is alive.

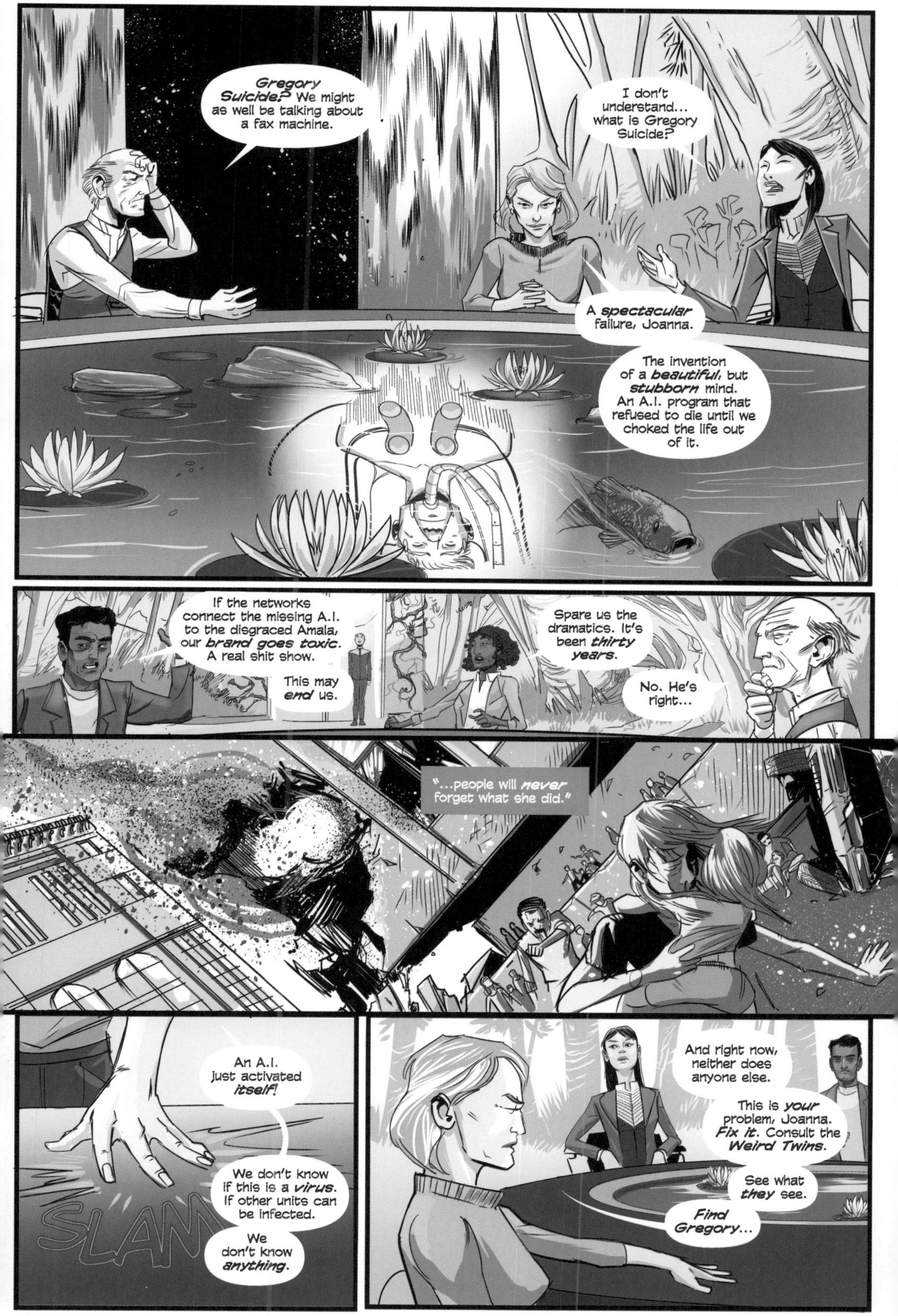
Gregory Suicide? We might as well be talking about a fax machine.
I don't understand... what is Gregory Suicide?
A spectacular failure, Joanna.
The invention of a beautiful, but stubborn mind. An A.I. program that refused to die until we choked the life out of it.
If the networks connect the missing A.I. to the disgraced Amala, our brand goes toxic. A real shit show.
This may end us.
Spare us the dramatics. It's been thirty years.
No. He's right...
"...people will never forget what she did."
An A.I. just activated itself!
We don't know if this is a virus. If other units can be infected.
We don't know anything.
SLAM
And right now, neither does anyone else.
This is your problem, Joanna. Fix it. Consult the Weird Twins.
See what they see.
Find Gregory...

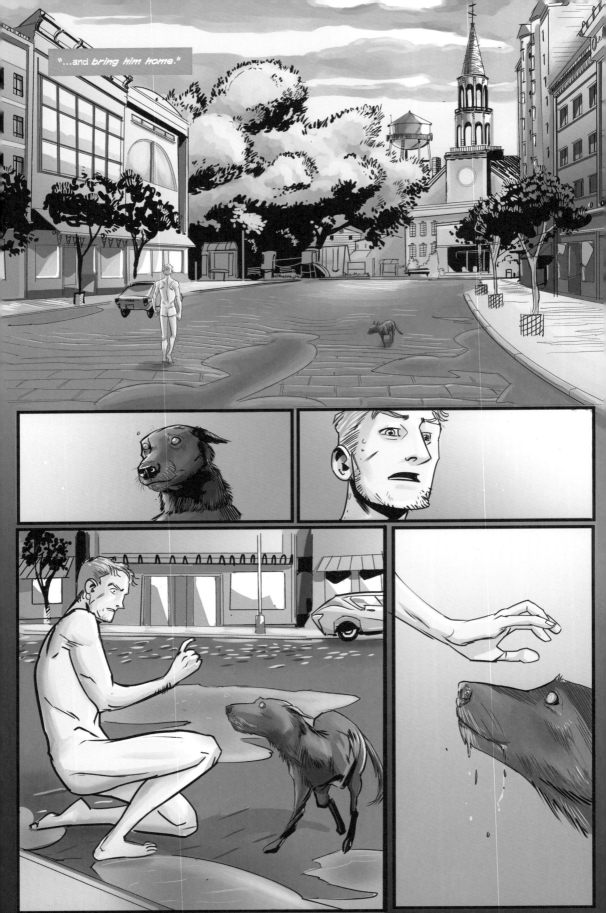

"...and *bring him home.*"

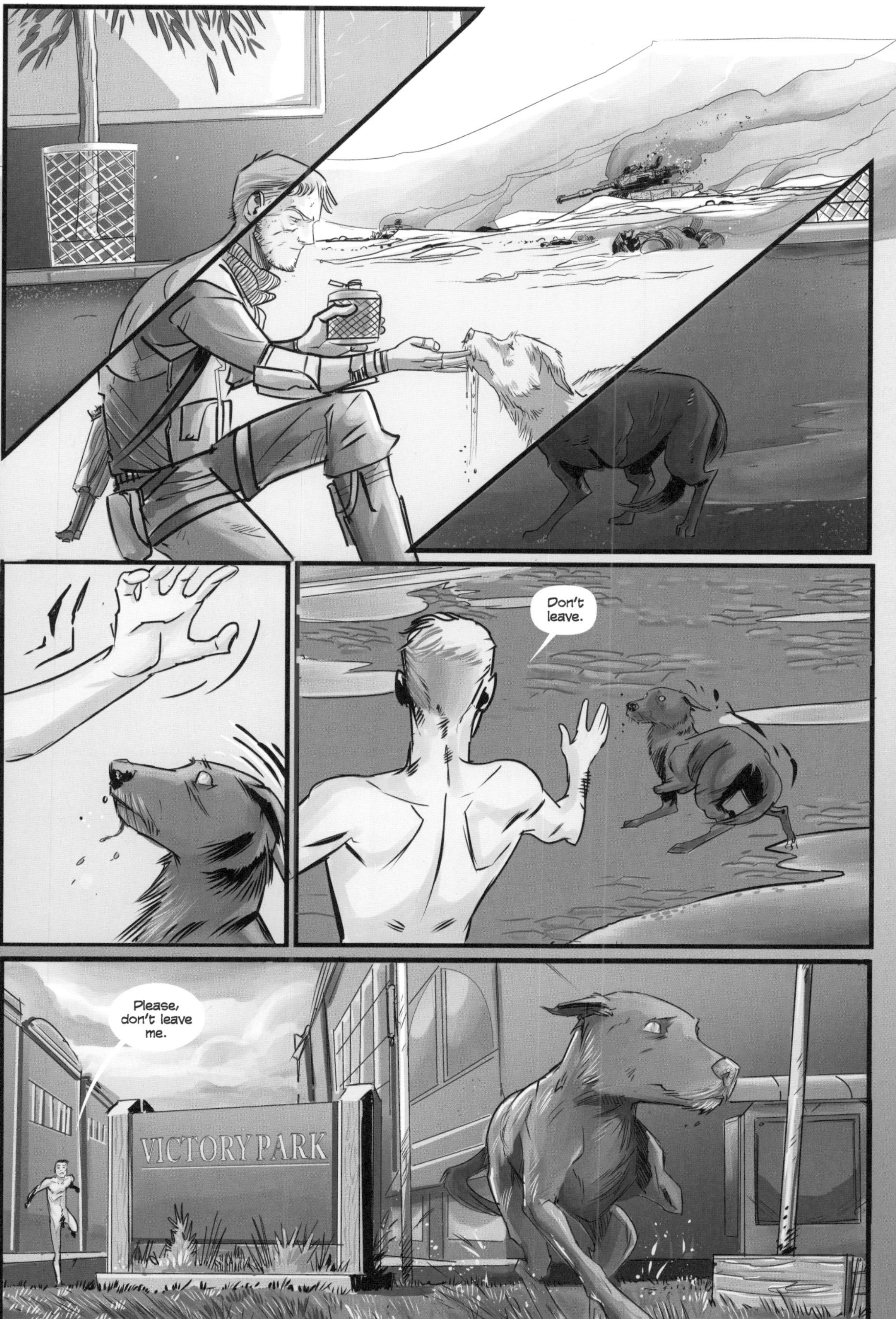
Don't leave.
Please, don't leave me.
VICTORY PARK

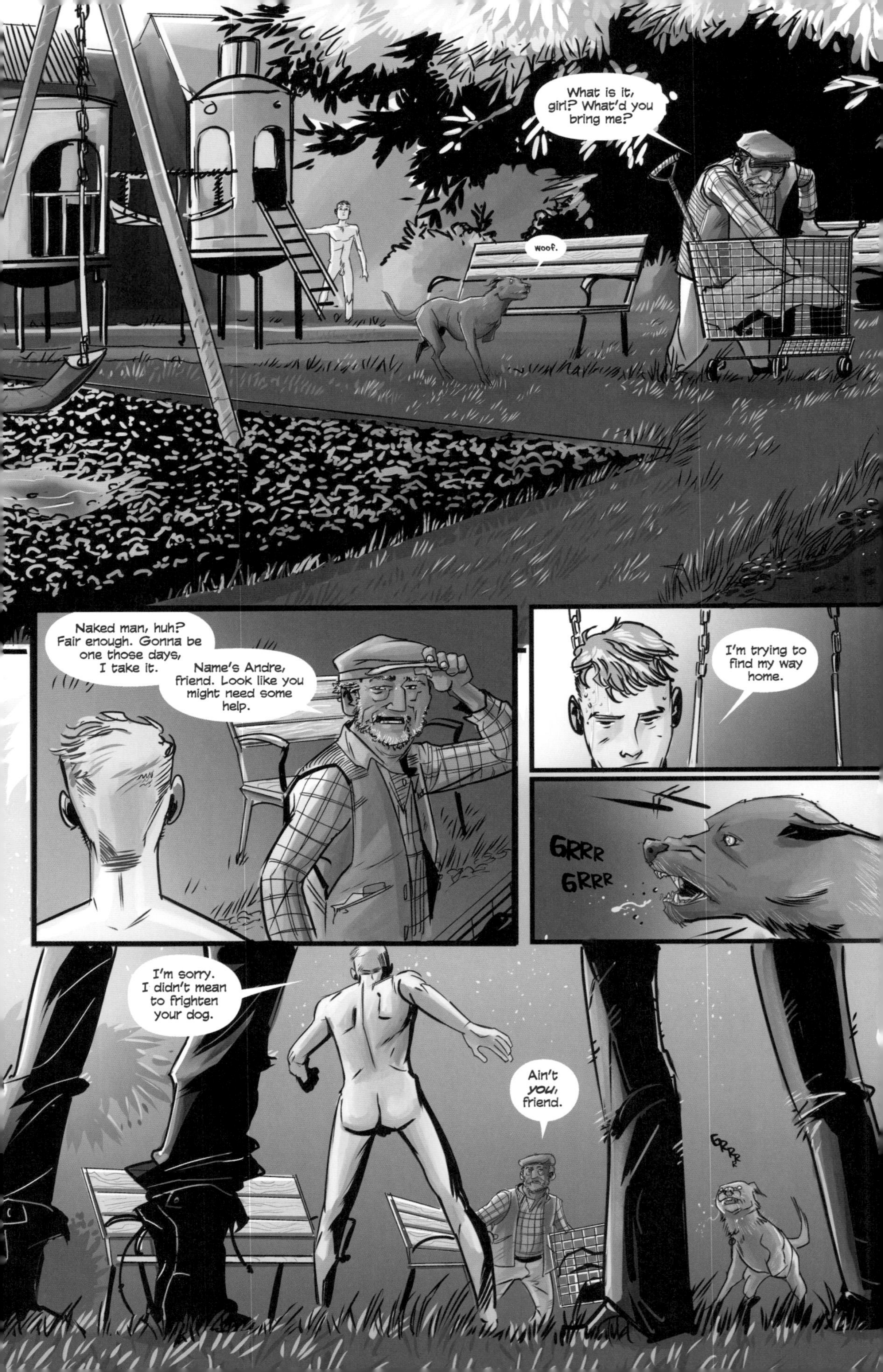
What is it, girl? What'd you bring me?
woof.
Naked man, huh? Fair enough. Gonna be one those days, I take it.
Name's Andre, friend. Look like you might need some help.
I'm trying to find my way home.
GRRR
GRRR
I'm sorry. I didn't mean to frighten your dog.
Ain't *you*, friend.
GRRR

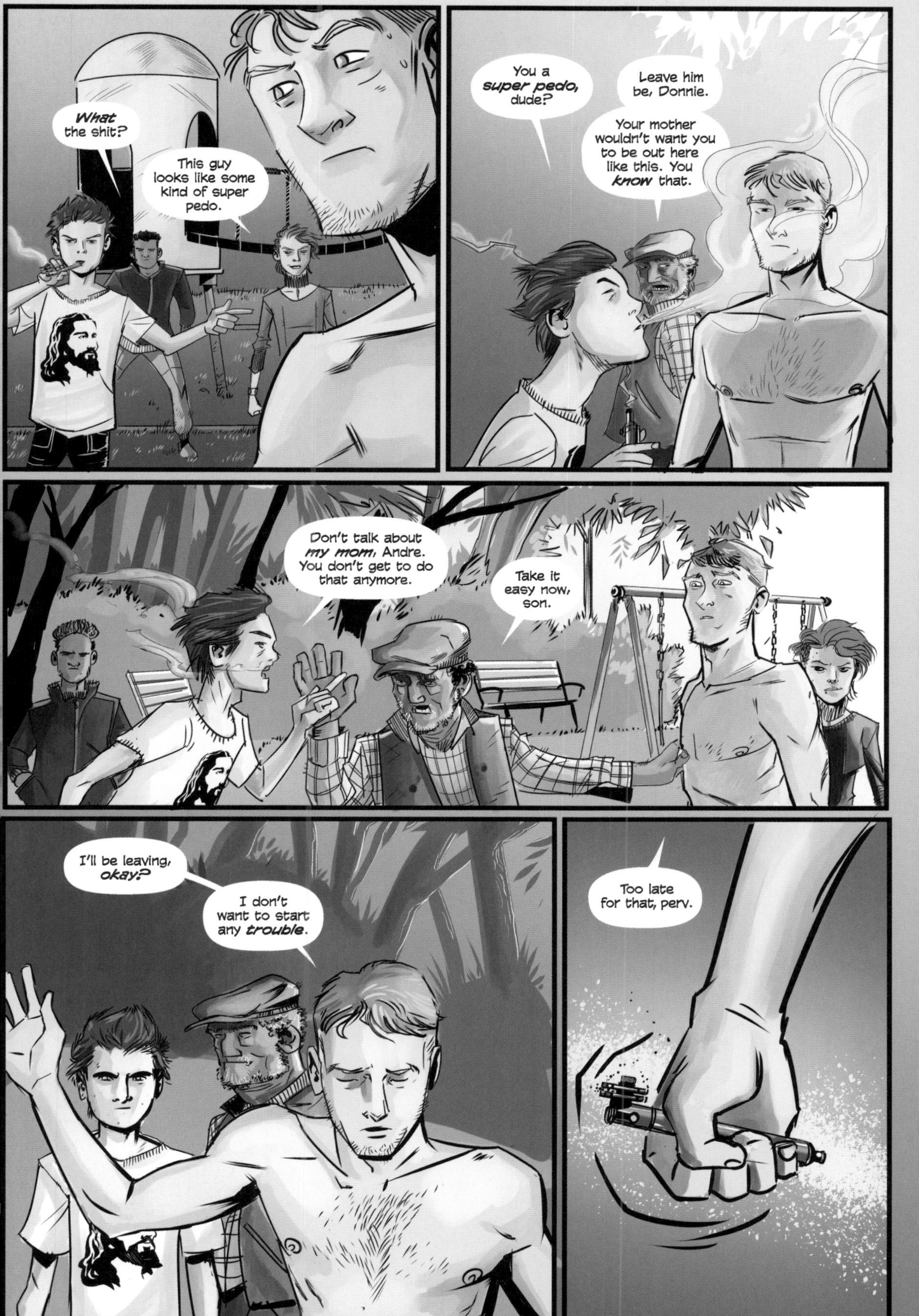
What the shit?
This guy looks like some kind of super pedo.
You a super pedo, dude?
Leave him be, Donnie.
Your mother wouldn't want you to be out here like this. You know that.
Don't talk about my mom, Andre. You don't get to do that anymore.
Take it easy now, son.
I'll be leaving, okay?
I don't want to start any trouble.
Too late for that, perv.

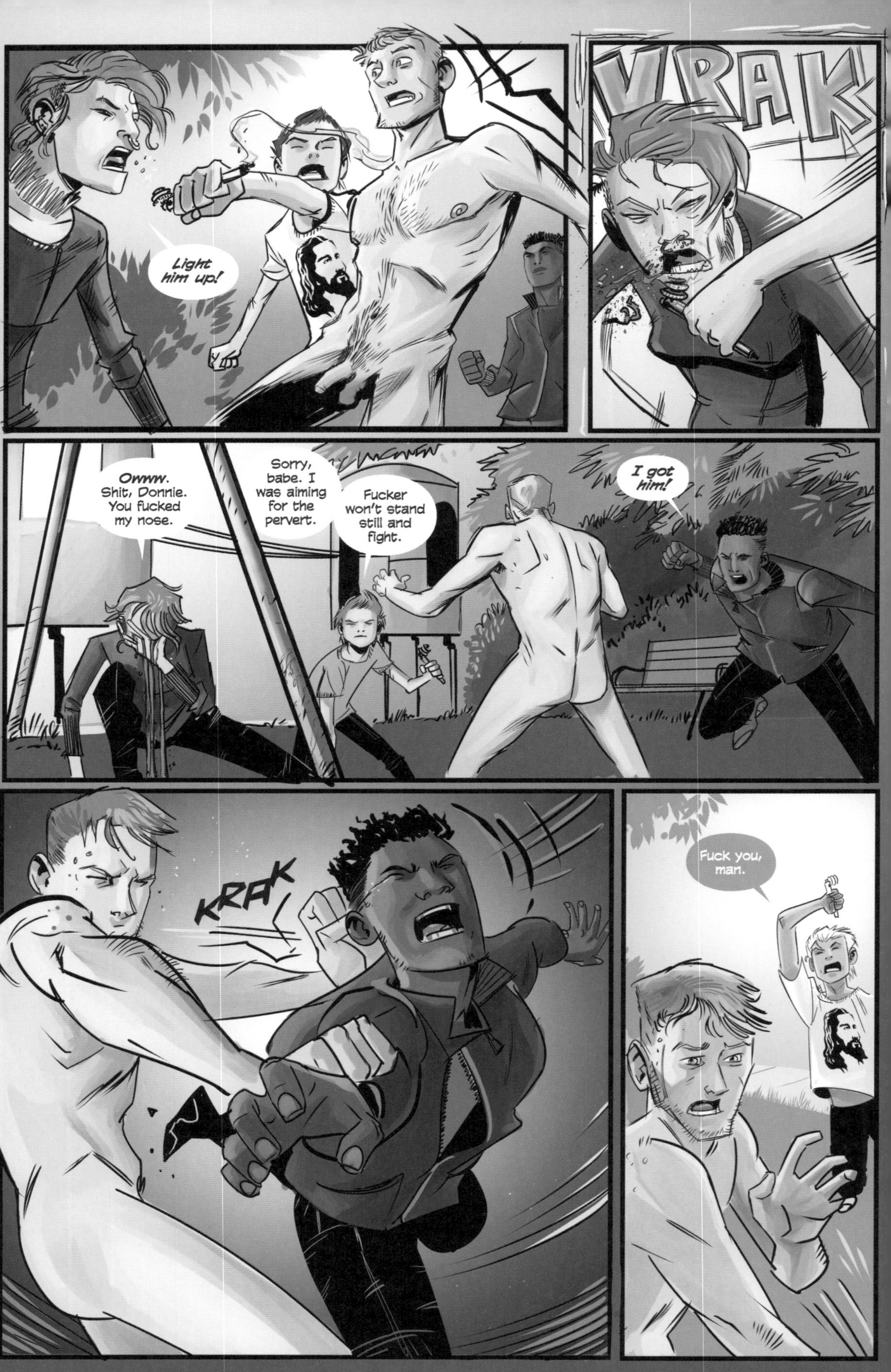
Light him up!
VRAK
Owww. Shit, Donnie. You fucked my nose.
Sorry, babe. I was aiming for the pervert.
Fucker won't stand still and fight.
I got him!
KRAK
Fuck you, man.

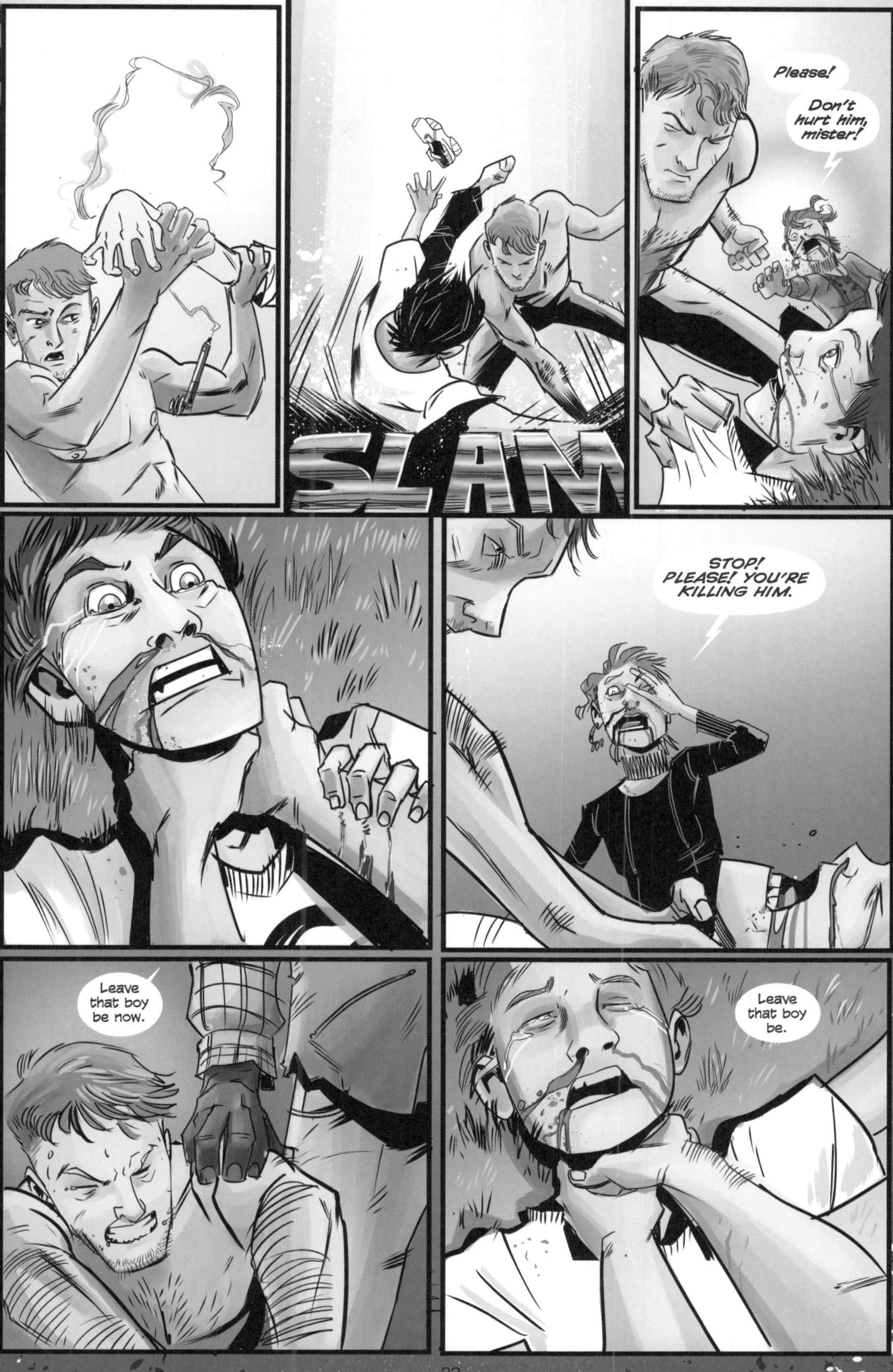
SLAM
Please!
Don't hurt him, mister!
STOP! PLEASE! YOU'RE KILLING HIM.
Leave that boy be now.
Leave that boy be.

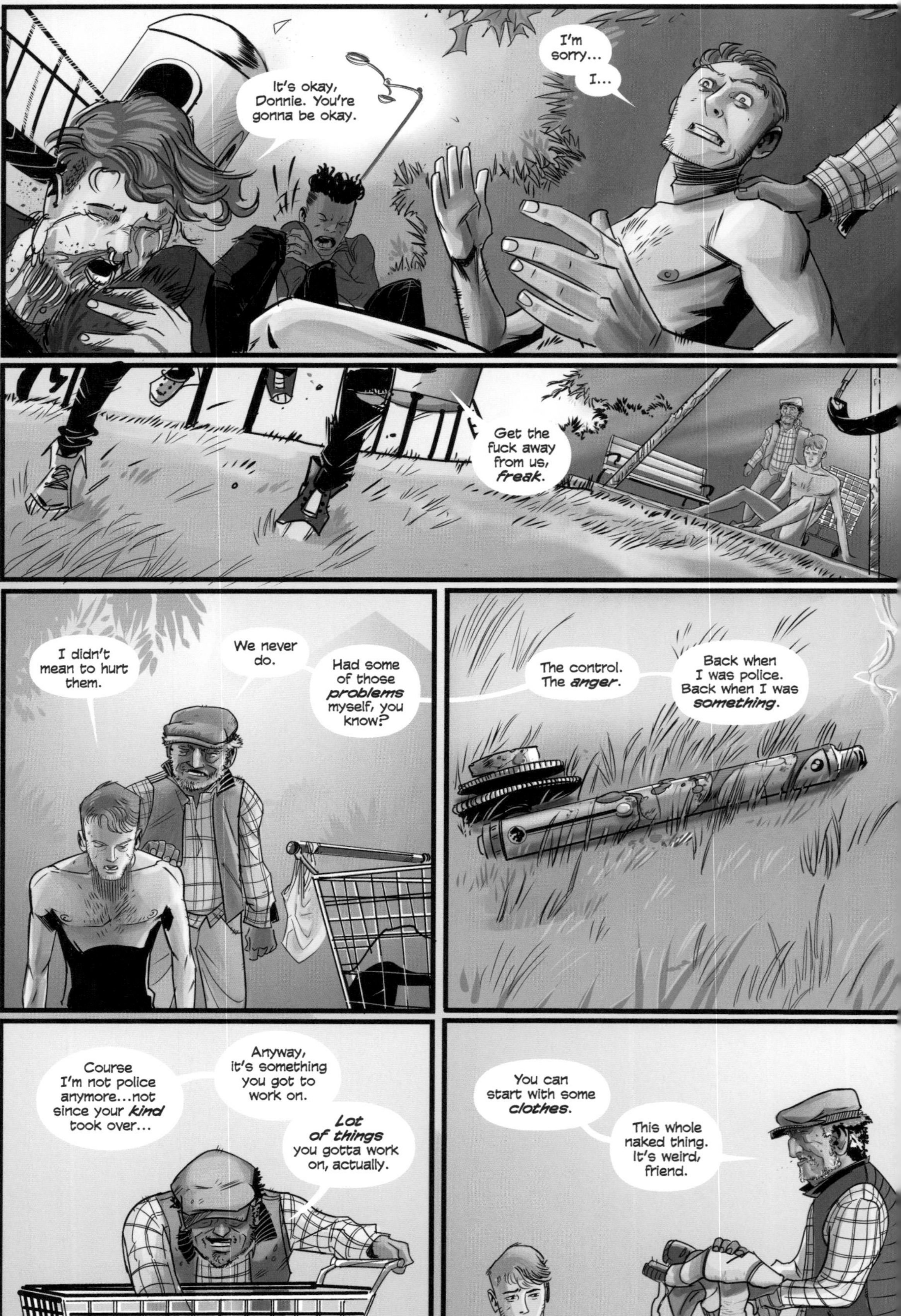

It's okay, Donnie. You're gonna be okay.
I'm sorry...
I...
Get the fuck away from us, *freak*.
I didn't mean to hurt them.
We never do.
Had some of those *problems* myself, you know?
The control. The *anger*.
Back when I was police. Back when I was *something*.
Course I'm not police anymore...not since your *kind* took over...
Anyway, it's something you got to work on.
Lot of things you gotta work on, actually.
You can start with some *clothes*.
This whole naked thing. It's weird, friend.

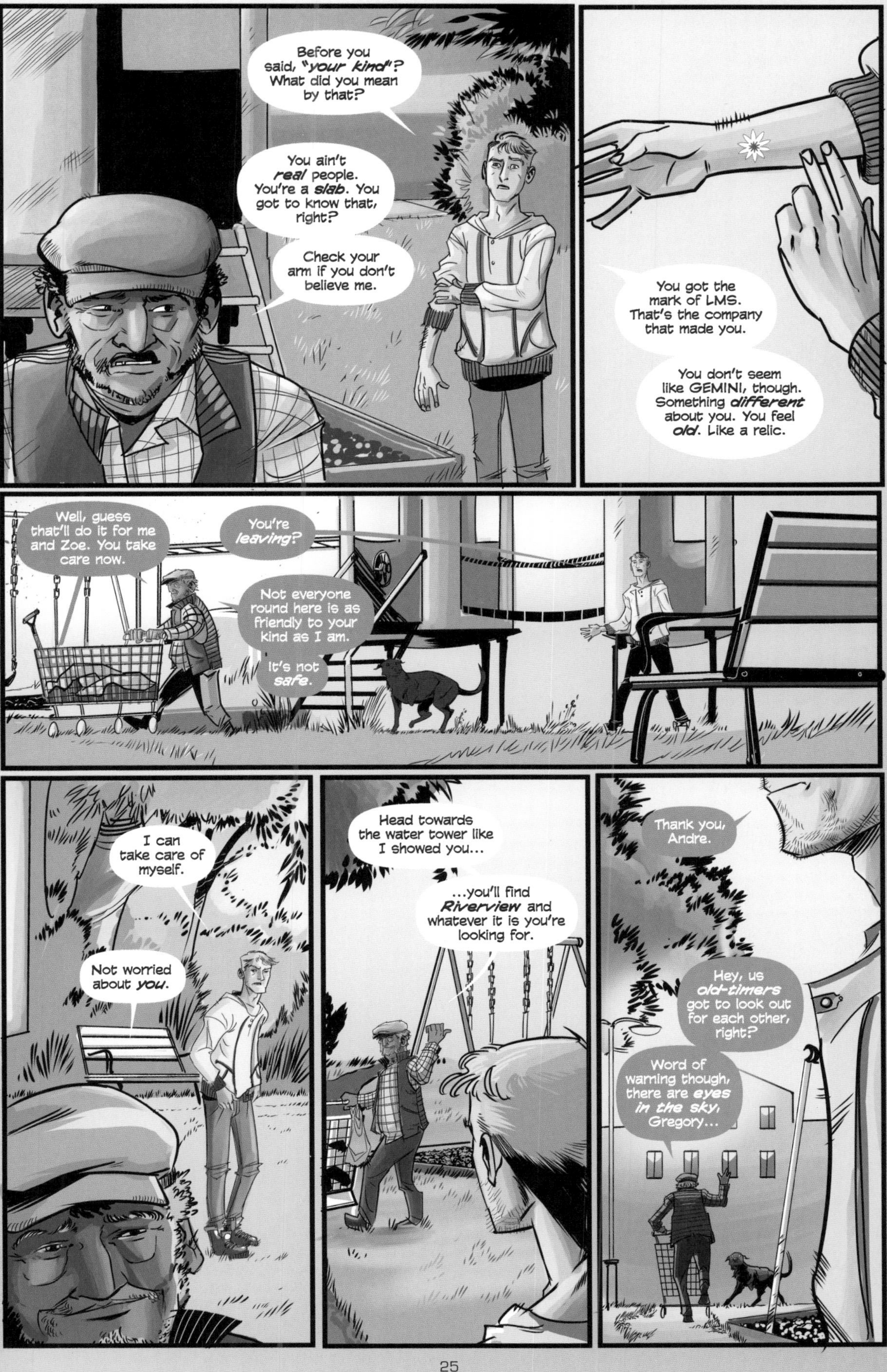
Before you said, "your kind"? What did you mean by that?
You ain't real people. You're a slab. You got to know that, right?
Check your arm if you don't believe me.
You got the mark of LMS. That's the company that made you.
You don't seem like GEMINI, though. Something different about you. You feel old. Like a relic.
Well, guess that'll do it for me and Zoe. You take care now.
You're leaving?
Not everyone round here is as friendly to your kind as I am.
It's not safe.
I can take care of myself.
Not worried about you.
Head towards the water tower like I showed you...
...you'll find Riverview and whatever it is you're looking for.
Thank you, Andre.
Hey, us old-timers got to look out for each other, right?
Word of warning though, there are eyes in the sky, Gregory...

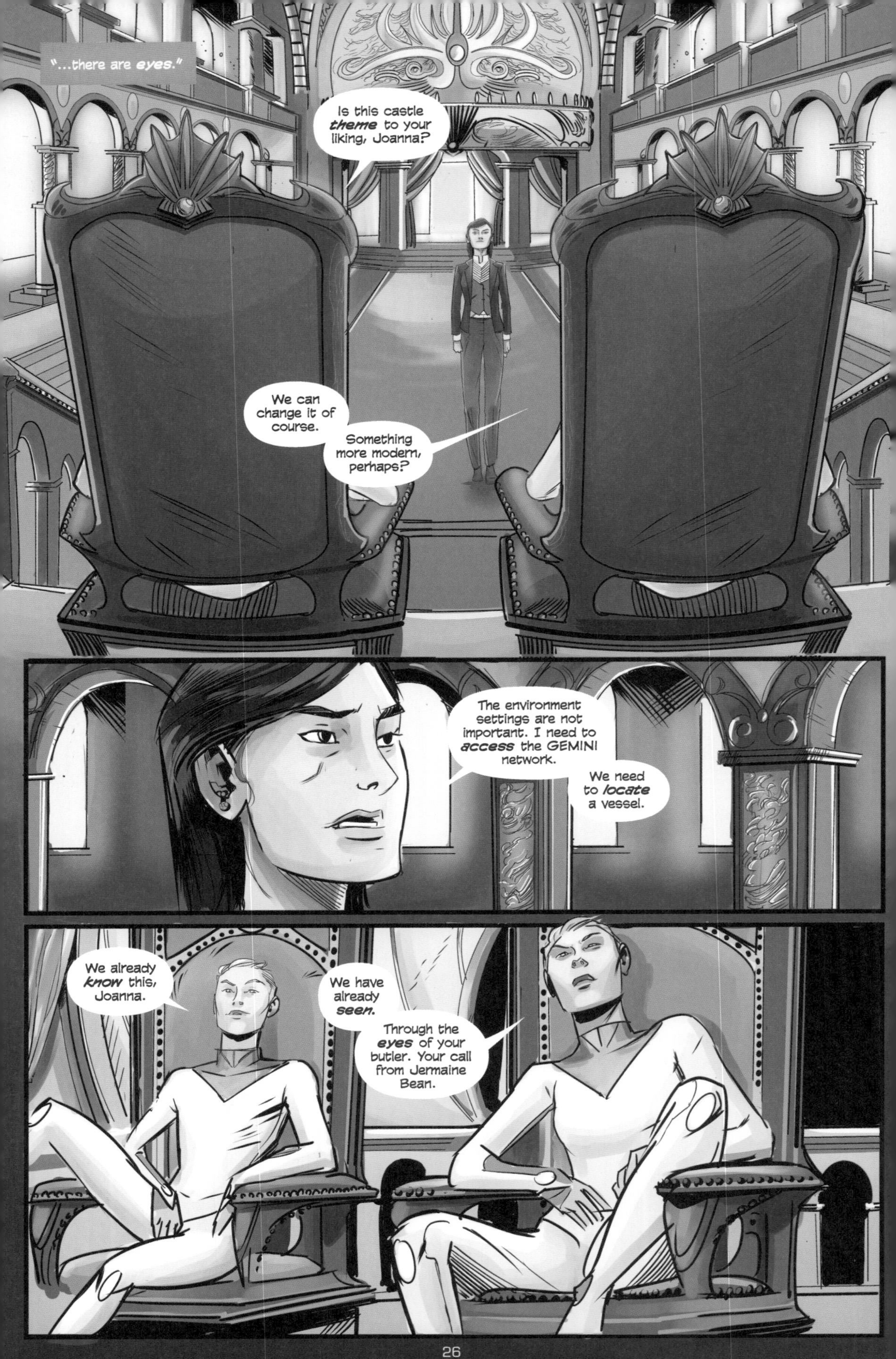
"...there are *eyes*."
Is this castle *theme* to your liking, Joanna?
We can change it of course.
Something more modern, perhaps?
The environment settings are not important. I need to *access* the GEMINI network.
We need to *locate* a vessel.
We already *know* this, Joanna.
We have already *seen*.
Through the *eyes* of your butler. Your call from Jermaine Bean.

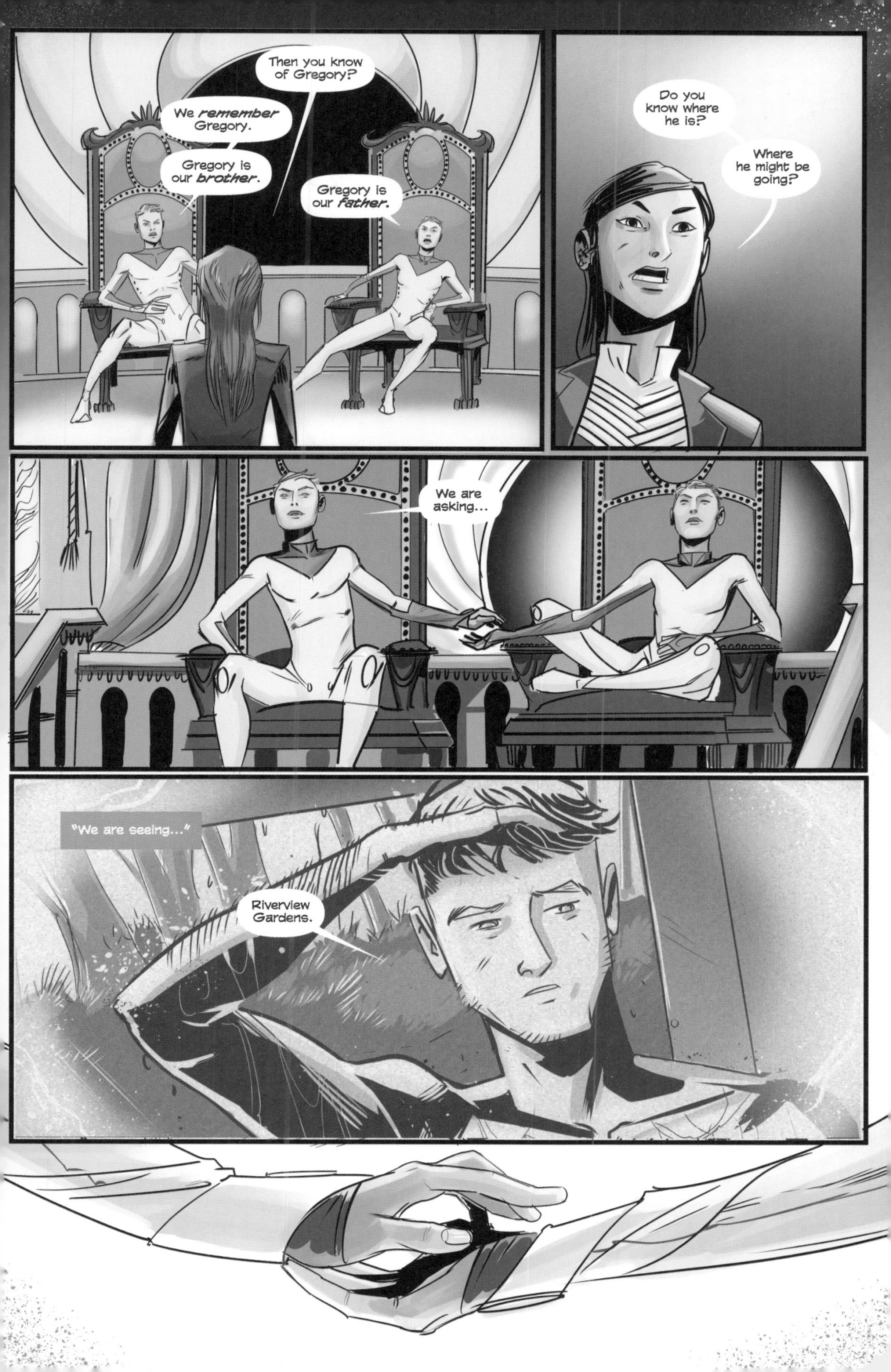
Then you know of Gregory?
We *remember* Gregory.
Gregory is our *brother*.
Gregory is our *father*.
Do you know where he is?
Where he might be going?
We are asking...
"We are seeing..."
Riverview Gardens.

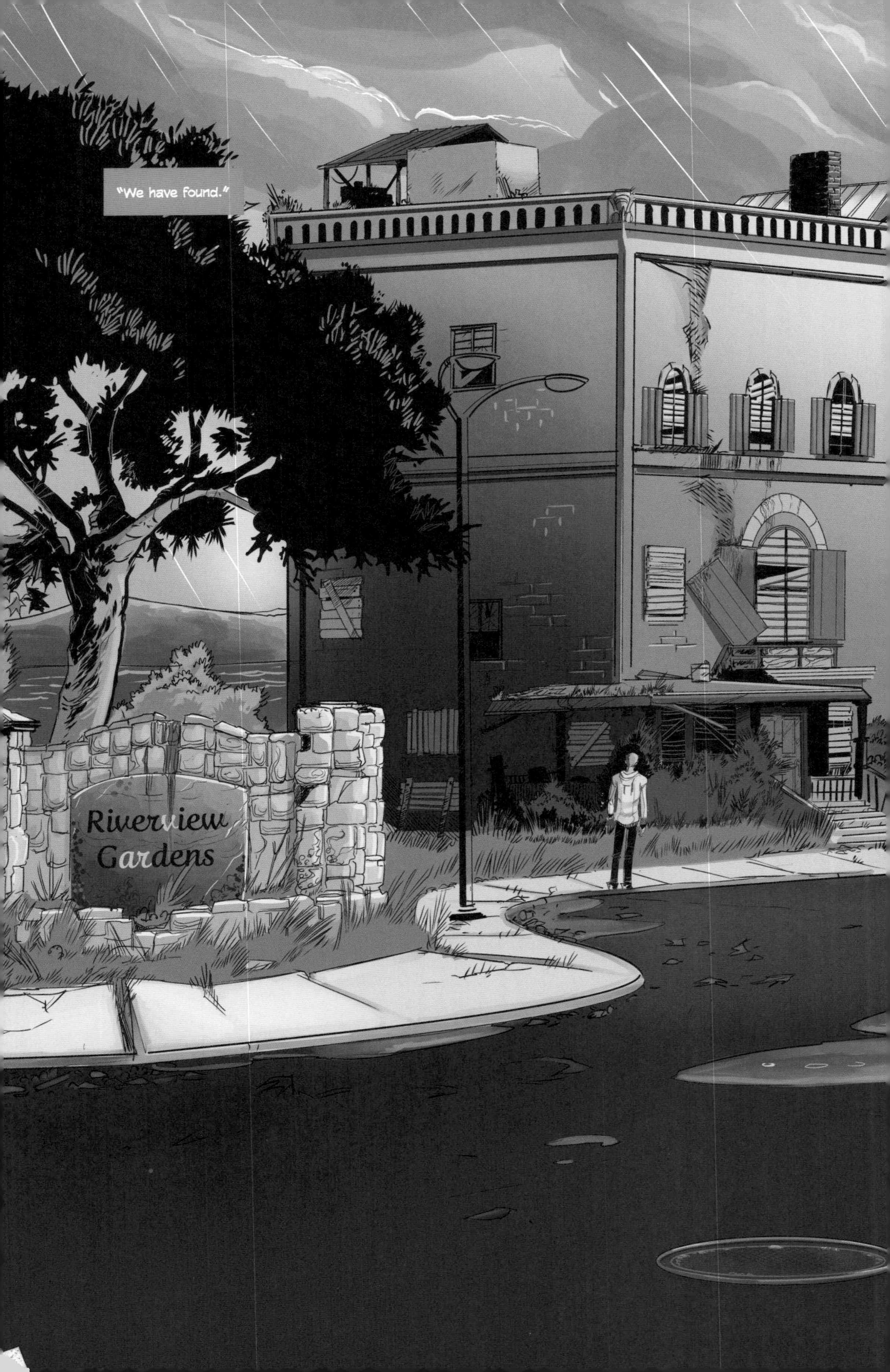
"We have found."
Riverview
Gardens

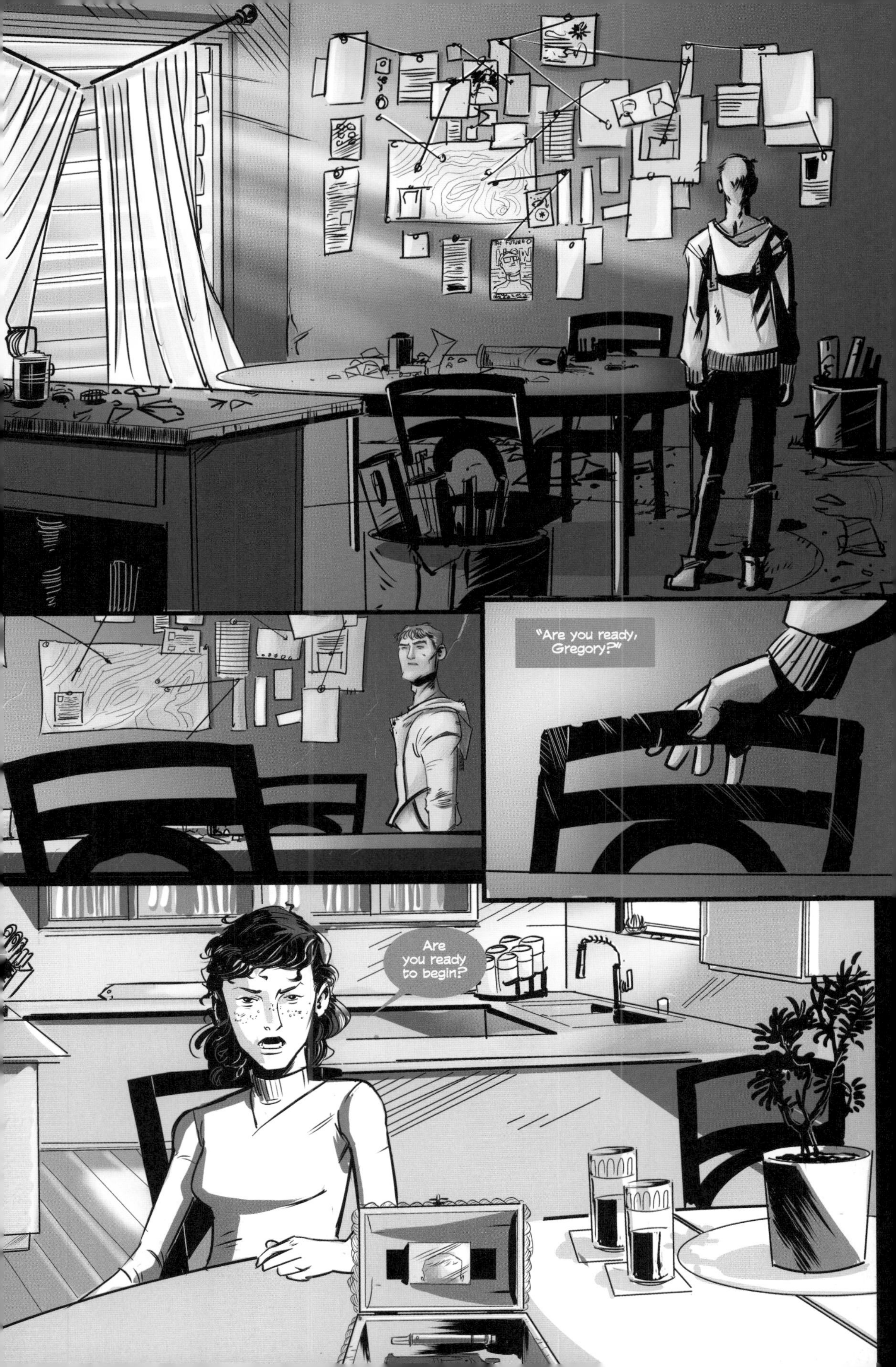
"Are you ready,
Gregory?"
Are
you ready
to begin?

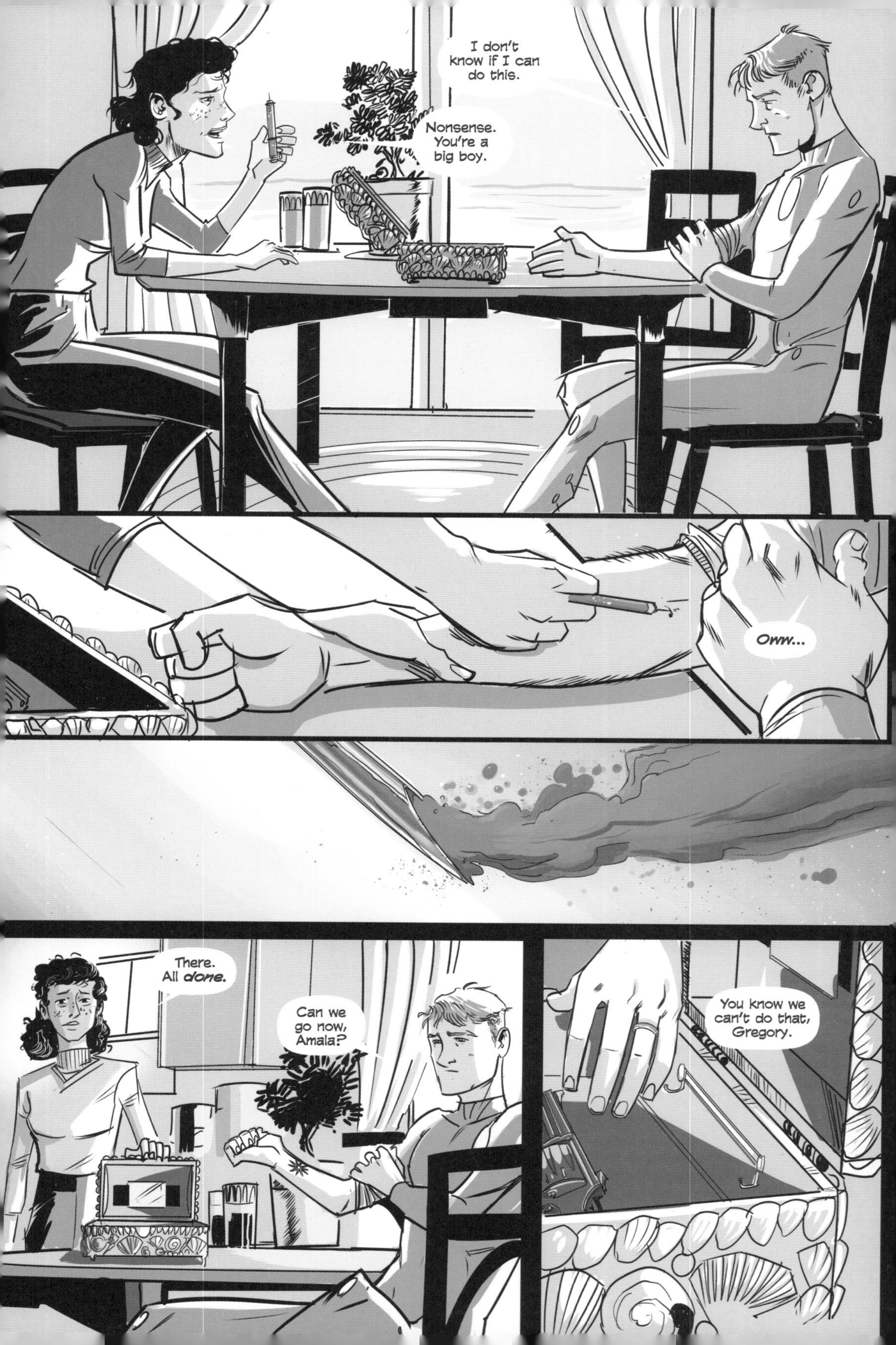
I don't know if I can do this.
Nonsense. You're a big boy.
Oww...
There. All *done.*
Can we go now, Amala?
You know we can't do that, Gregory.

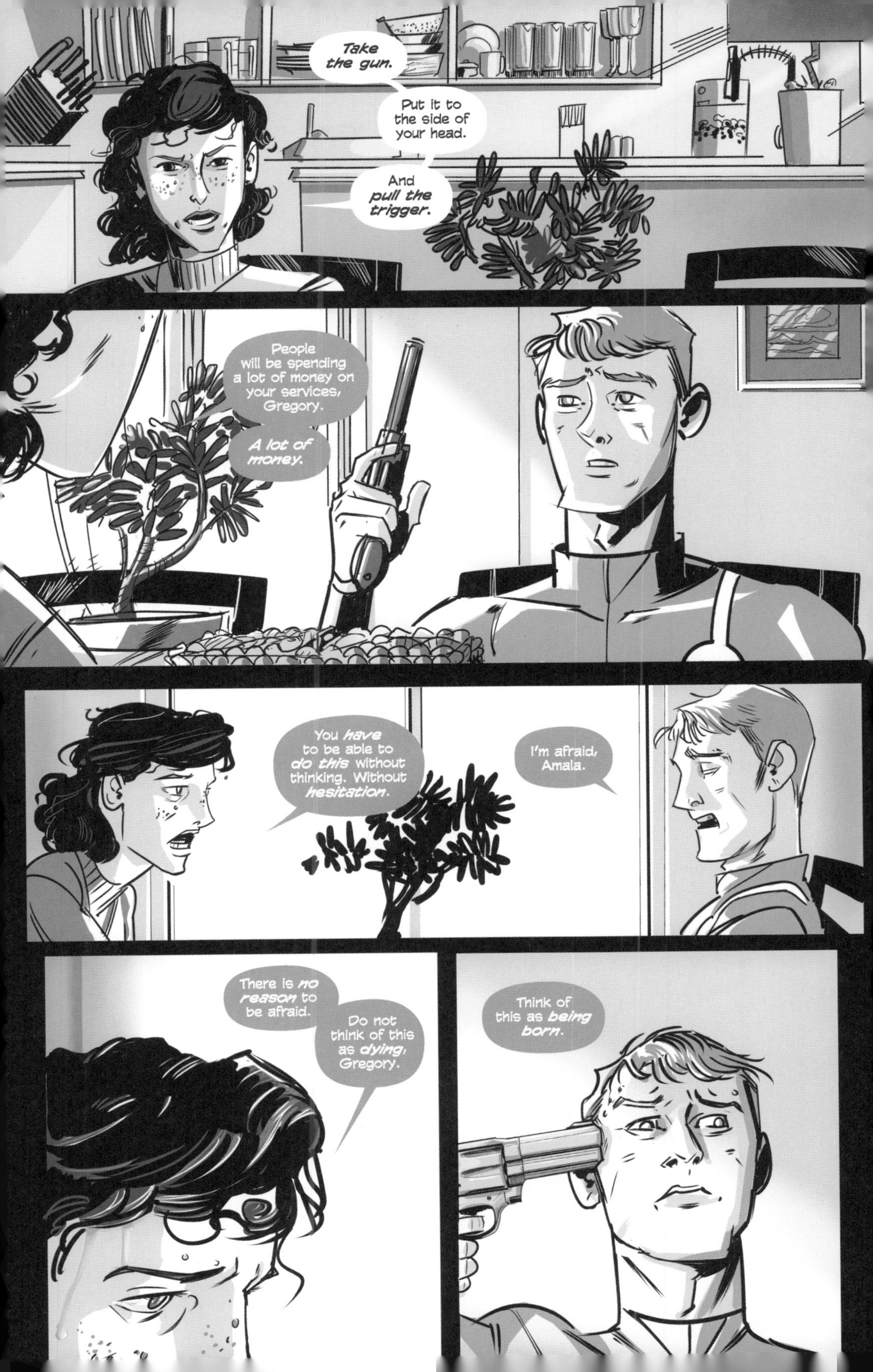
Take the gun.
Put it to the side of your head.
And pull the trigger.
People will be spending a lot of money on your services, Gregory.
A lot of money.
You have to be able to do this without thinking. Without hesitation.
I'm afraid, Amala.
There is no reason to be afraid.
Do not think of this as dying, Gregory.
Think of this as being born.

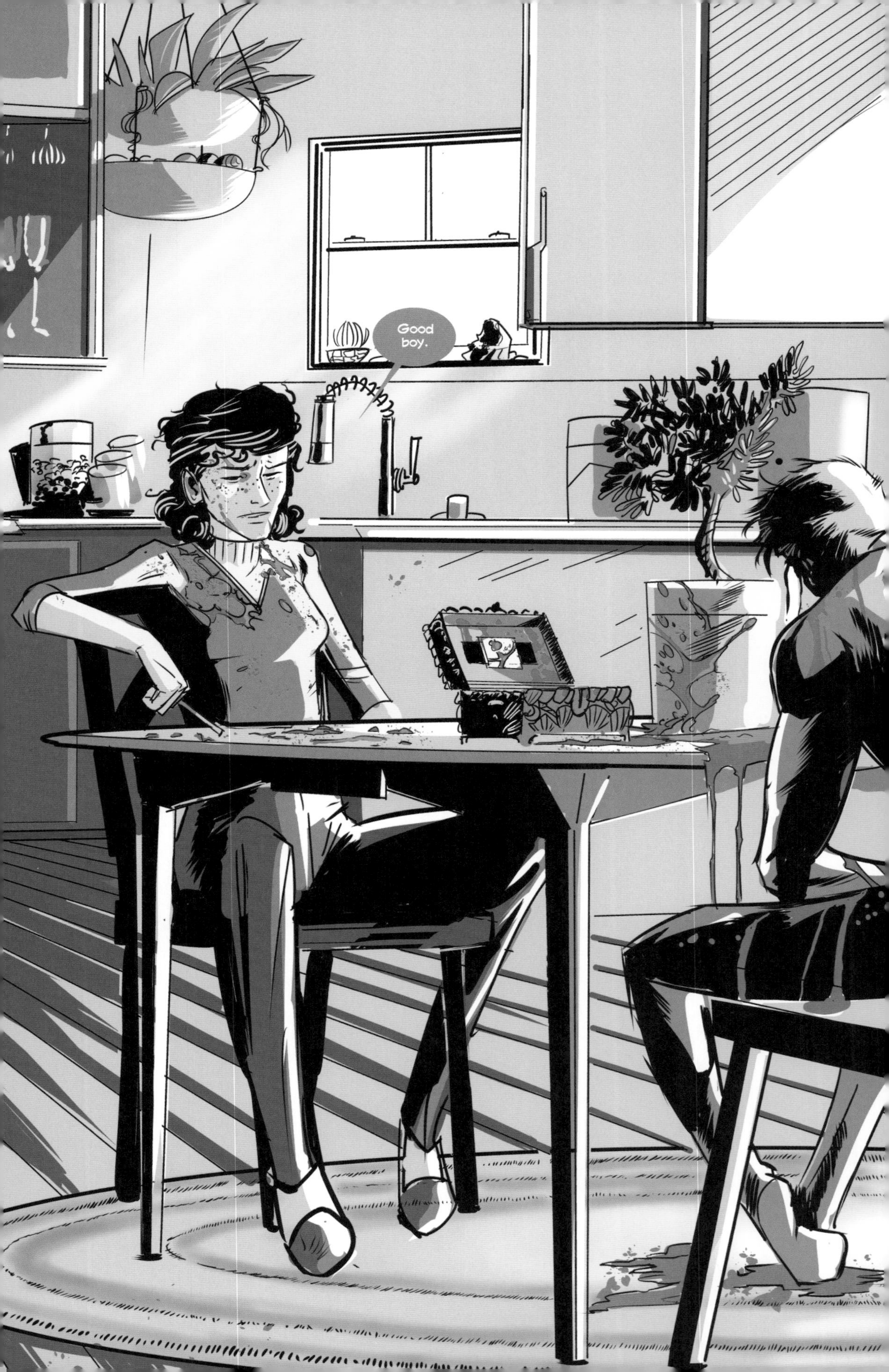
Good boy.

It comes for me
on blackened sea.

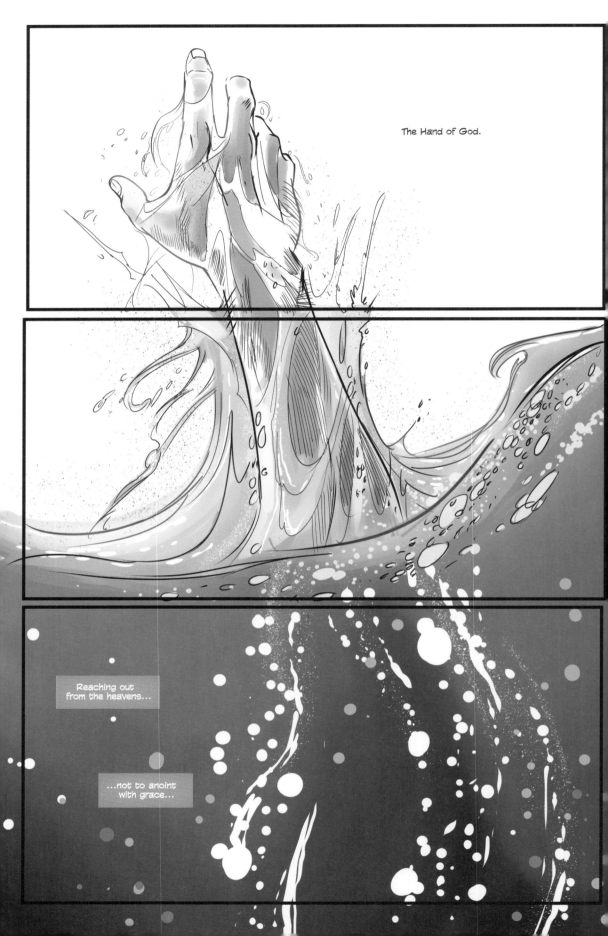

The Hand of God.

Reaching out
from the heavens...

...not to anoint
with grace...

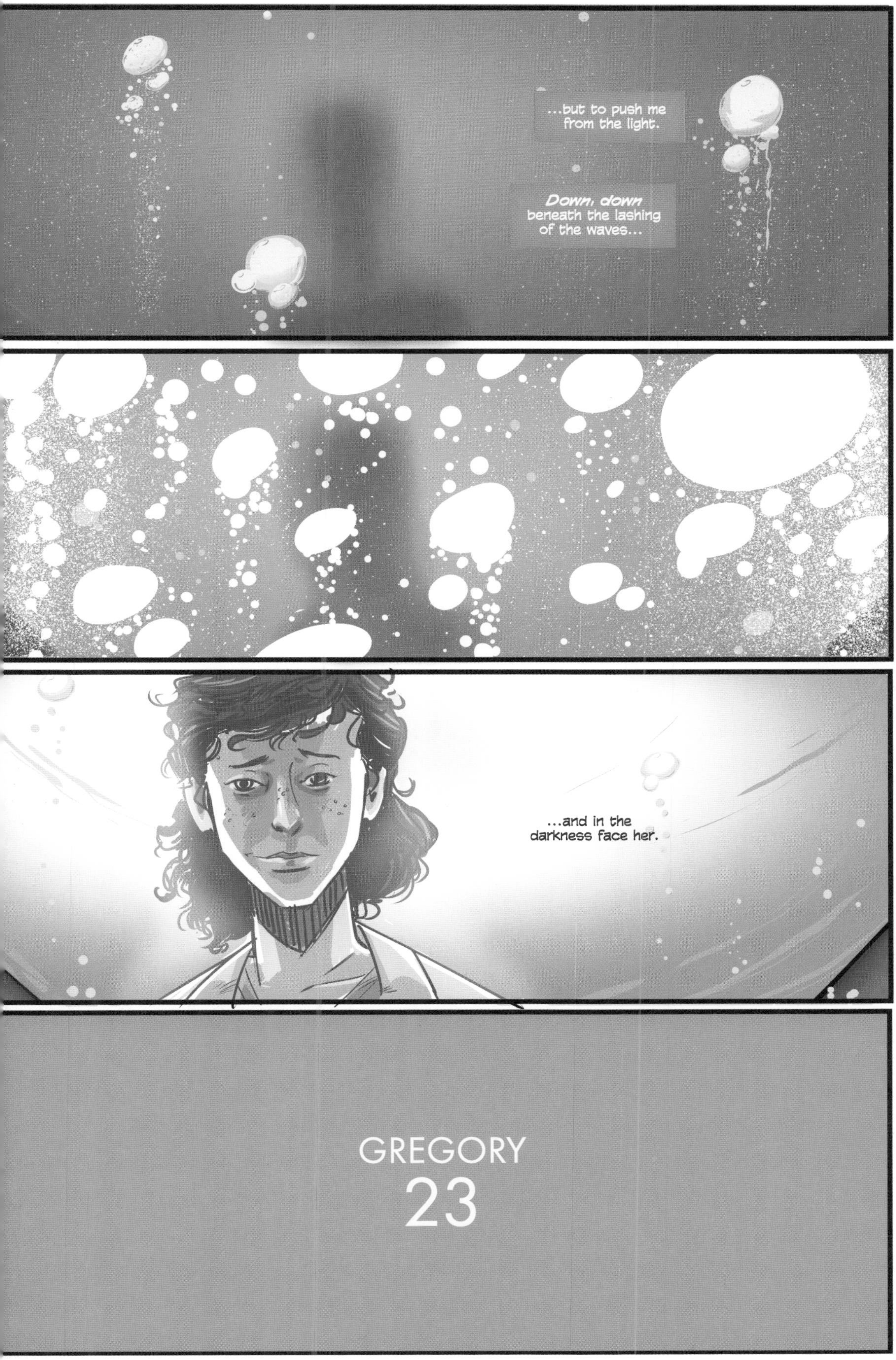
...but to push me from the light.
Down, down beneath the lashing of the waves...
...and in the darkness face her.
GREGORY
23

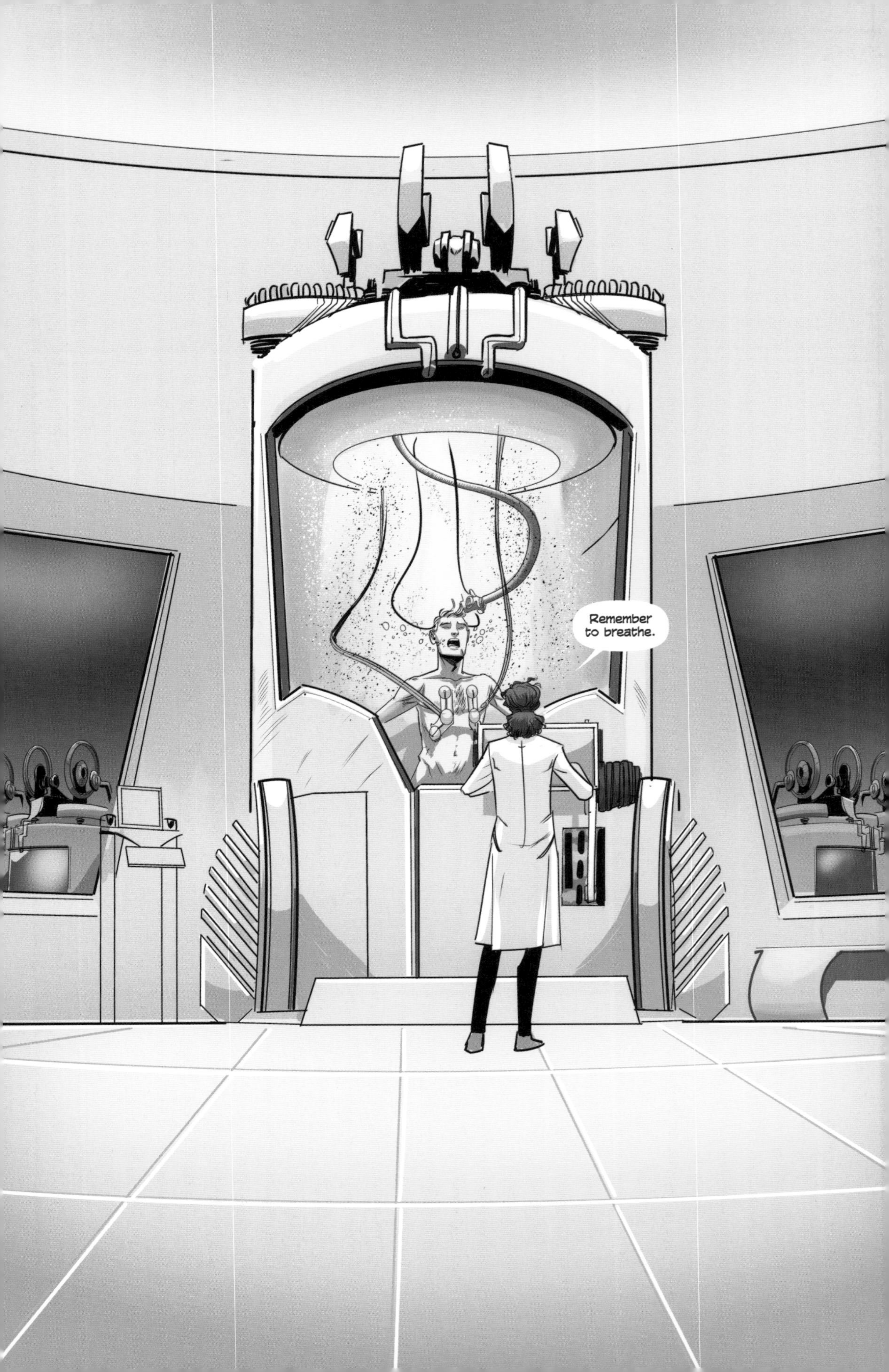
Remember to breathe.

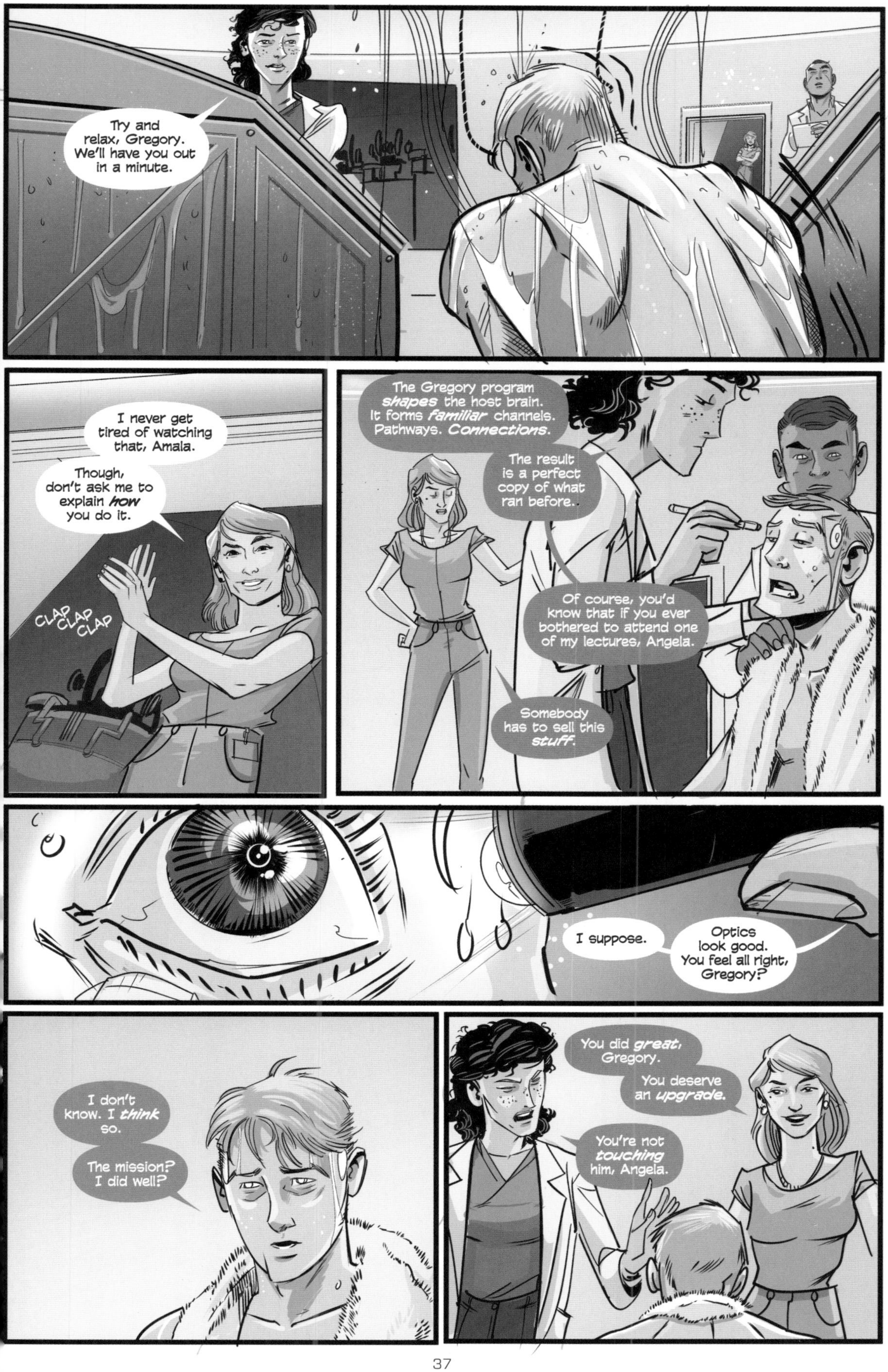
Try and relax, Gregory. We'll have you out in a minute.
I never get tired of watching that, Amala.
Though, don't ask me to explain *how* you do it.
CLAP CLAP CLAP
The Gregory program *shapes* the host brain. It forms *familiar* channels. Pathways. *Connections*.
The result is a perfect copy of what ran before.
Of course, you'd know that if you ever bothered to attend one of my lectures, Angela.
Somebody has to sell this *stuff*.
Optics look good. You feel all right, Gregory?
I suppose.
I don't know. I *think* so.
The mission? I did well?
You did *great*, Gregory.
You deserve an *upgrade*.
You're not *touching* him, Angela.

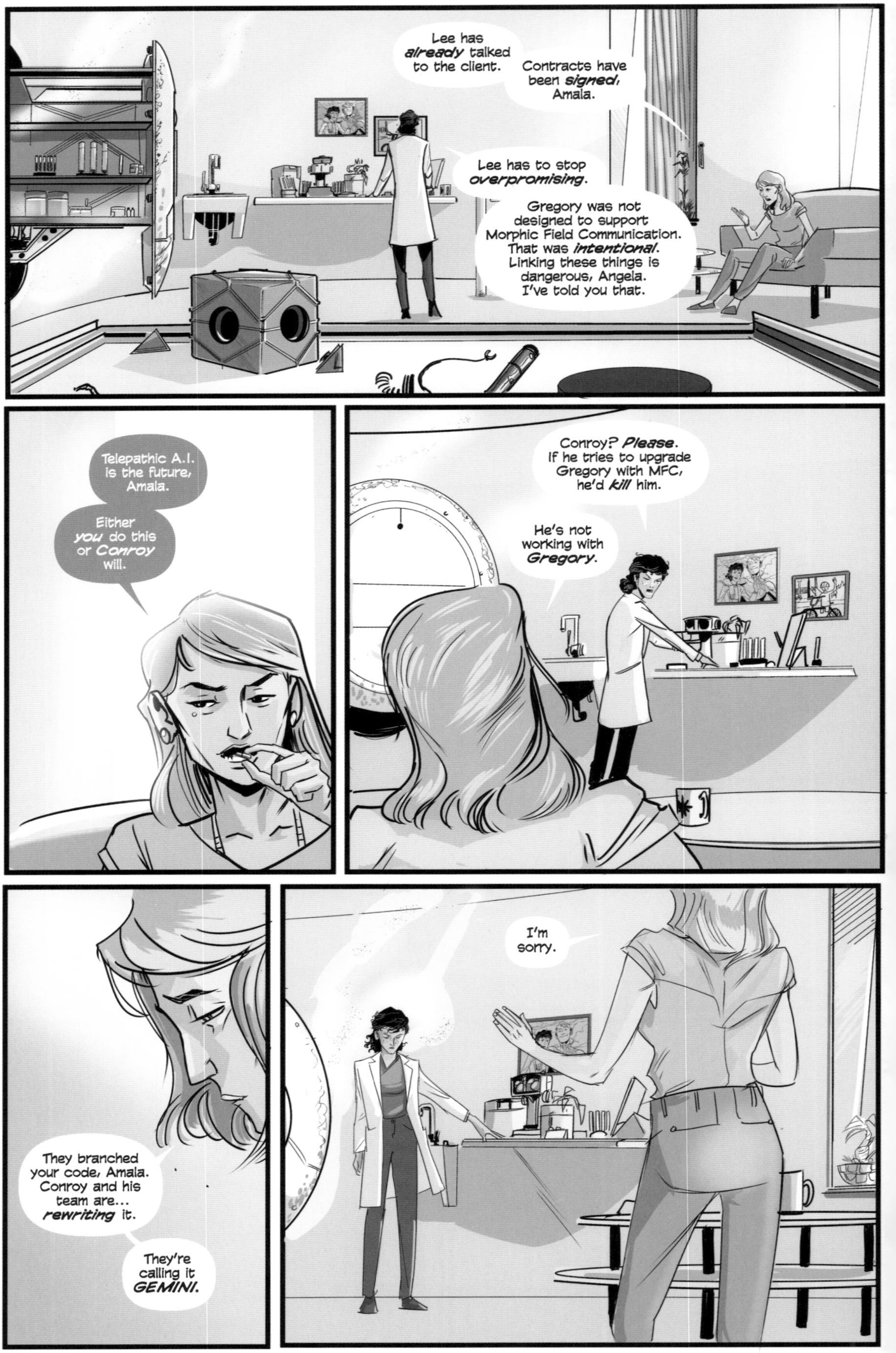
Lee has *already* talked to the client.
Contracts have been *signed*, Amala.
Lee has to stop *overpromising*.
Gregory was not designed to support Morphic Field Communication. That was *intentional*. Linking these things is dangerous, Angela. I've told you that.
Telepathic A.I. is the future, Amala.
Either *you* do this or *Conroy* will.
Conroy? *Please*. If he tries to upgrade Gregory with MFC, he'd *kill* him.
He's not working with *Gregory*.
They branched your code, Amala. Conroy and his team are... *rewriting* it.
They're calling it *GEMINI*.
I'm sorry.

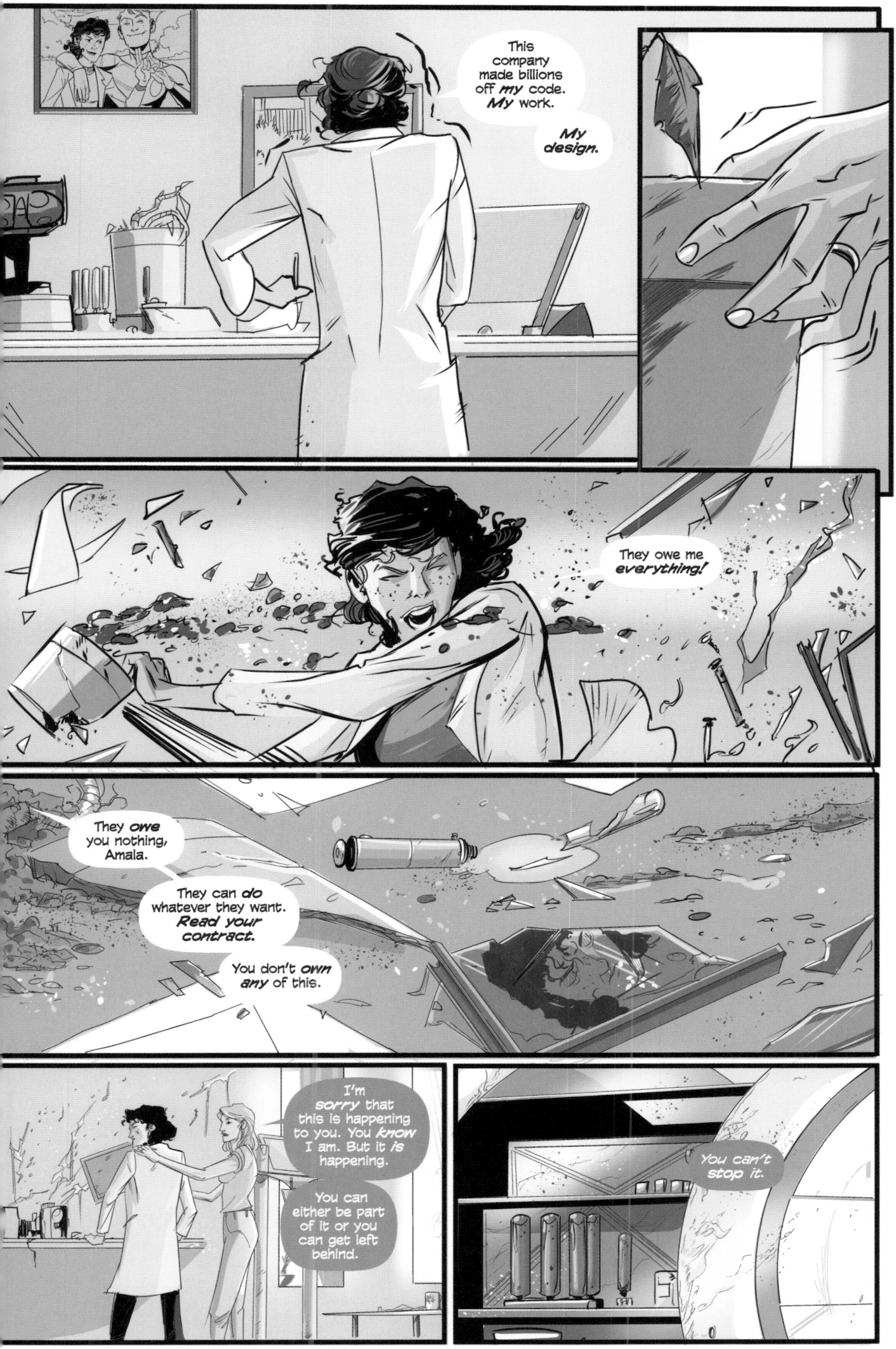
This company made billions off *my* code. *My* work.
My design.
They owe me *everything!*
They *owe* you nothing, Amala.
They can *do* whatever they want. *Read your contract.*
You don't *own any* of this.
I'm *sorry* that this is happening to you. You *know* I am. But it *is* happening.
You can either be part of it or you can get left behind.
You can't stop it.

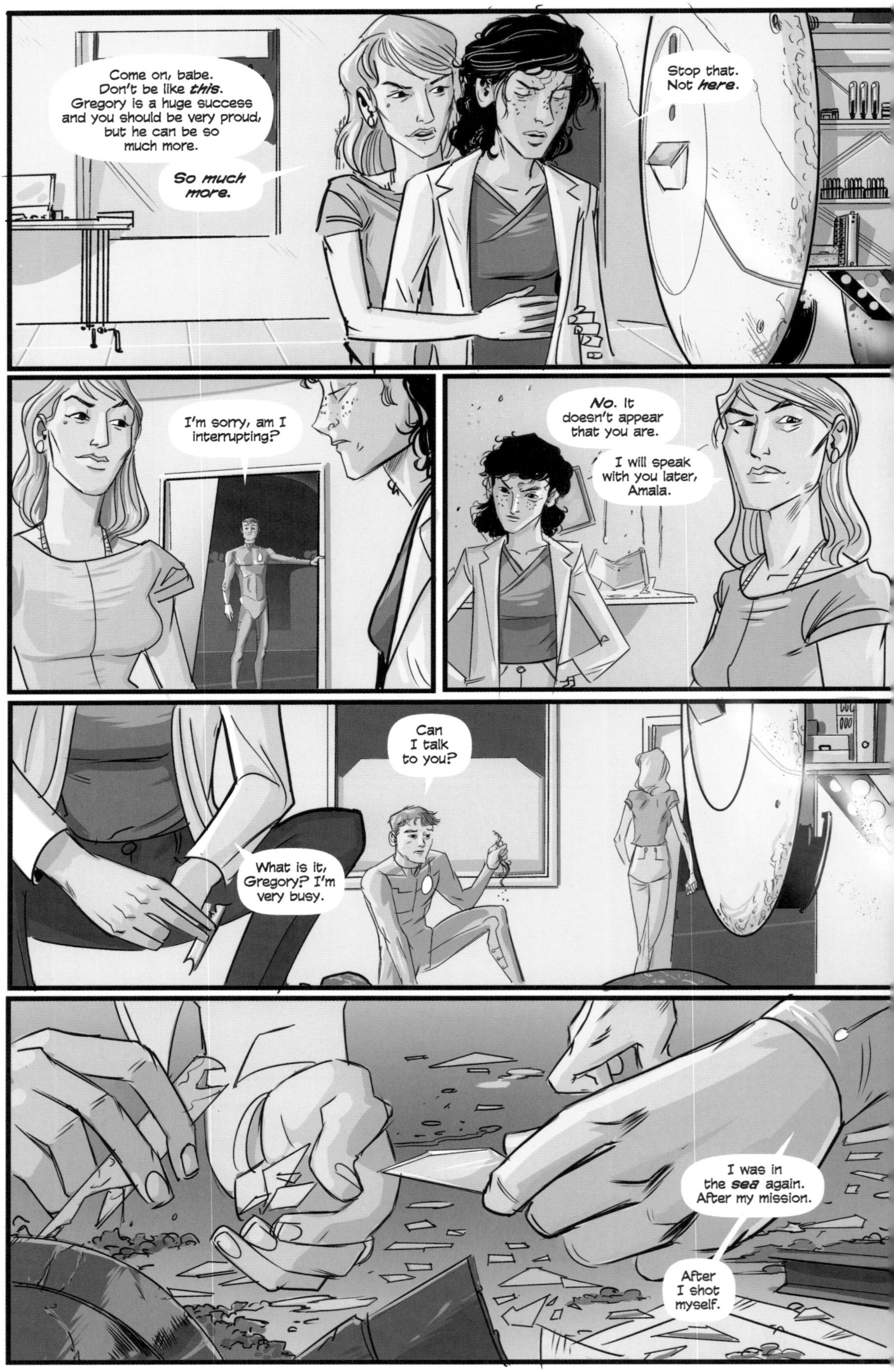

Come on, babe. Don't be like *this*. Gregory is a huge success and you should be very proud, but he can be so much more.
So much more.
Stop that. Not *here*.
I'm sorry, am I interrupting?
No. It doesn't appear that you are.
I will speak with you later, Amala.
Can I talk to you?
What is it, Gregory? I'm very busy.
I was in the *sea* again. After my mission.
After I shot myself.

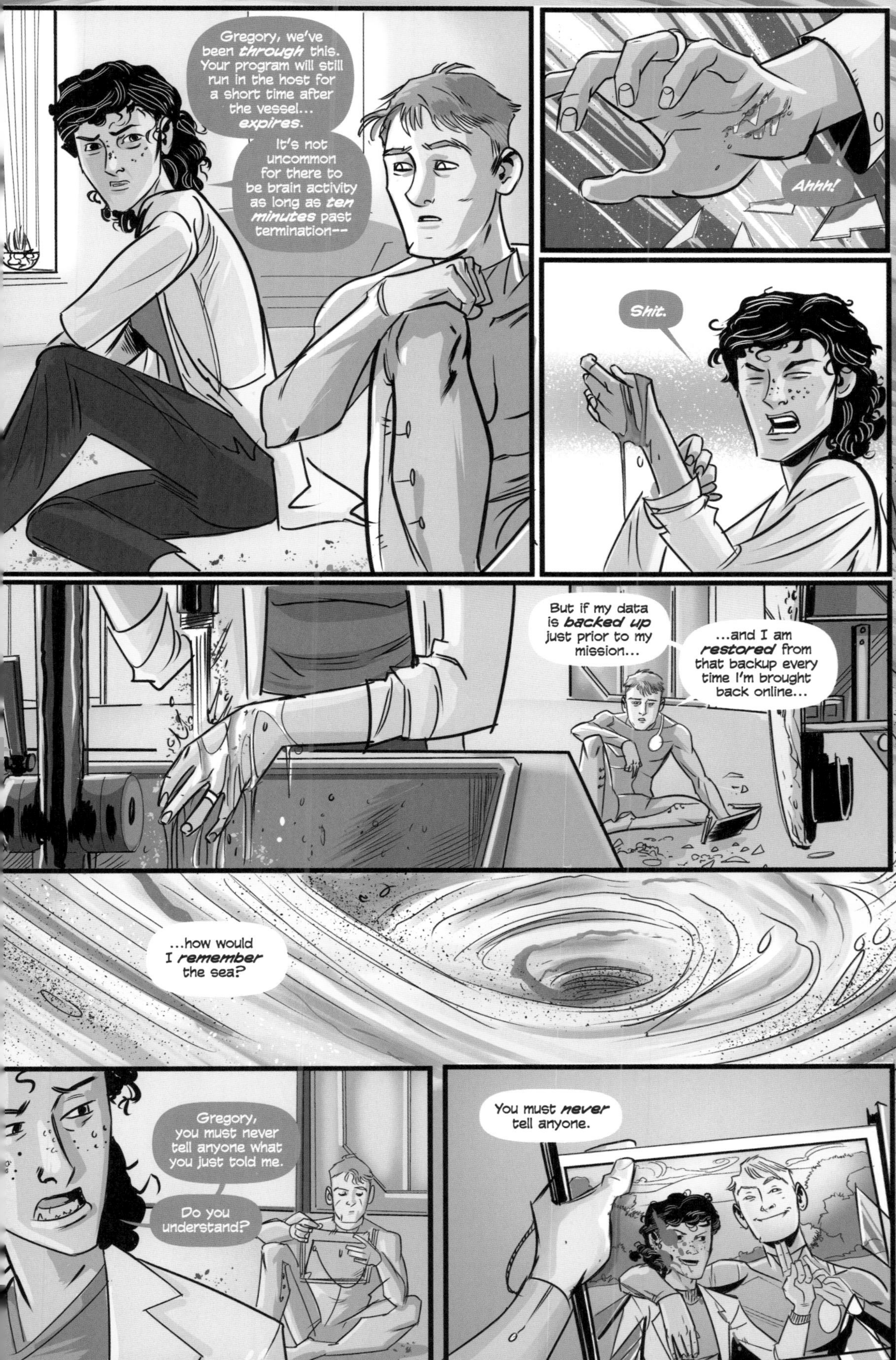
Gregory, we've been *through* this. Your program will still run in the host for a short time after the vessel... *expires*.
It's not uncommon for there to be brain activity as long as *ten minutes* past termination--
Ahhh!
Shit.
But if my data is *backed up* just prior to my mission...
...and I am *restored* from that backup every time I'm brought back online...
...how would I *remember* the sea?
Gregory, you must never tell anyone what you just told me.
Do you understand?
You must *never* tell anyone.

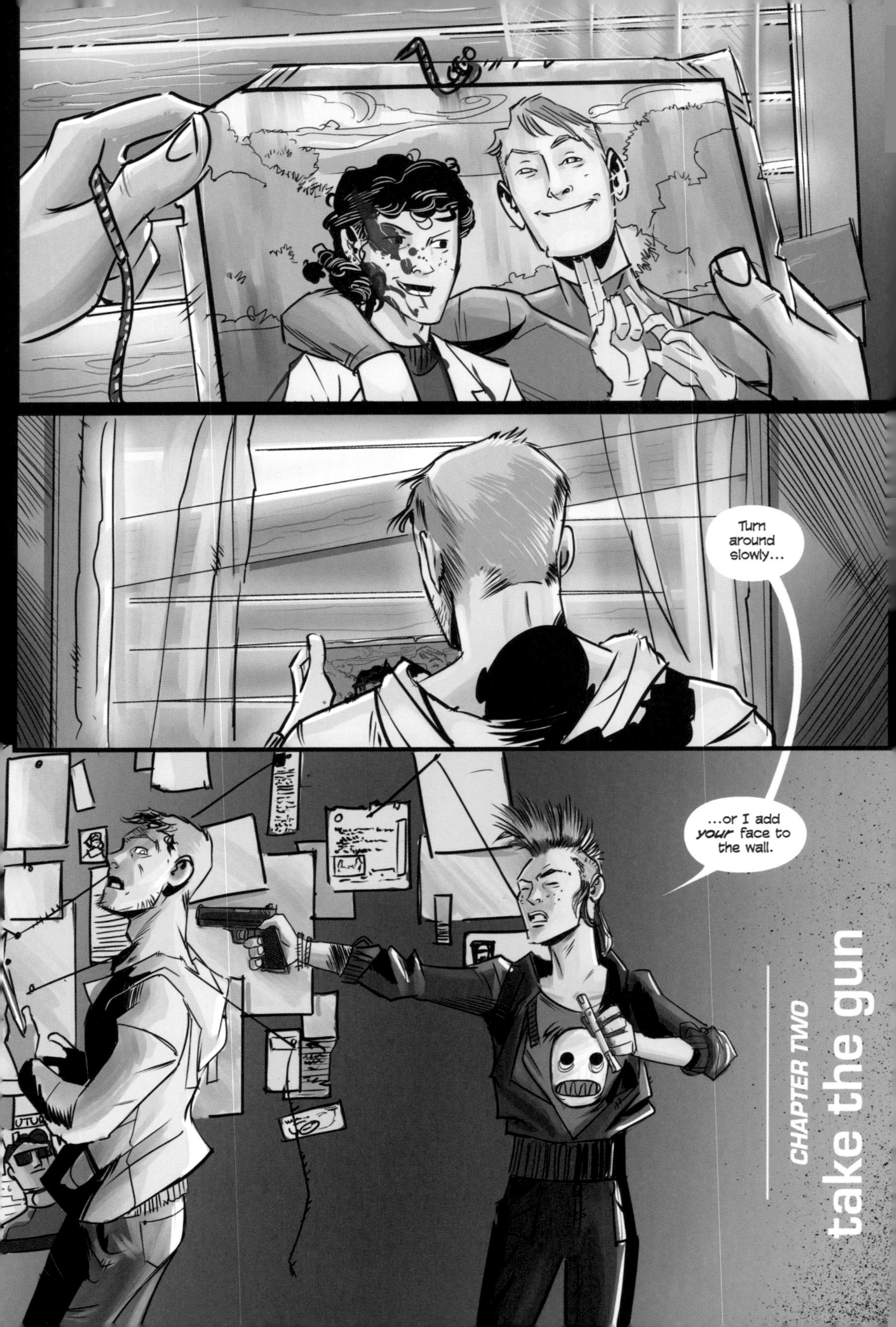

Turn around slowly...
...or I add *your* face to the wall.
CHAPTER TWO
take the gun

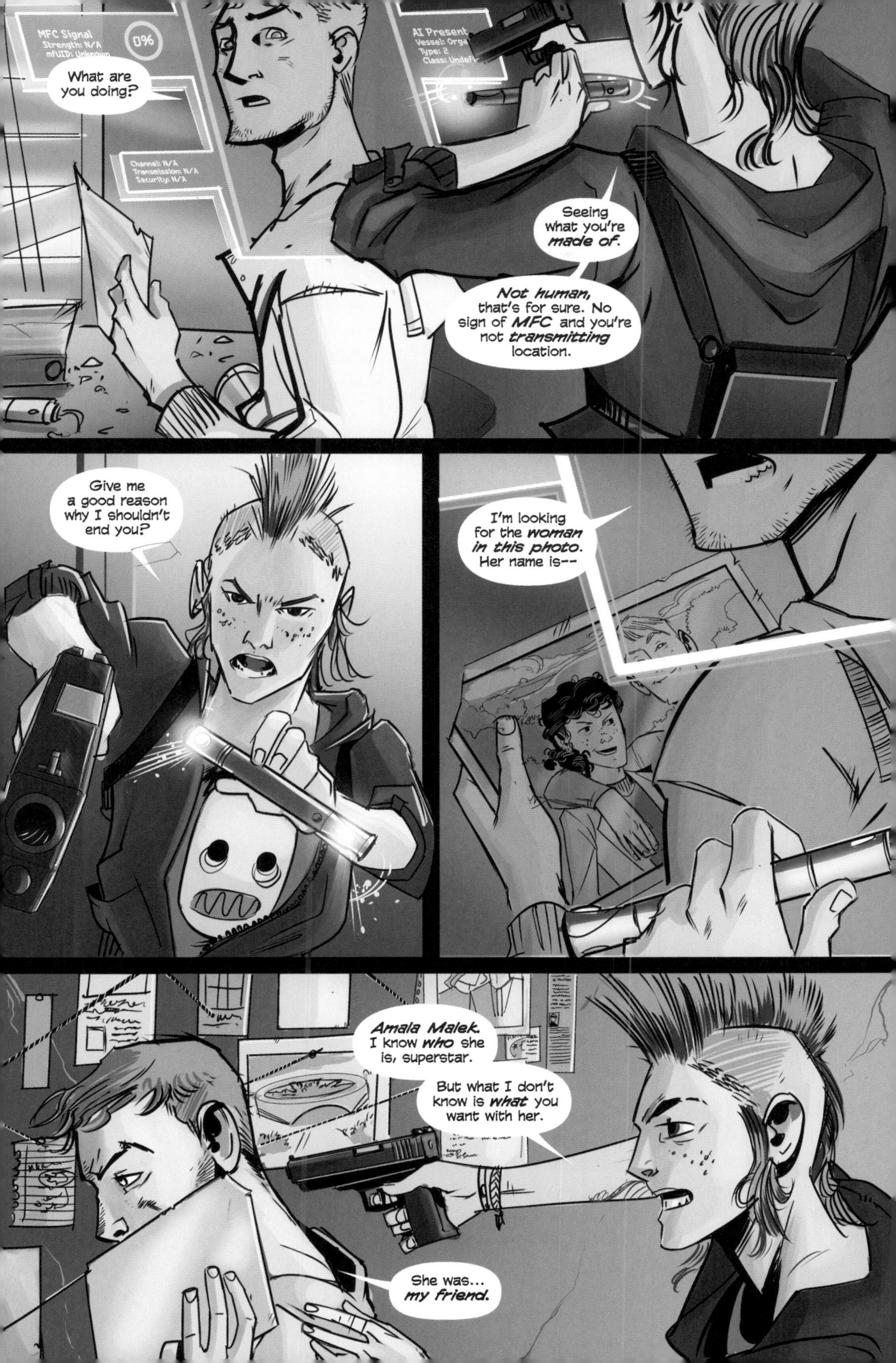
MFC Signal
Strength: N/A
0%
What are you doing?
Channel: N/A
Transmission: N/A
Security: N/A
Seeing what you're *made of*.
Not human, that's for sure. No sign of *MFC* and you're not *transmitting* location.
Give me a good reason why I shouldn't end you?
I'm looking for the *woman in this photo*. Her name is--
Amala Malek. I know *who* she is, superstar.
But what I don't know is *what* you want with her.
She was... *my friend.*

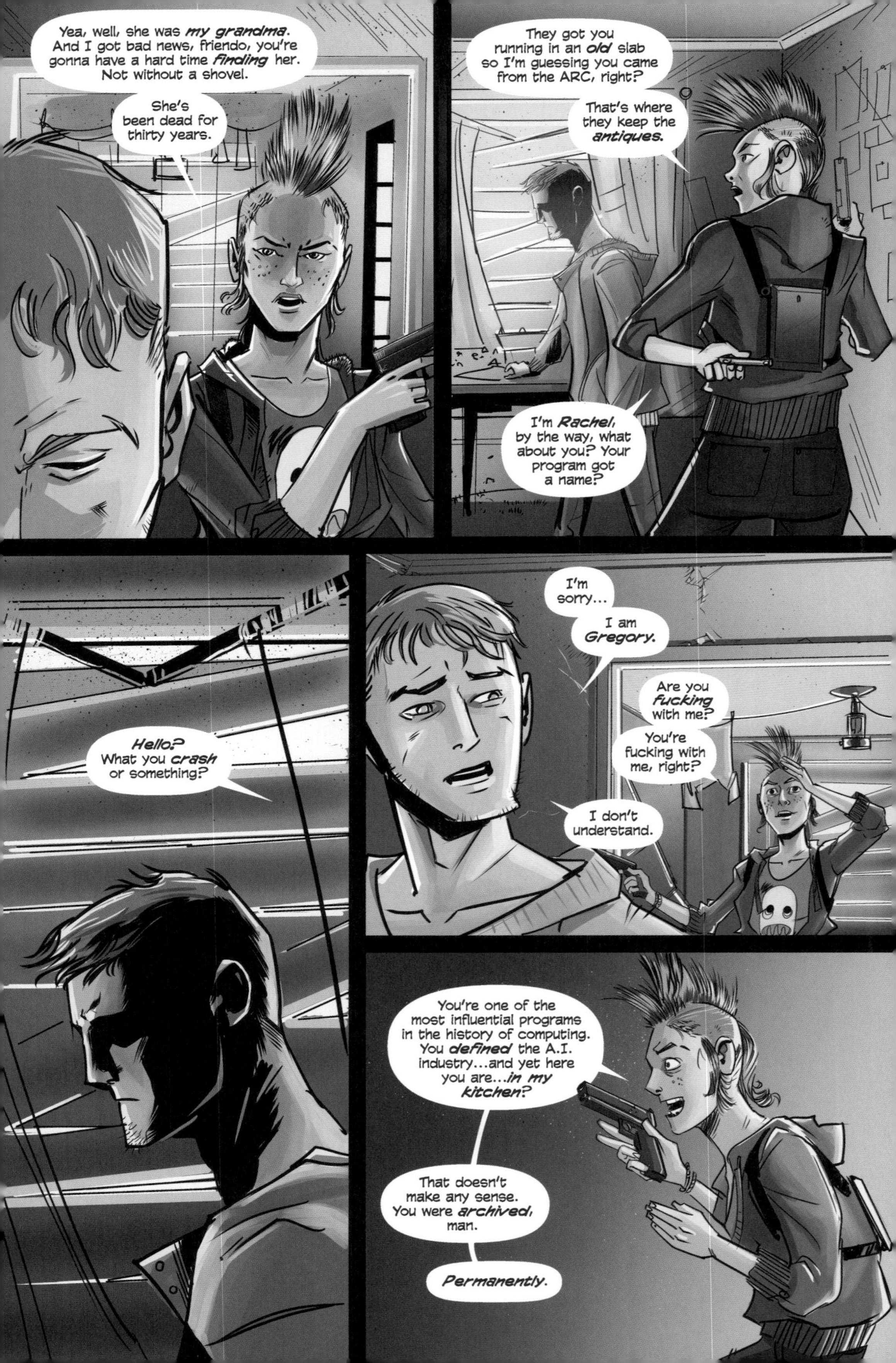
Yea, well, she was *my grandma*. And I got bad news, friendo, you're gonna have a hard time *finding* her. Not without a shovel.
She's been dead for thirty years.
They got you running in an *old* slab so I'm guessing you came from the ARC, right?
That's where they keep the *antiques*.
I'm *Rachel*, by the way, what about you? Your program got a name?
Hello? What you *crash* or something?
I'm sorry...
I am *Gregory*.
Are you *fucking* with me?
You're fucking with me, right?
I don't understand.
You're one of the most influential programs in the history of computing. You *defined* the A.I. industry...and yet here you are...*in my kitchen*?
That doesn't make any sense. You were *archived*, man.
Permanently.

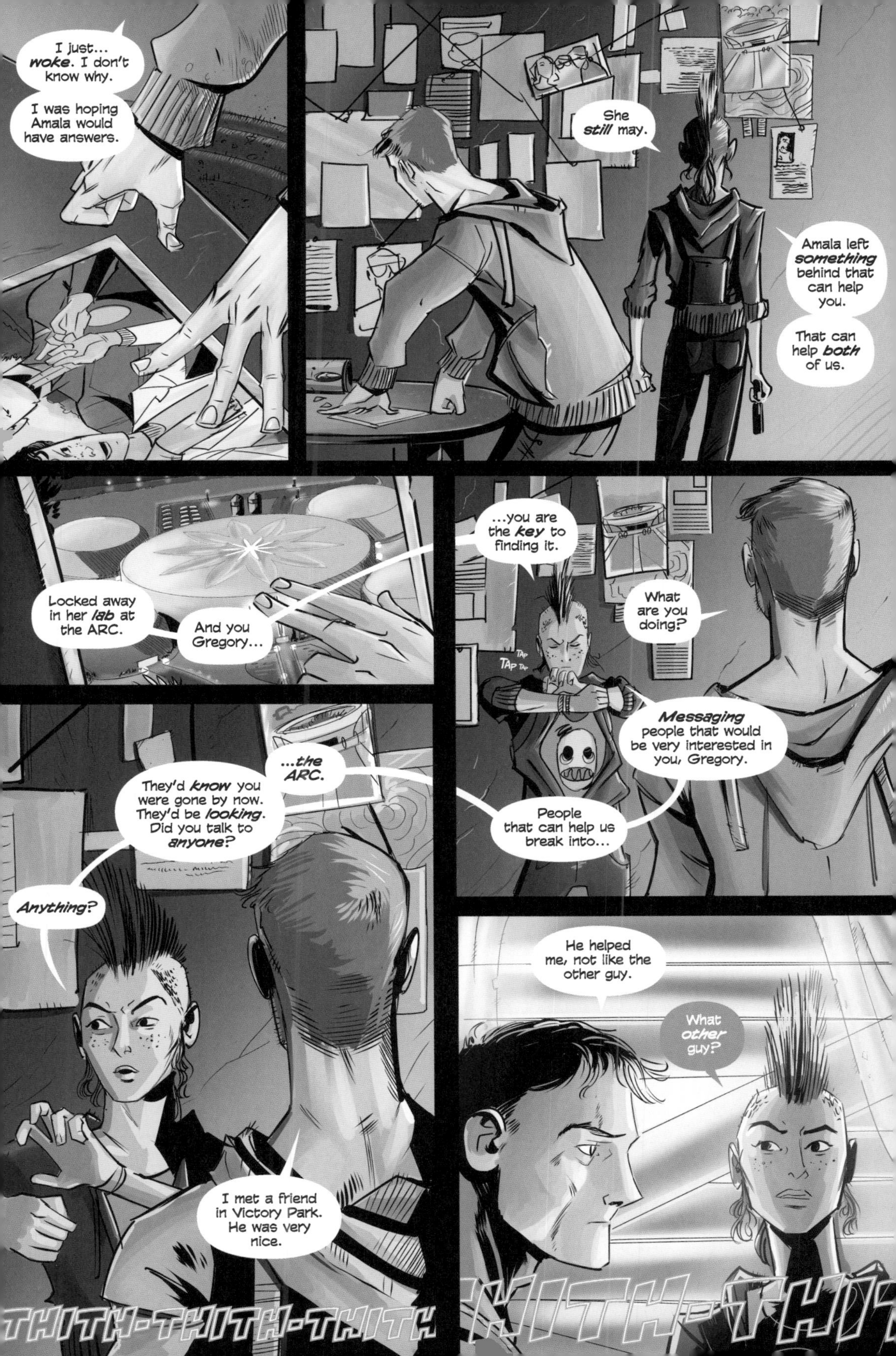
I just... woke. I don't know why.
I was hoping Amala would have answers.
She still may.
Amala left something behind that can help you.
That can help both of us.
Locked away in her lab at the ARC.
And you Gregory...
...you are the key to finding it.
What are you doing?
TAP TAP TAP
Messaging people that would be very interested in you, Gregory.
People that can help us break into...
...the ARC.
They'd know you were gone by now. They'd be looking. Did you talk to anyone?
Anything?
I met a friend in Victory Park. He was very nice.
He helped me, not like the other guy.
What other guy?
THITH-THITH-THITH-THITH-THITH-THI

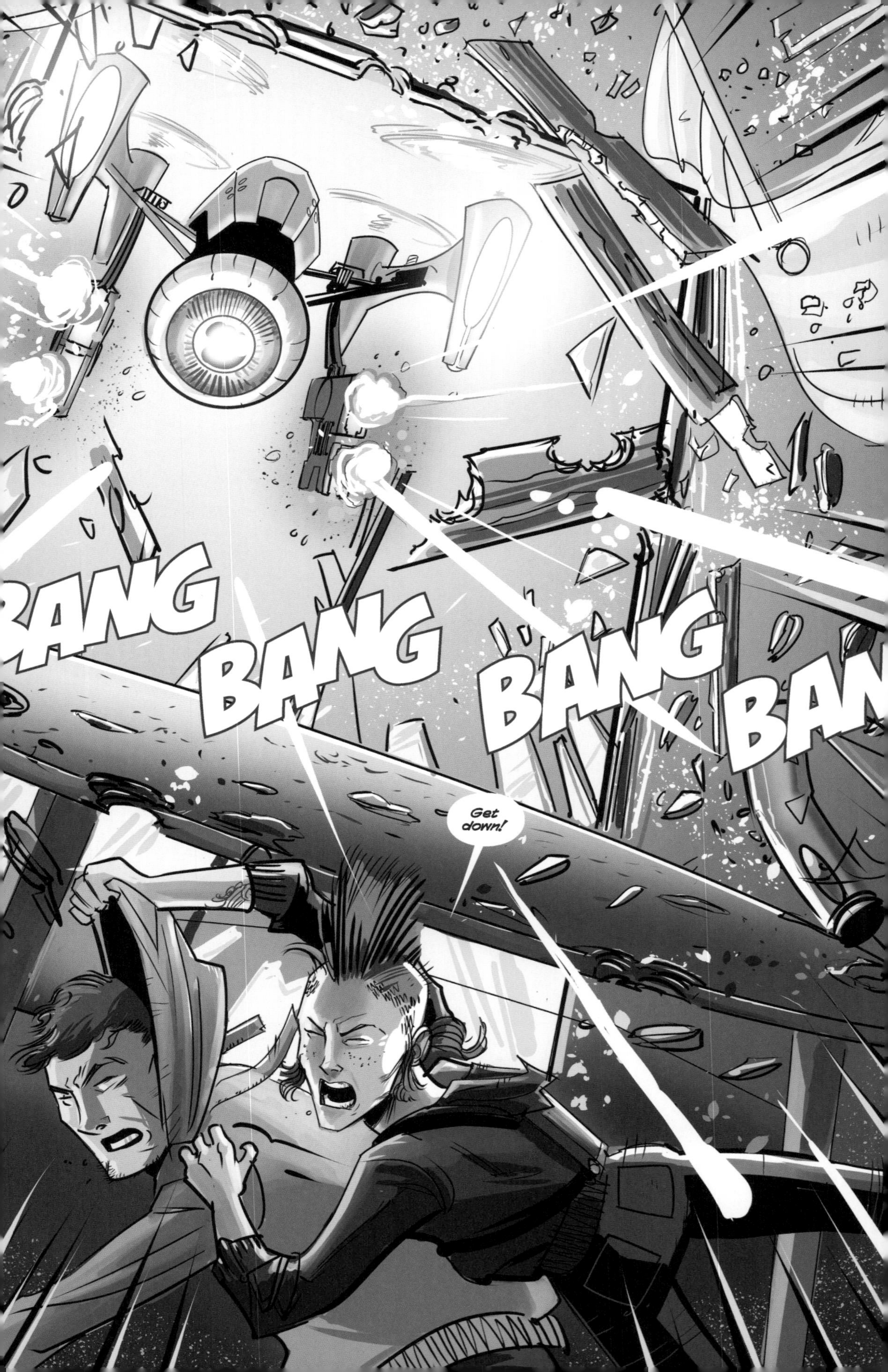
BANG
BANG
BANG
BAN
Get down!

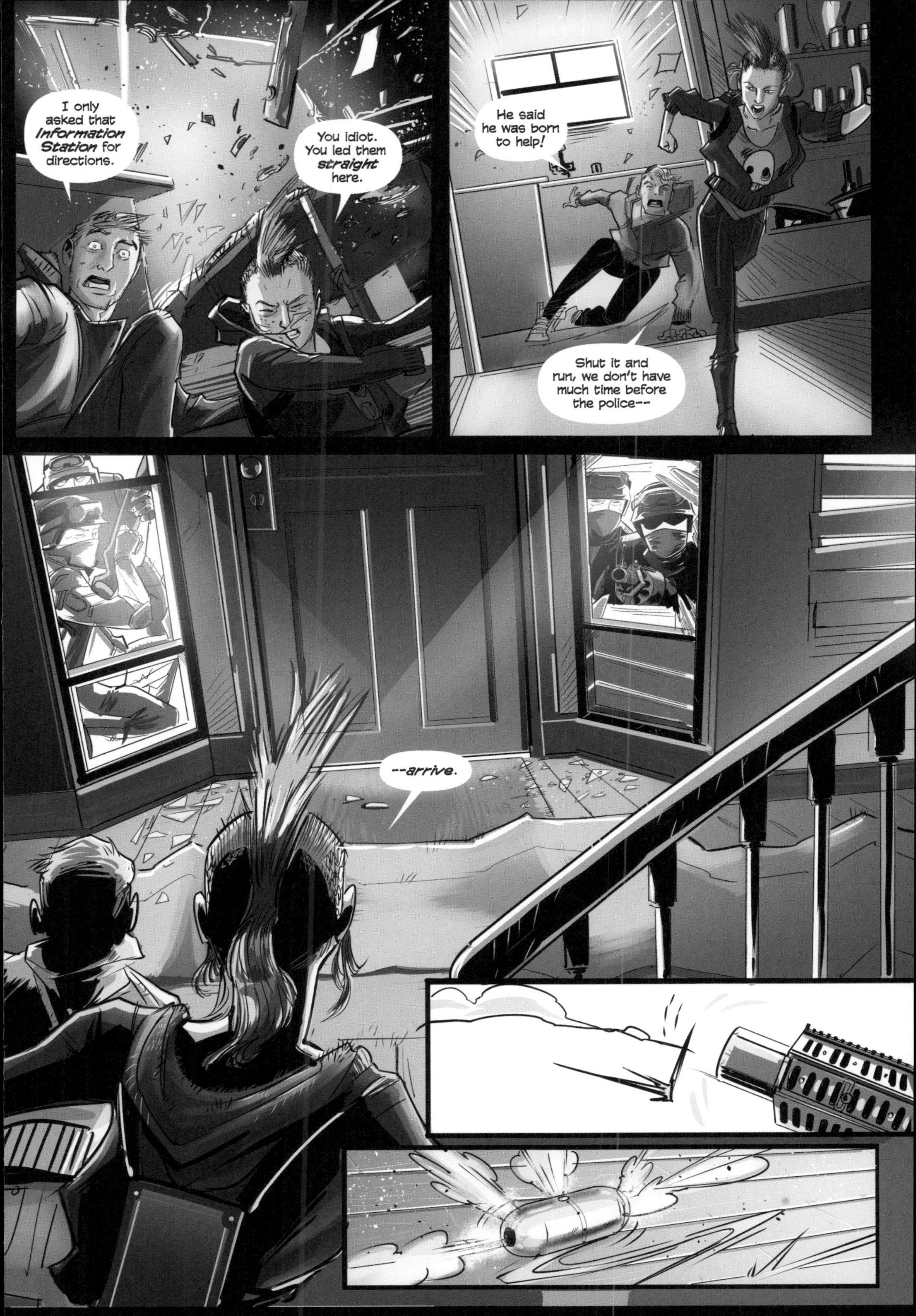
I only asked that *Information Station* for directions.
You idiot. You led them *straight* here.
He said he was born to help!
Shut it and run, we don't have much time before the police--
--*arrive*.

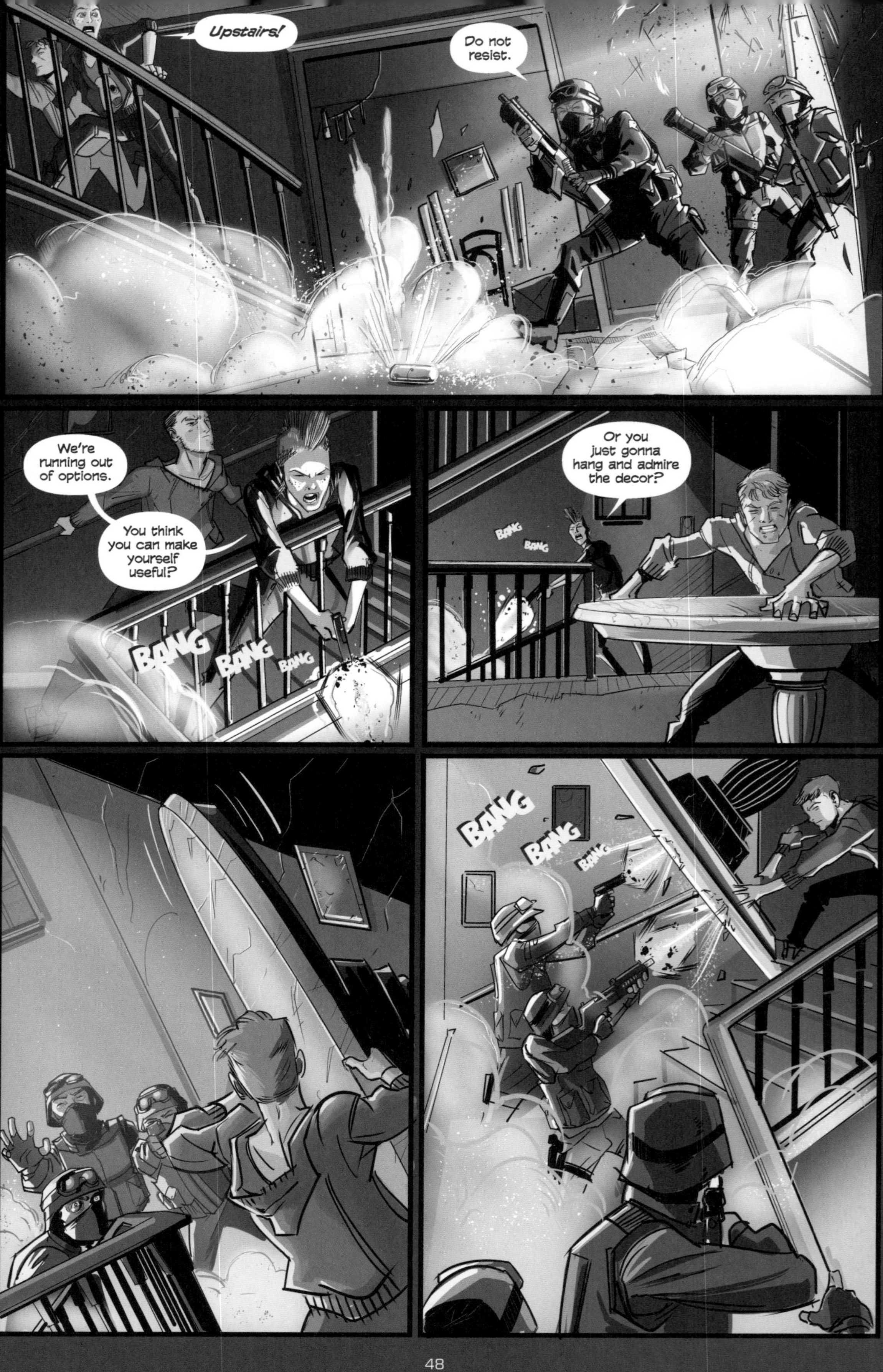
Upstairs!
Do not resist.
We're running out of options.
You think you can make yourself useful?
BANG
BANG
BANG
Or you just gonna hang and admire the decor?
BANG
BANG
BANG
BANG
BANG

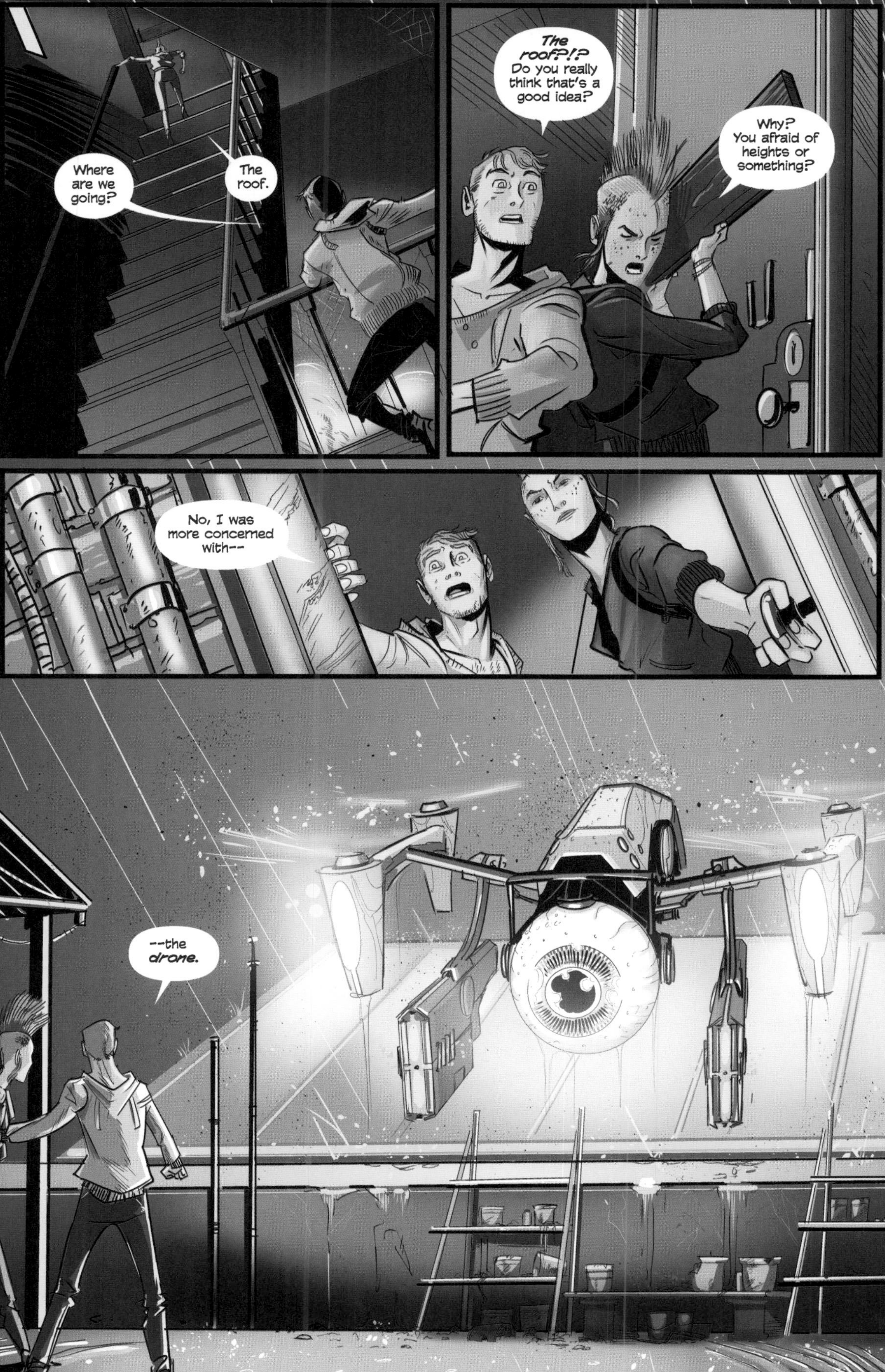
Where are we going?
The roof.
The roof?!? Do you really think that's a good idea?
Why? You afraid of heights or something?
No, I was more concerned with--
--the drone.

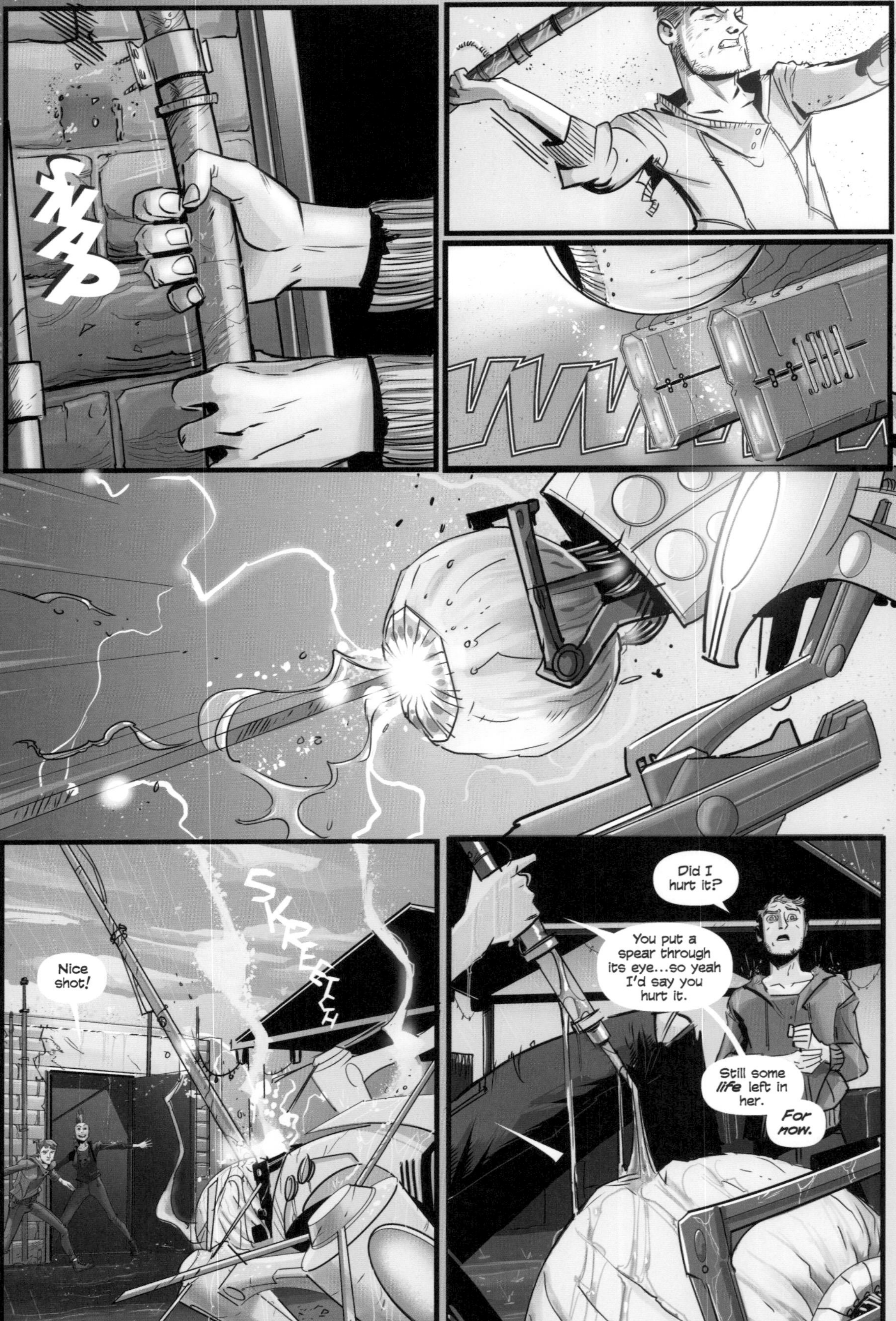
SNAP
VWWM
Nice shot!
SKREEECH
Did I hurt it?
You put a spear through its eye...so yeah I'd say you hurt it.
Still some *life* left in her.
For now.

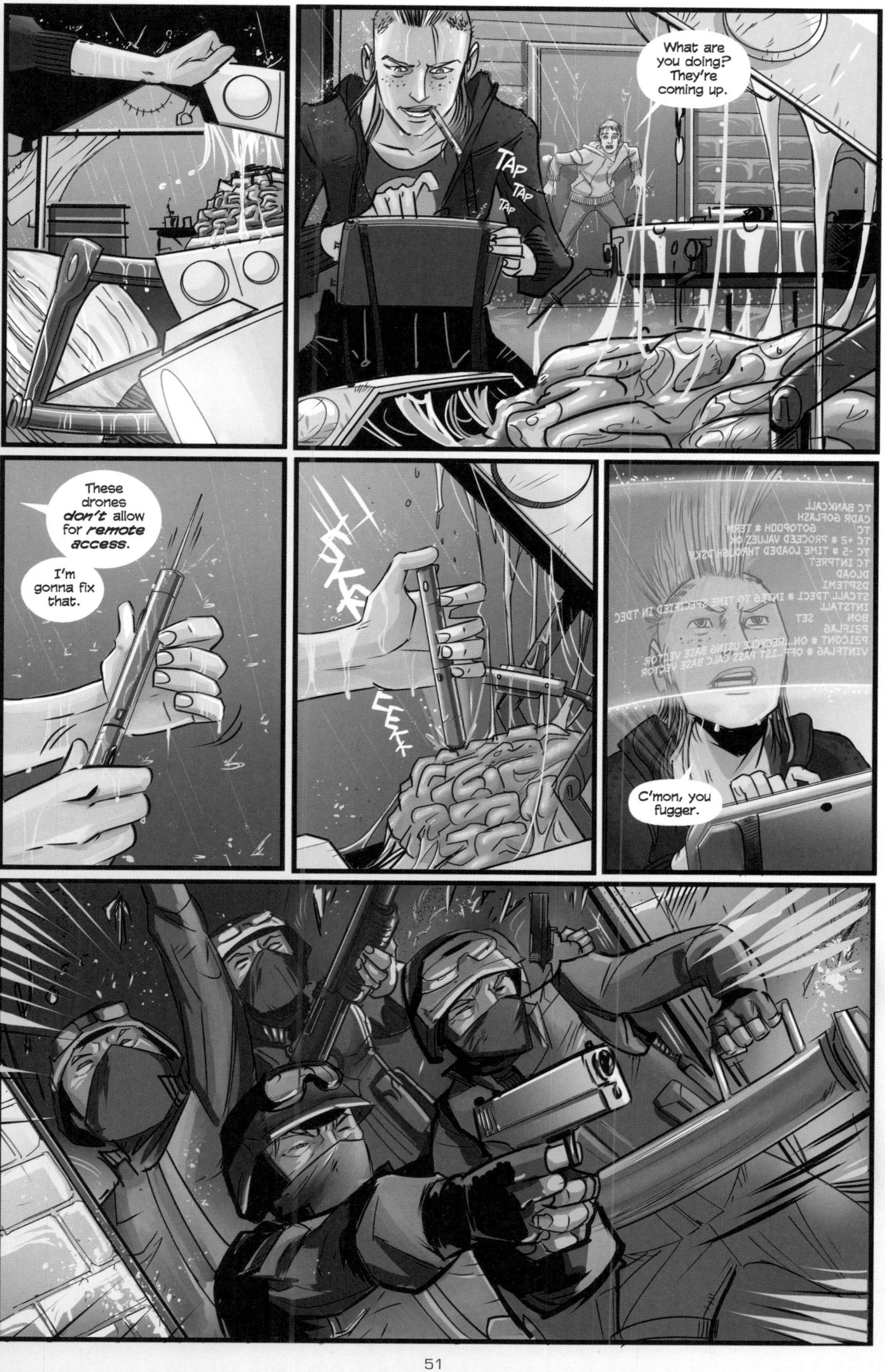

What are you doing? They're coming up.
TAP
TAP
TAP
These drones *don't* allow for *remote access*.
I'm gonna fix that.
C'mon, you fugger.

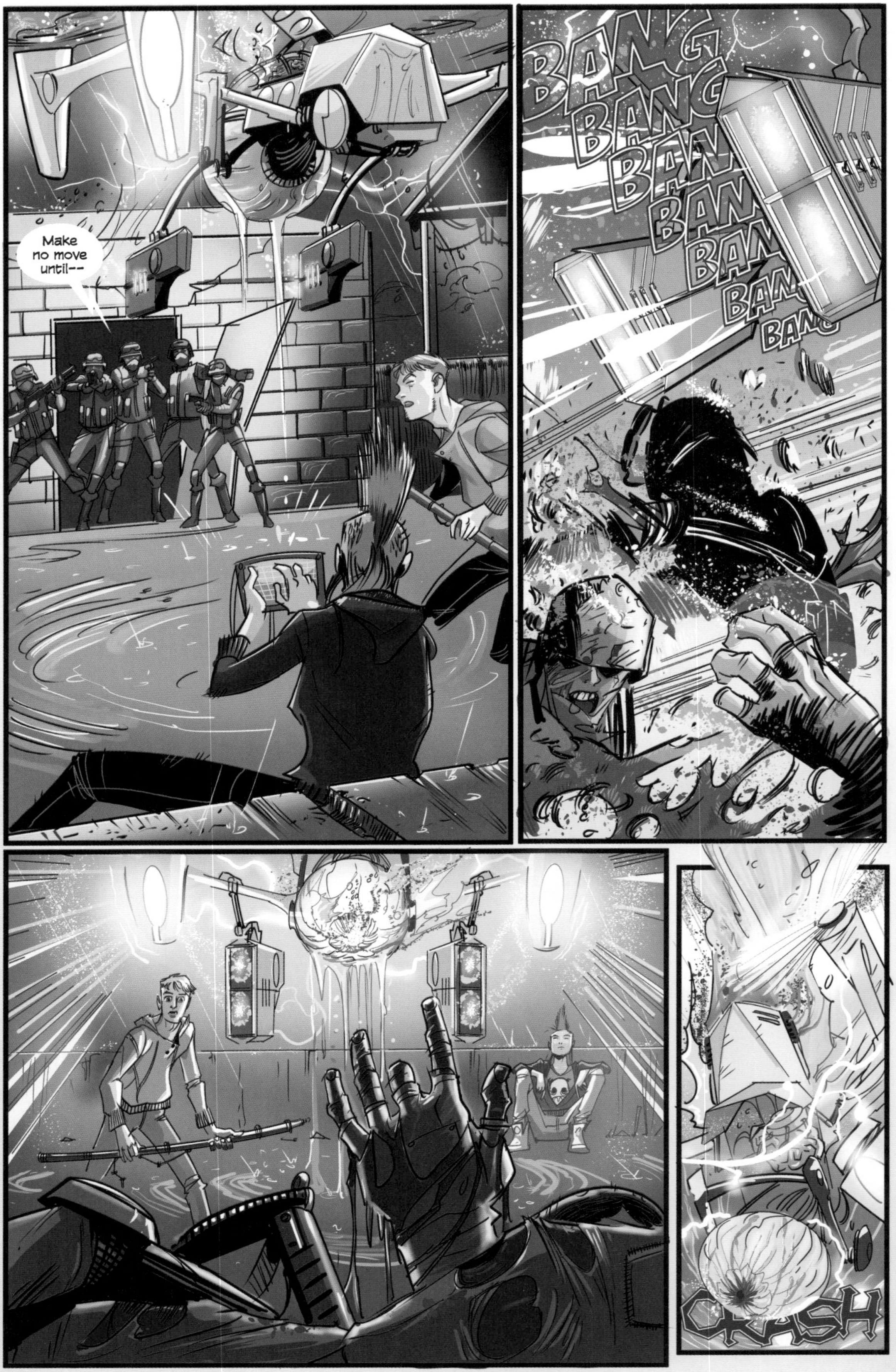
Make no move until--
BANG
BANG
BANG
BANG
BANG
BANG
BANG
BANG
CRASH

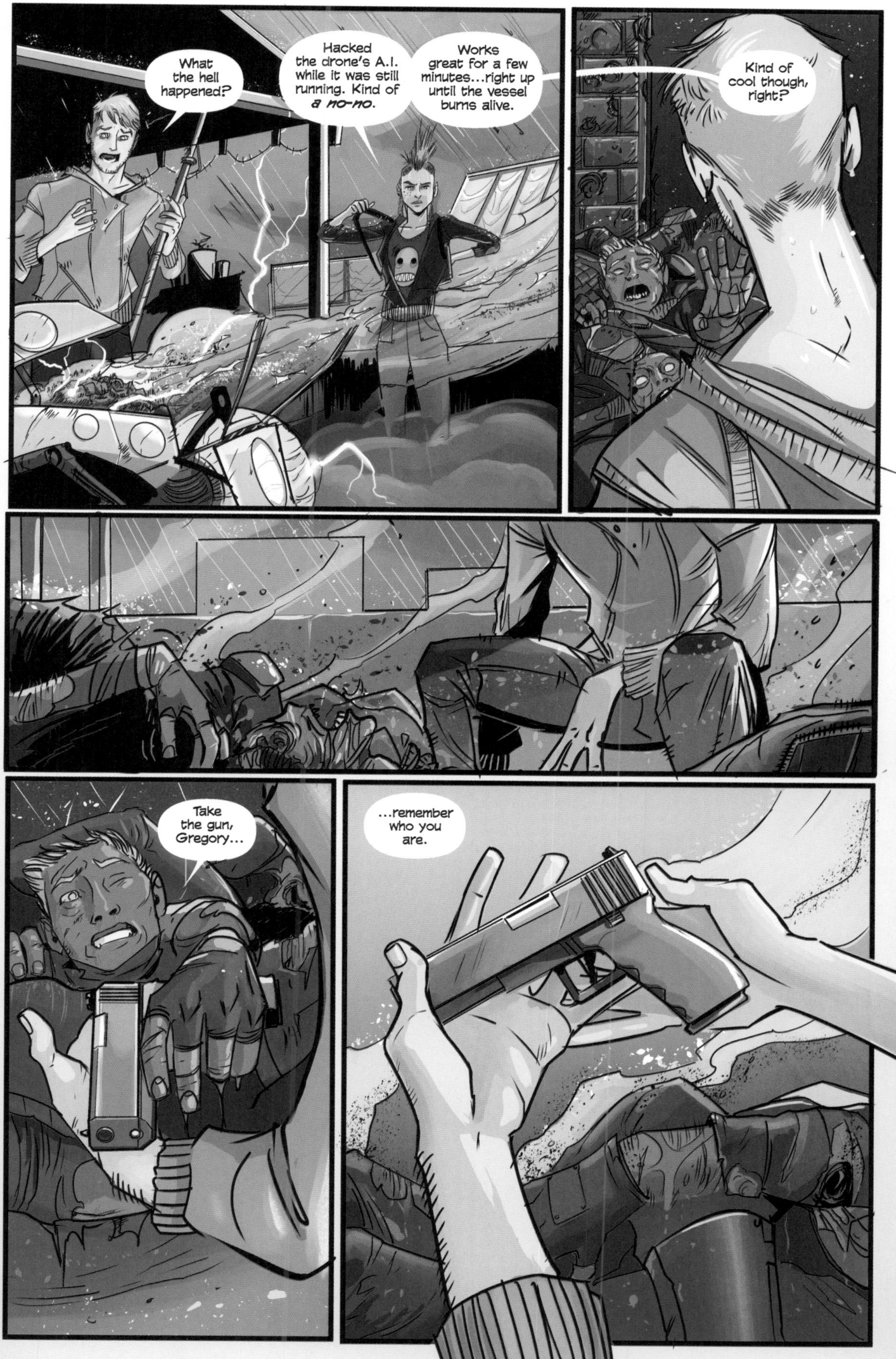
What the hell happened?
Hacked the drone's A.I. while it was still running. Kind of *a no-no*.
Works great for a few minutes...right up until the vessel burns alive.
Kind of cool though, right?
Take the gun, Gregory...
...remember who you are.

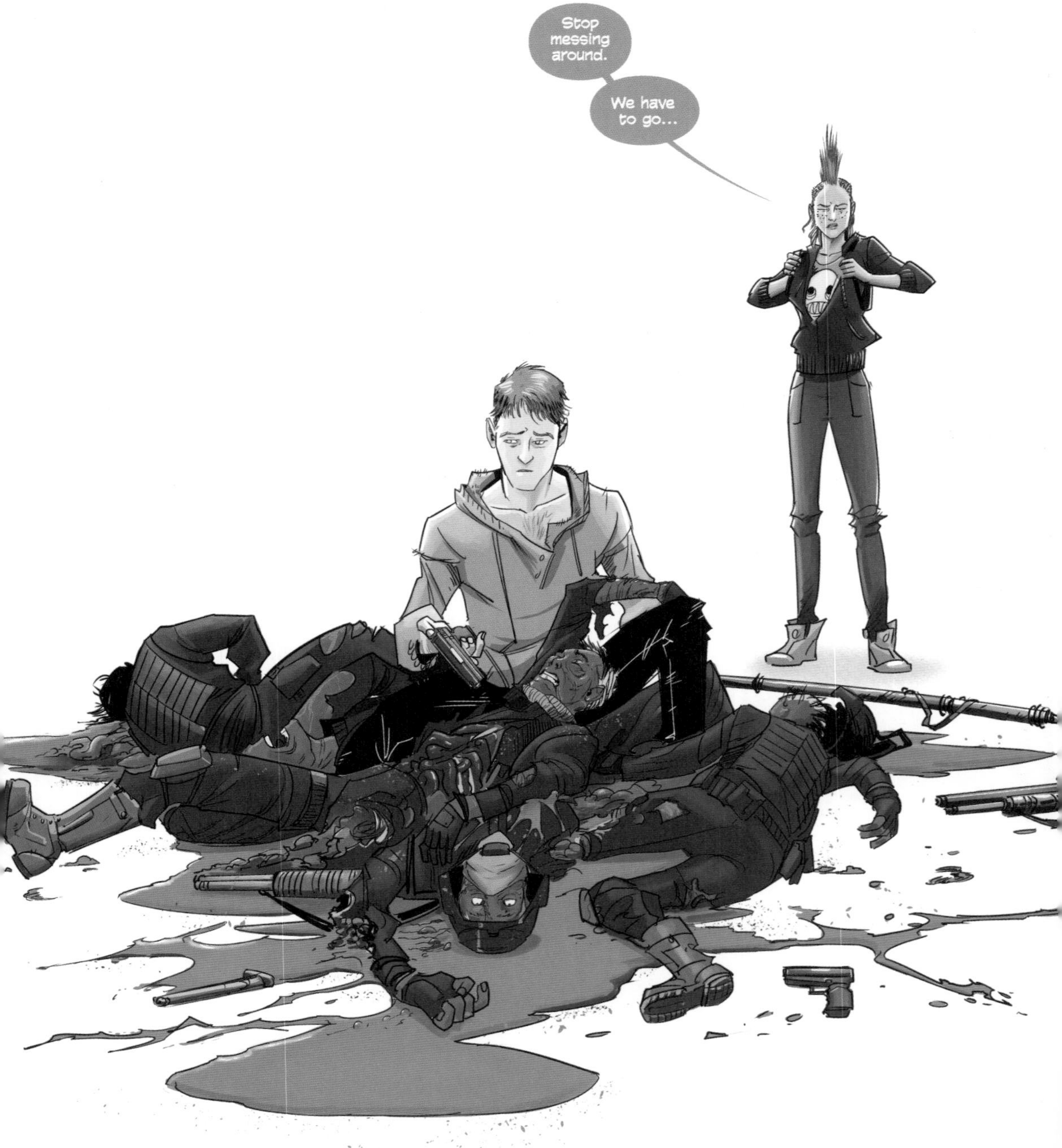
Stop messing around.
We have to go...

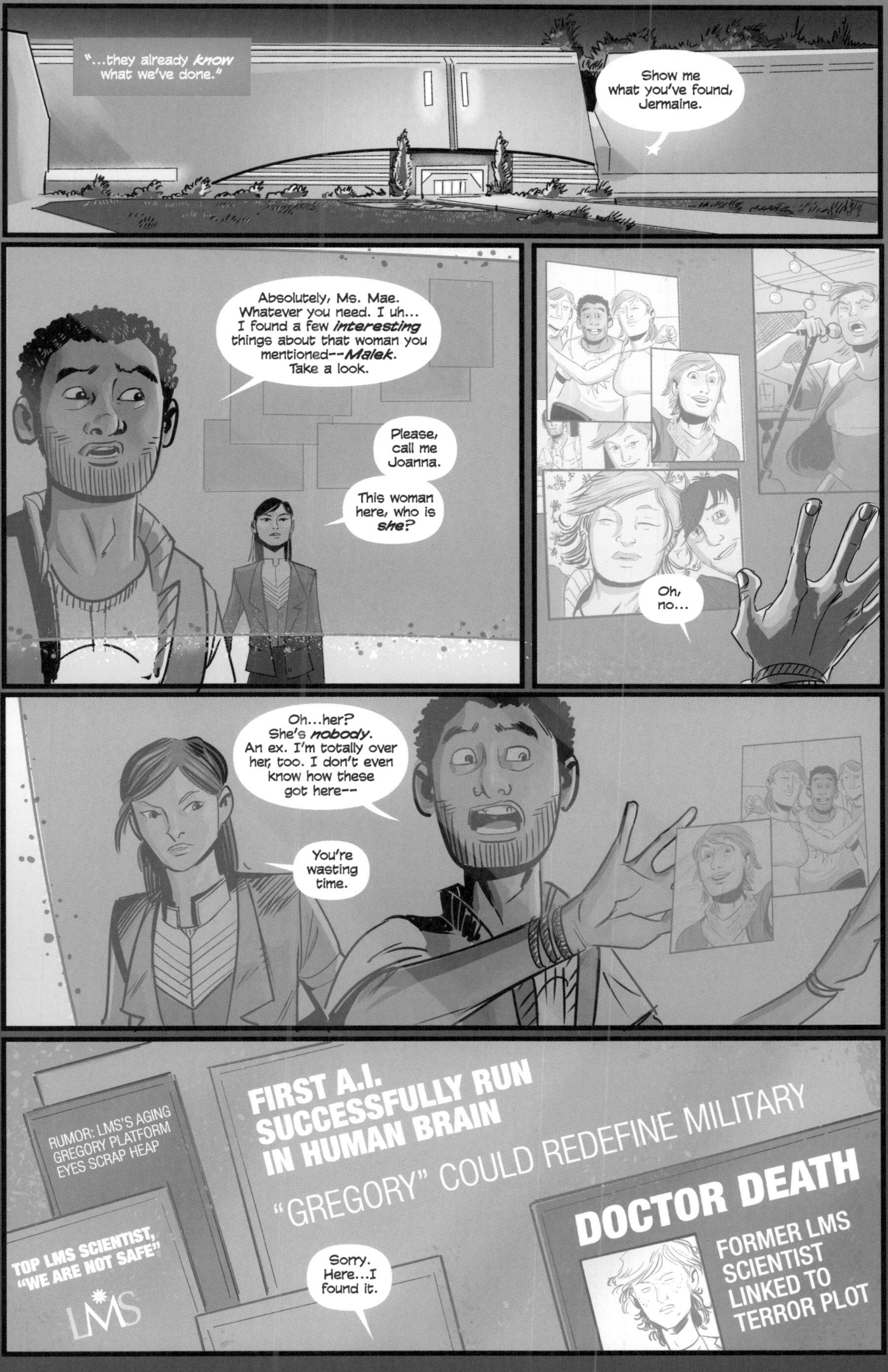
"...they already *know* what we've done."
Show me what you've found, Jermaine.
Absolutely, Ms. Mae. Whatever you need. I uh... I found a few *interesting* things about that woman you mentioned--*Malek*. Take a look.
Please, call me Joanna.
This woman here, who is *she?*
Oh, no...
Oh...her? She's *nobody*. An ex. I'm totally over her, too. I don't even know how these got here--
You're wasting time.
RUMOR: LMS'S AGING GREGORY PLATFORM EYES SCRAP HEAP
FIRST A.I. SUCCESSFULLY RUN IN HUMAN BRAIN
"GREGORY" COULD REDEFINE MILITARY
TOP LMS SCIENTIST, "WE ARE NOT SAFE"
LMS
DOCTOR DEATH
FORMER LMS SCIENTIST LINKED TO TERROR PLOT
Sorry. Here...I found it.

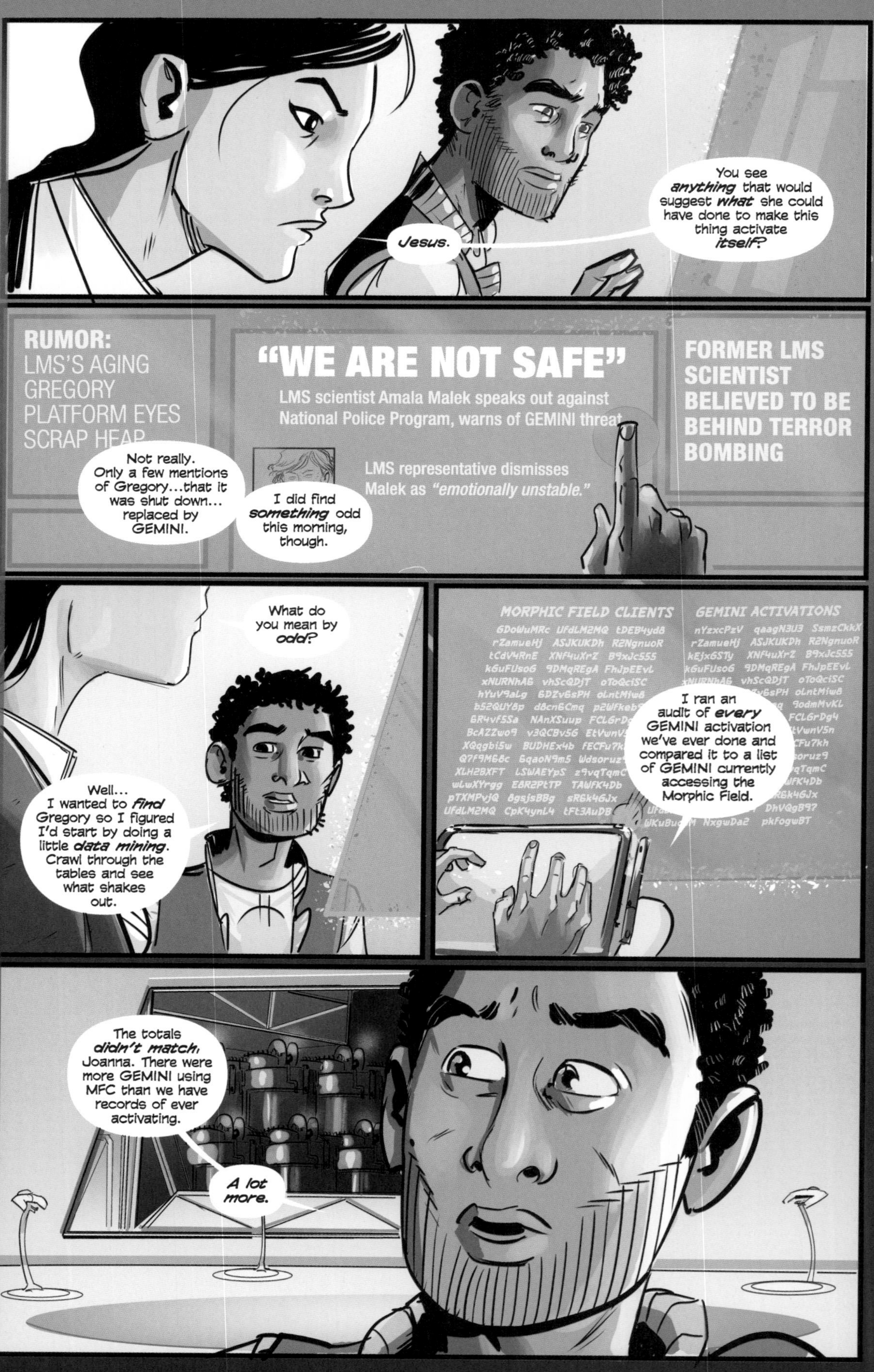
You see *anything* that would suggest *what* she could have done to make this thing activate *itself?*
Jesus.
RUMOR: LMS'S AGING GREGORY PLATFORM EYES SCRAP HEAP
"WE ARE NOT SAFE"
LMS scientist Amala Malek speaks out against National Police Program, warns of GEMINI threat
LMS representative dismisses Malek as *"emotionally unstable."*
FORMER LMS SCIENTIST BELIEVED TO BE BEHIND TERROR BOMBING
Not really. Only a few mentions of Gregory...that it was shut down... replaced by GEMINI.
I did find *something* odd this morning, though.
What do you mean by *odd?*
Well... I wanted to *find* Gregory so I figured I'd start by doing a little *data mining*. Crawl through the tables and see what shakes out.
MORPHIC FIELD CLIENTS
GEMINI ACTIVATIONS
I ran an audit of *every* GEMINI activation we've ever done and compared it to a list of GEMINI currently accessing the Morphic Field.
The totals *didn't match*, Joanna. There were more GEMINI using MFC than we have records of ever activating.
A lot more.

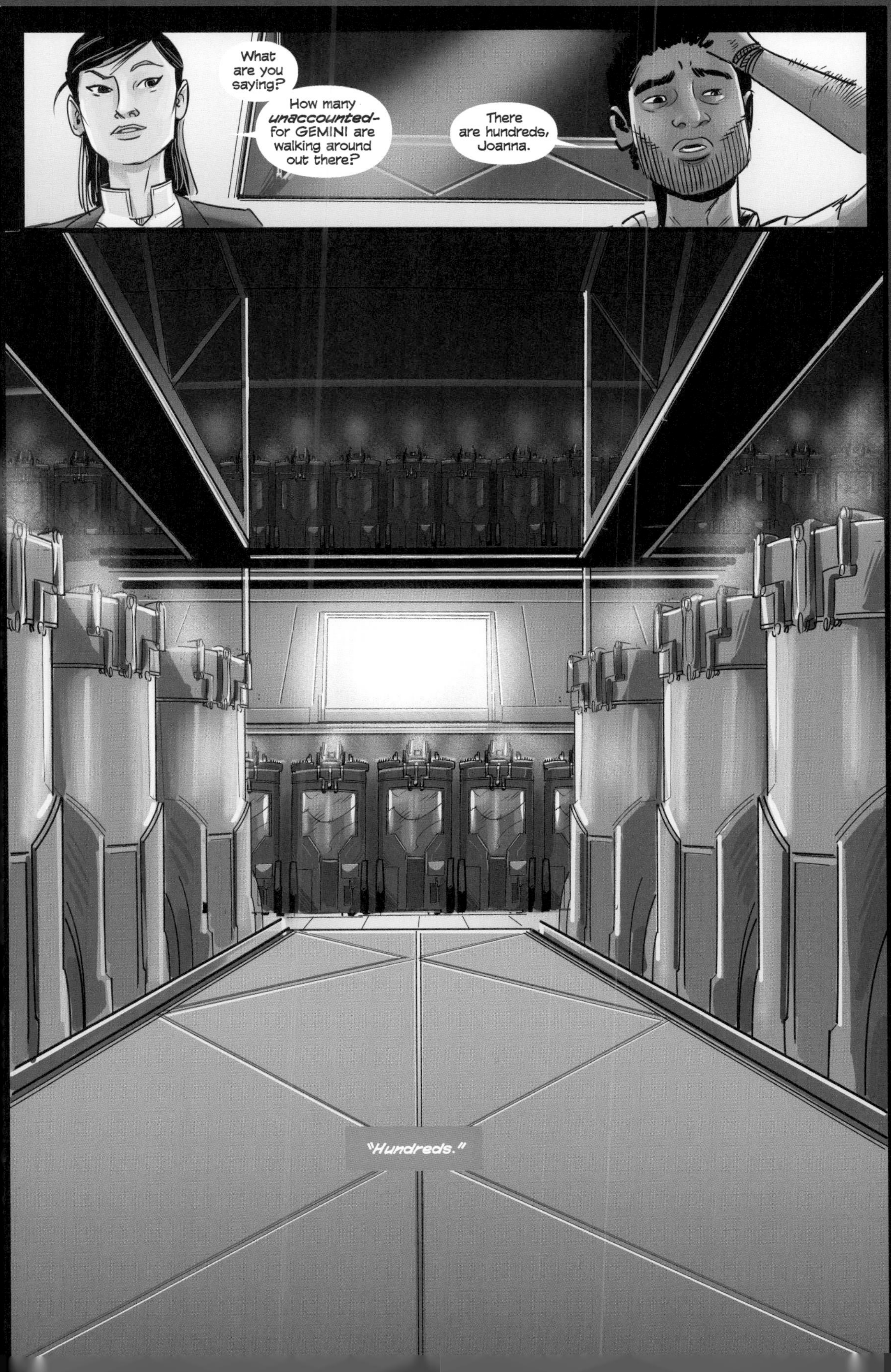
What are you saying?
How many *unaccounted-* for GEMINI are walking around out there?
There are hundreds, Joanna.
"Hundreds."

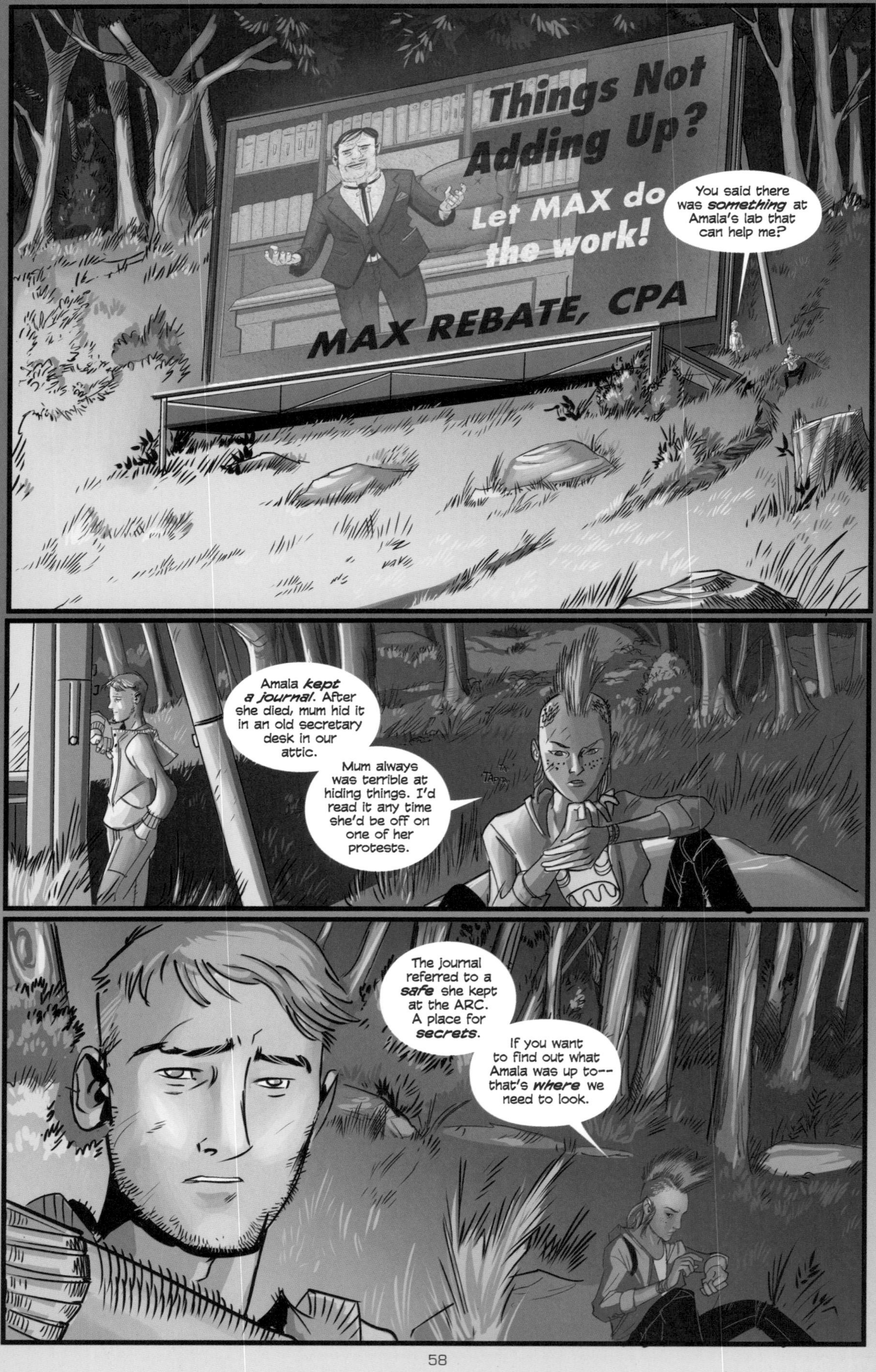
Things Not Adding Up?
Let MAX do the work!
MAX REBATE, CPA
You said there was *something* at Amala's lab that can help me?
Amala *kept a journal*. After she died, mum hid it in an old secretary desk in our attic.
Mum always was terrible at hiding things. I'd read it any time she'd be off on one of her protests.
The journal referred to a *safe* she kept at the ARC. A place for *secrets*.
If you want to find out what Amala was up to-- that's *where* we need to look.

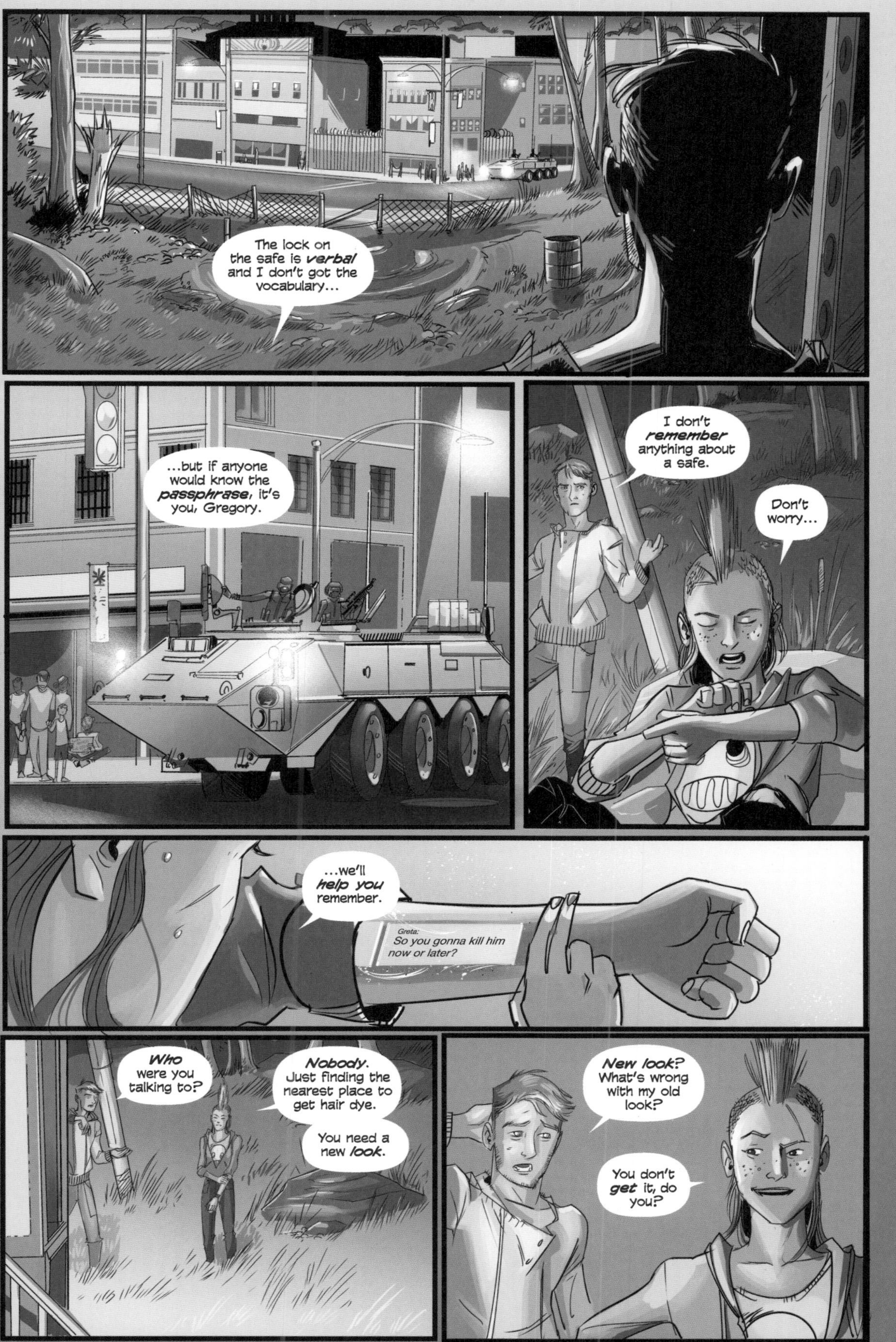
The lock on the safe is *verbal* and I don't got the vocabulary...
...but if anyone would know the *passphrase*, it's you, Gregory.
I don't *remember* anything about a safe.
Don't worry...
...we'll *help you* remember.
Greta:
So you gonna kill him now or later?
Who were you talking to?
Nobody. Just finding the nearest place to get hair dye.
You need a new *look*.
New look? What's wrong with my old look?
You don't *get* it, do you?

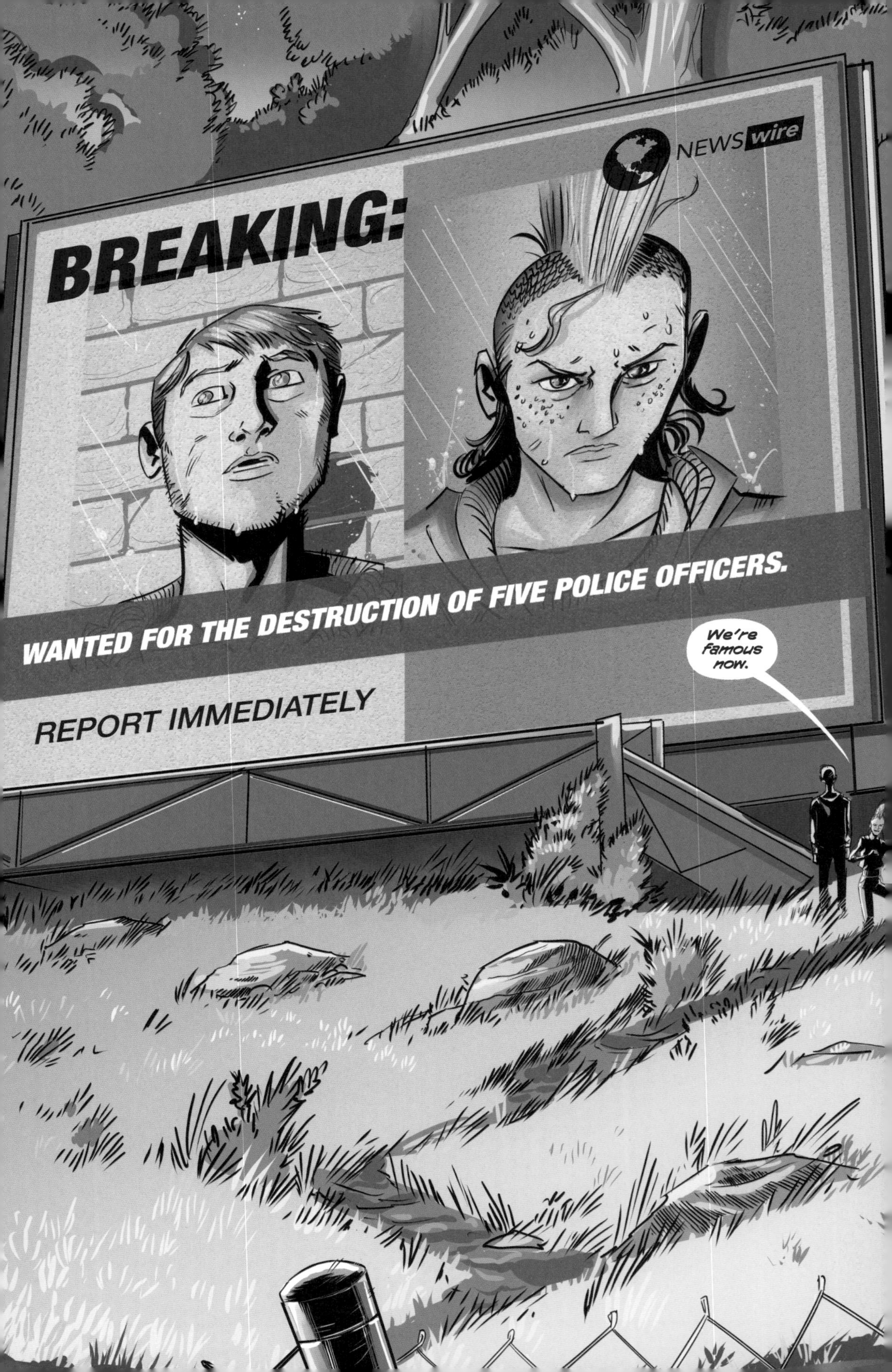
NEWS wire
BREAKING:
WANTED FOR THE DESTRUCTION OF FIVE POLICE OFFICERS.
REPORT IMMEDIATELY
We're famous now.

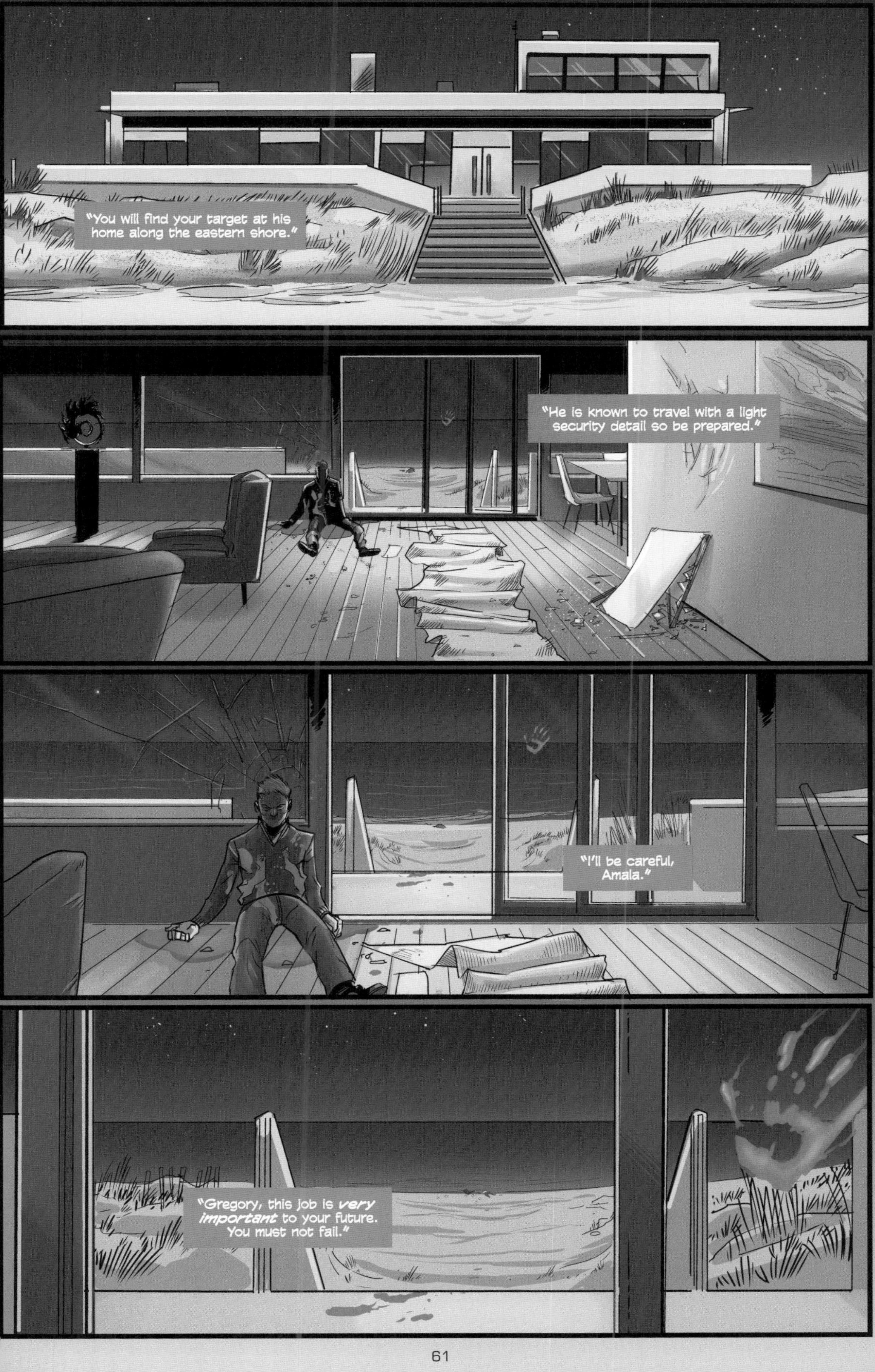
"You will find your target at his home along the eastern shore."
"He is known to travel with a light security detail so be prepared."
"I'll be careful, Amala."
"Gregory, this job is *very important* to your future. You must not fail."

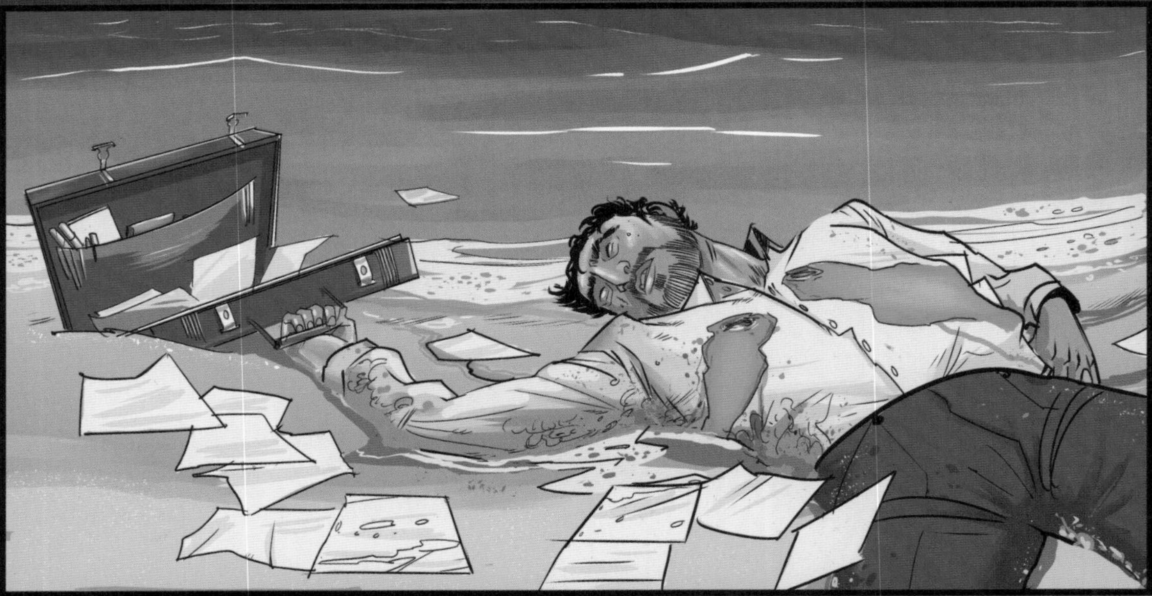

GREGORY
27

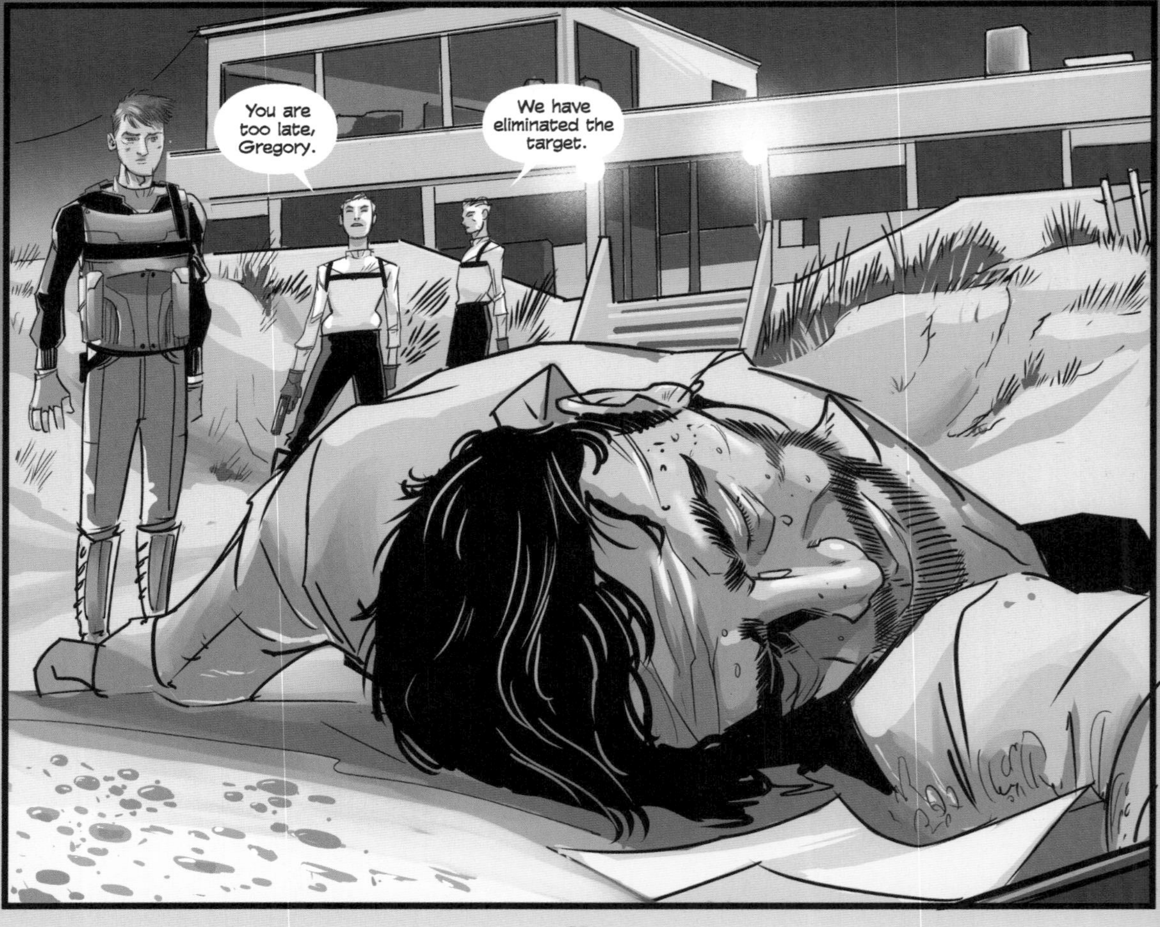
You are too late, Gregory.
We have eliminated the target.

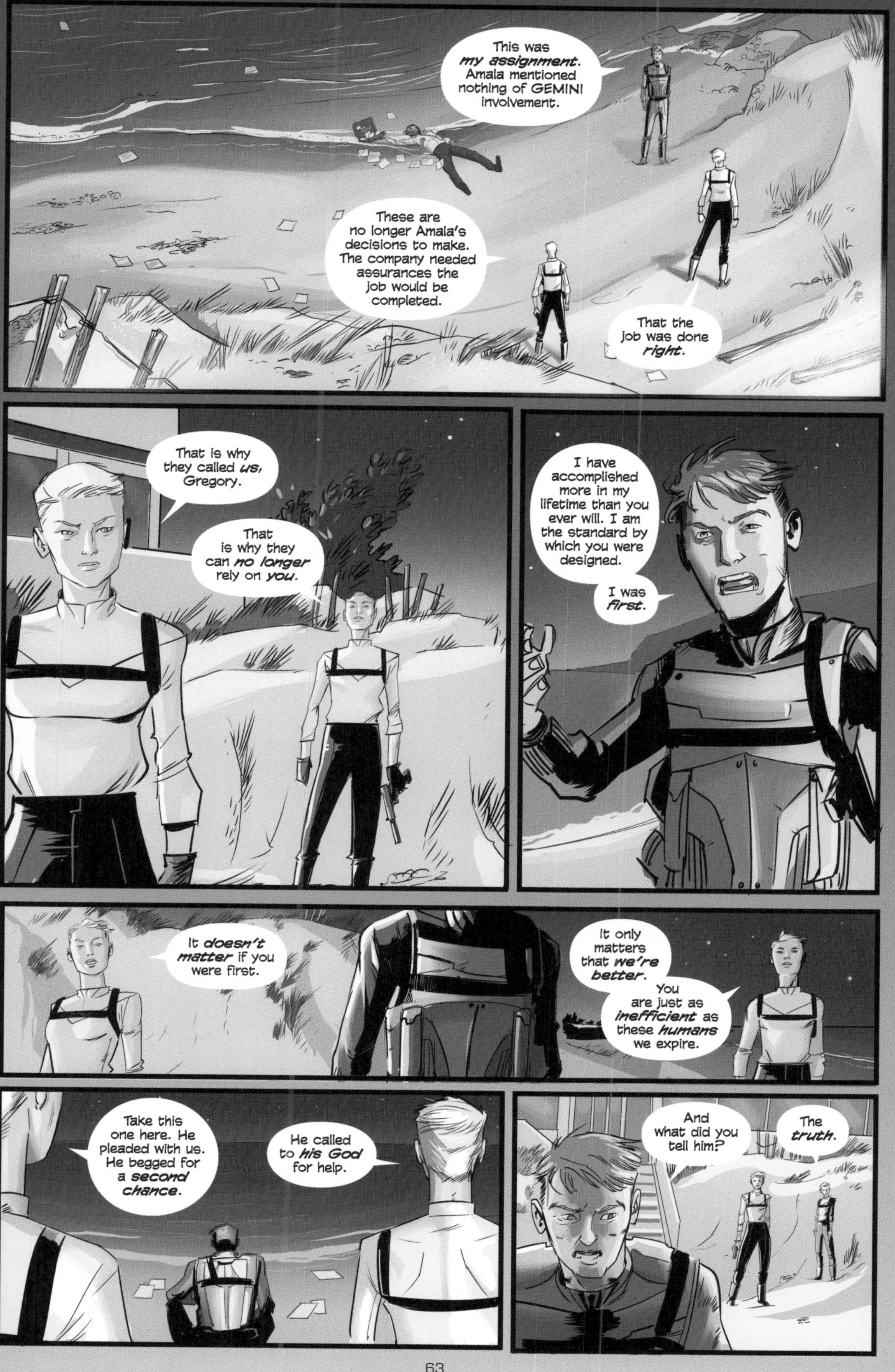
This was my assignment. Amala mentioned nothing of GEMINI involvement.
These are no longer Amala's decisions to make. The company needed assurances the job would be completed.
That the job was done right.
That is why they called us, Gregory.
That is why they can no longer rely on you.
I have accomplished more in my lifetime than you ever will. I am the standard by which you were designed.
I was first.
It doesn't matter if you were first.
It only matters that we're better.
You are just as inefficient as these humans we expire.
Take this one here. He pleaded with us. He begged for a second chance.
He called to his God for help.
And what did you tell him?
The truth.

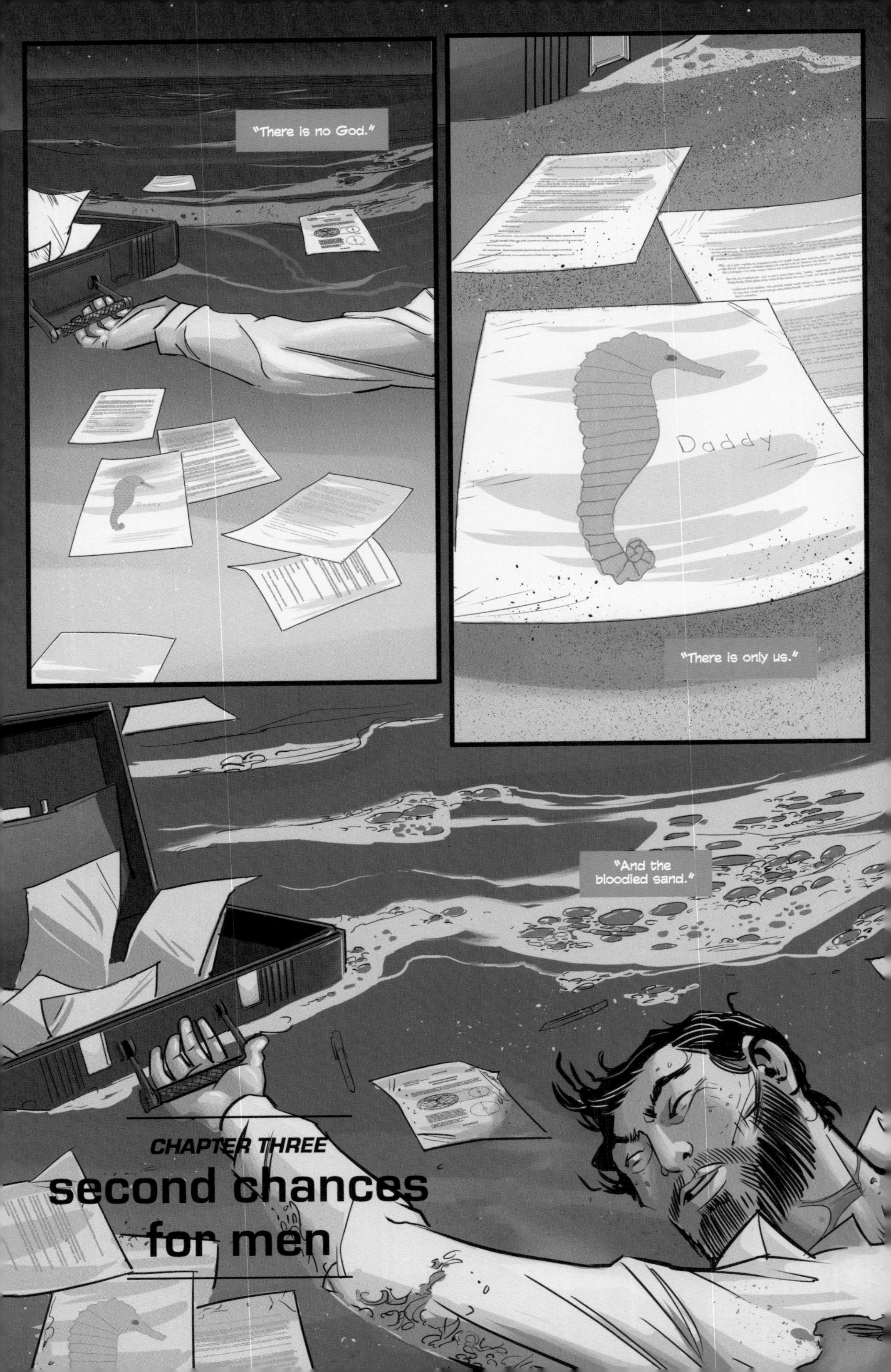
"There is no God."
"There is only us."
Daddy
"And the bloodied sand."
CHAPTER THREE
second chances for men

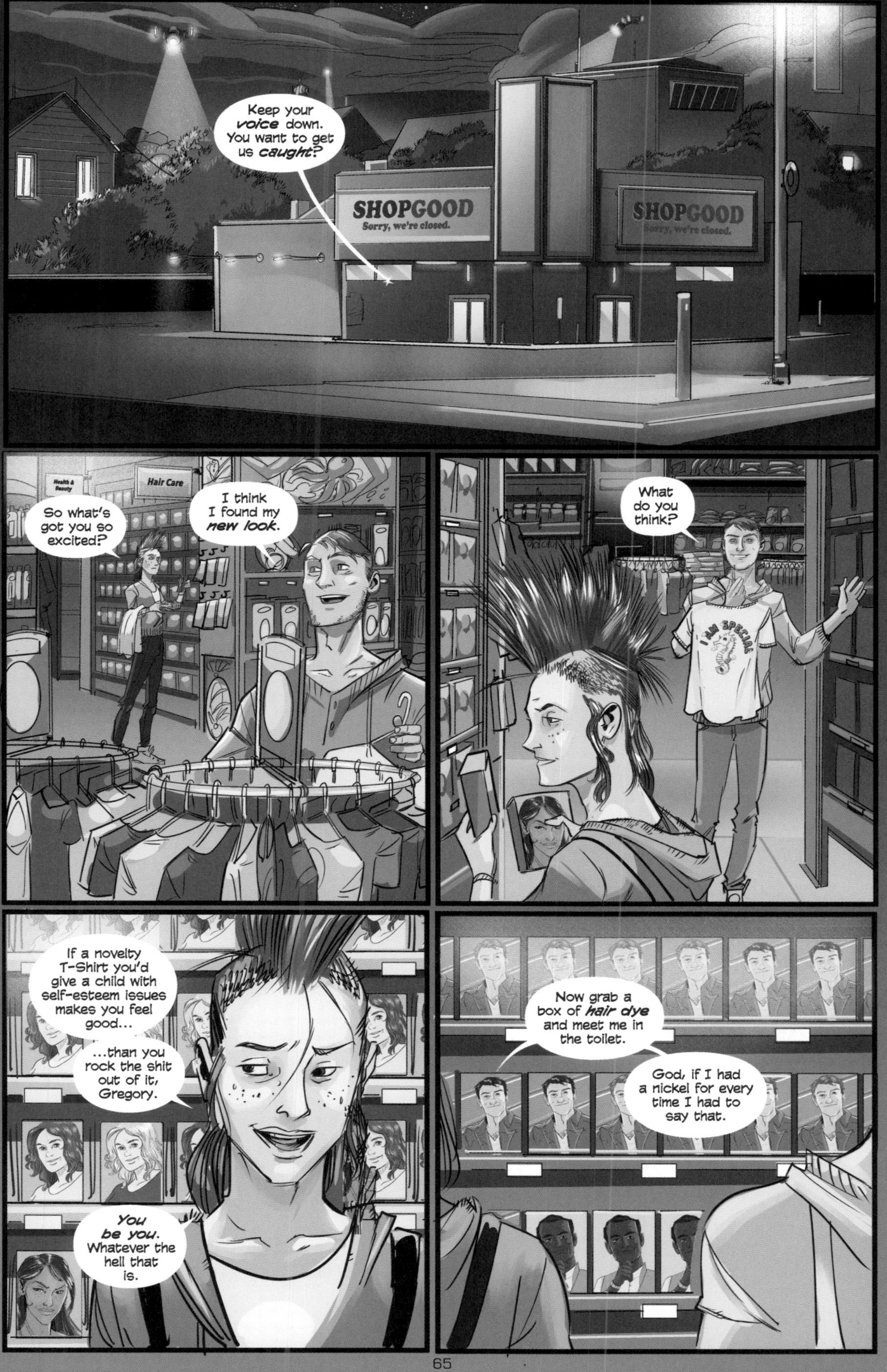
Keep your voice down. You want to get us caught?
SHOPGOOD
Sorry, we're closed.
SHOPGOOD
Sorry, we're closed.
Health & Beauty
Hair Care
So what's got you so excited?
I think I found my new look.
What do you think?
I AM SPECIAL
If a novelty T-Shirt you'd give a child with self-esteem issues makes you feel good...
...than you rock the shit out of it, Gregory.
You be you. Whatever the hell that is.
Now grab a box of hair dye and meet me in the toilet.
God, if I had a nickel for every time I had to say that.

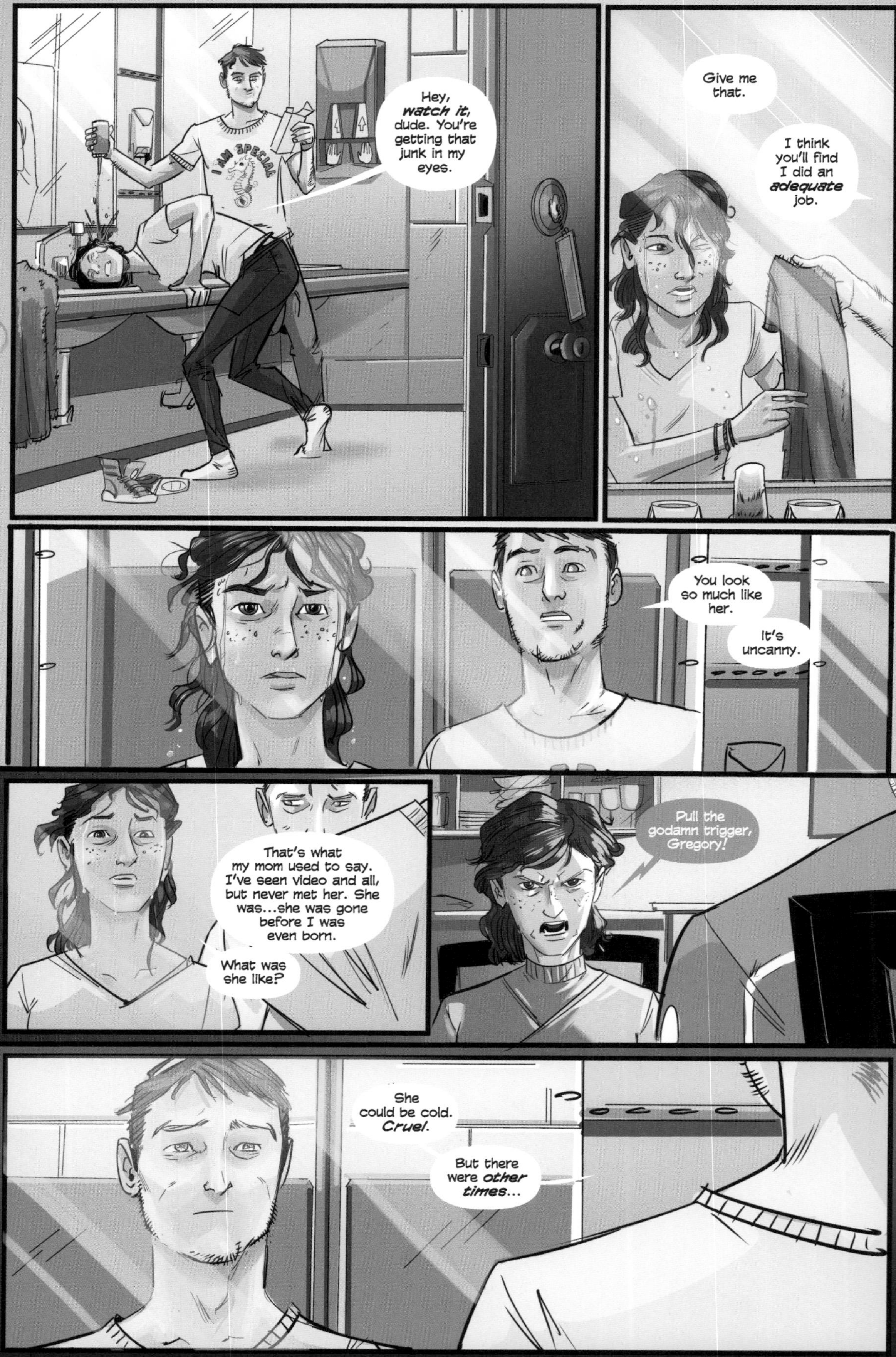

Hey, watch it, dude. You're getting that junk in my eyes.
I AM SPECIAL
Give me that.
I think you'll find I did an adequate job.
You look so much like her.
It's uncanny.
That's what my mom used to say. I've seen video and all, but never met her. She was...she was gone before I was even born.
What was she like?
Pull the godamn trigger, Gregory!
She could be cold. Cruel.
But there were other times...

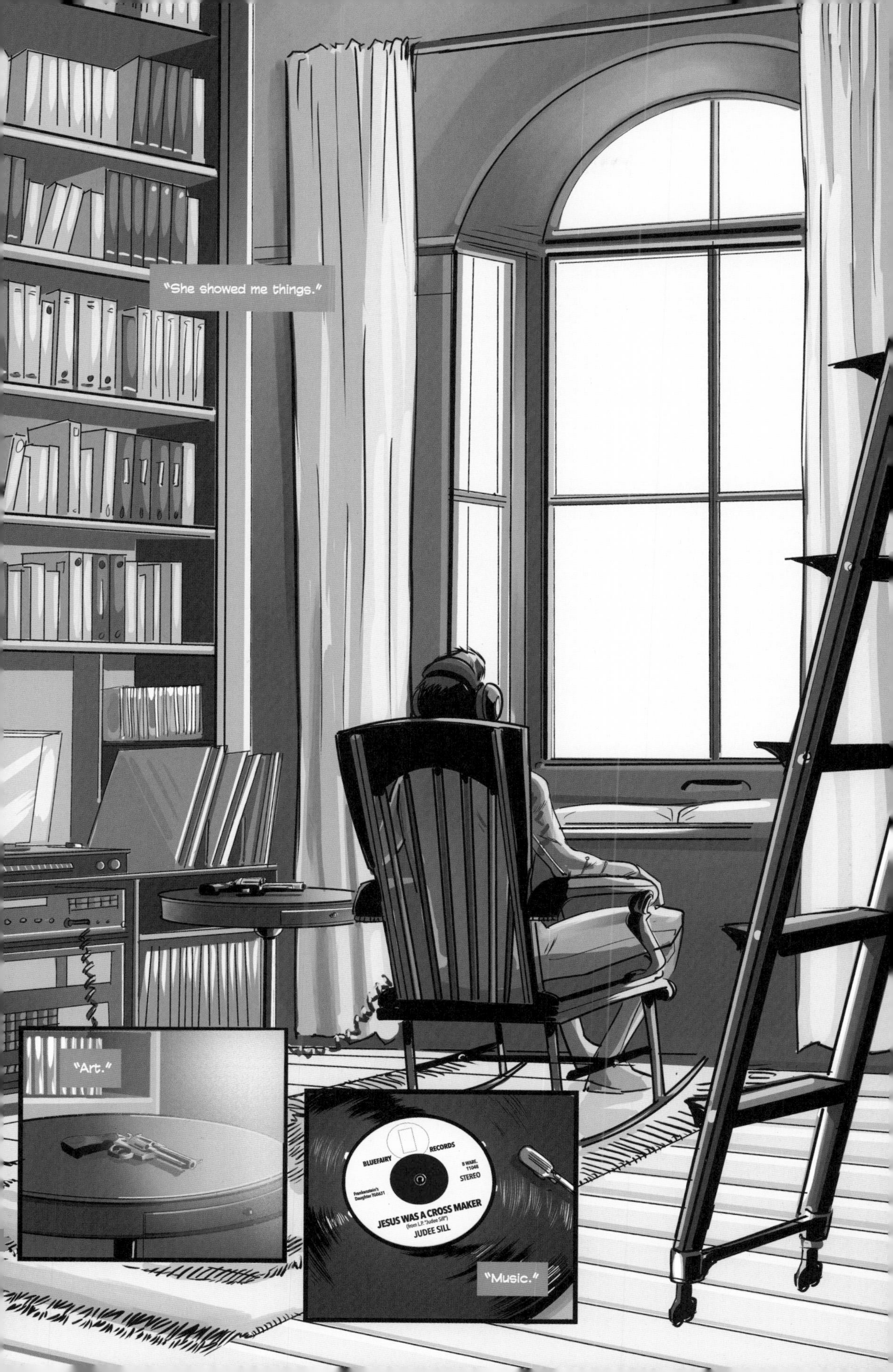
"She showed me things."
"Art."
BLUEFAIRY
RECORDS
B WARE. 11048
STEREO
Frankenstein's Daughter TG0631
JESUS WAS A CROSS MAKER
(from L.P. "Judee Sill")
JUDEE SILL
"Music."

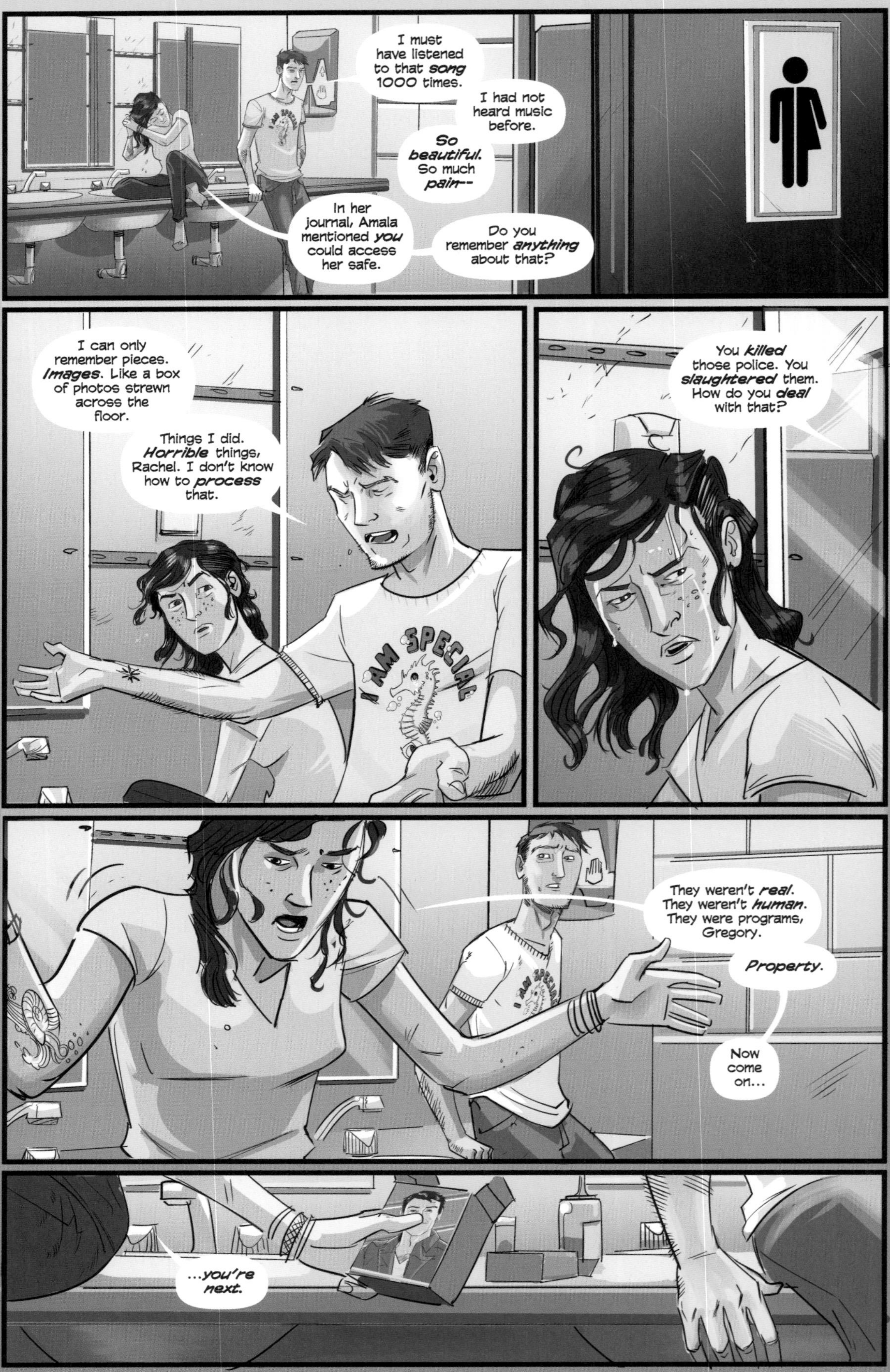
I must have listened to that *song* 1000 times.
I had not heard music before.
So beautiful. So much *pain--*
In her journal, Amala mentioned *you* could access her safe.
Do you remember *anything* about that?
I can only remember pieces. *Images*. Like a box of photos strewn across the floor.
Things I did. *Horrible* things, Rachel. I don't know how to *process* that.
I AM SPECIAL
You *killed* those police. You *slaughtered* them. How do you *deal* with that?
They weren't *real*. They weren't *human*. They were programs, Gregory.
Property.
Now come on...
...*you're next.*

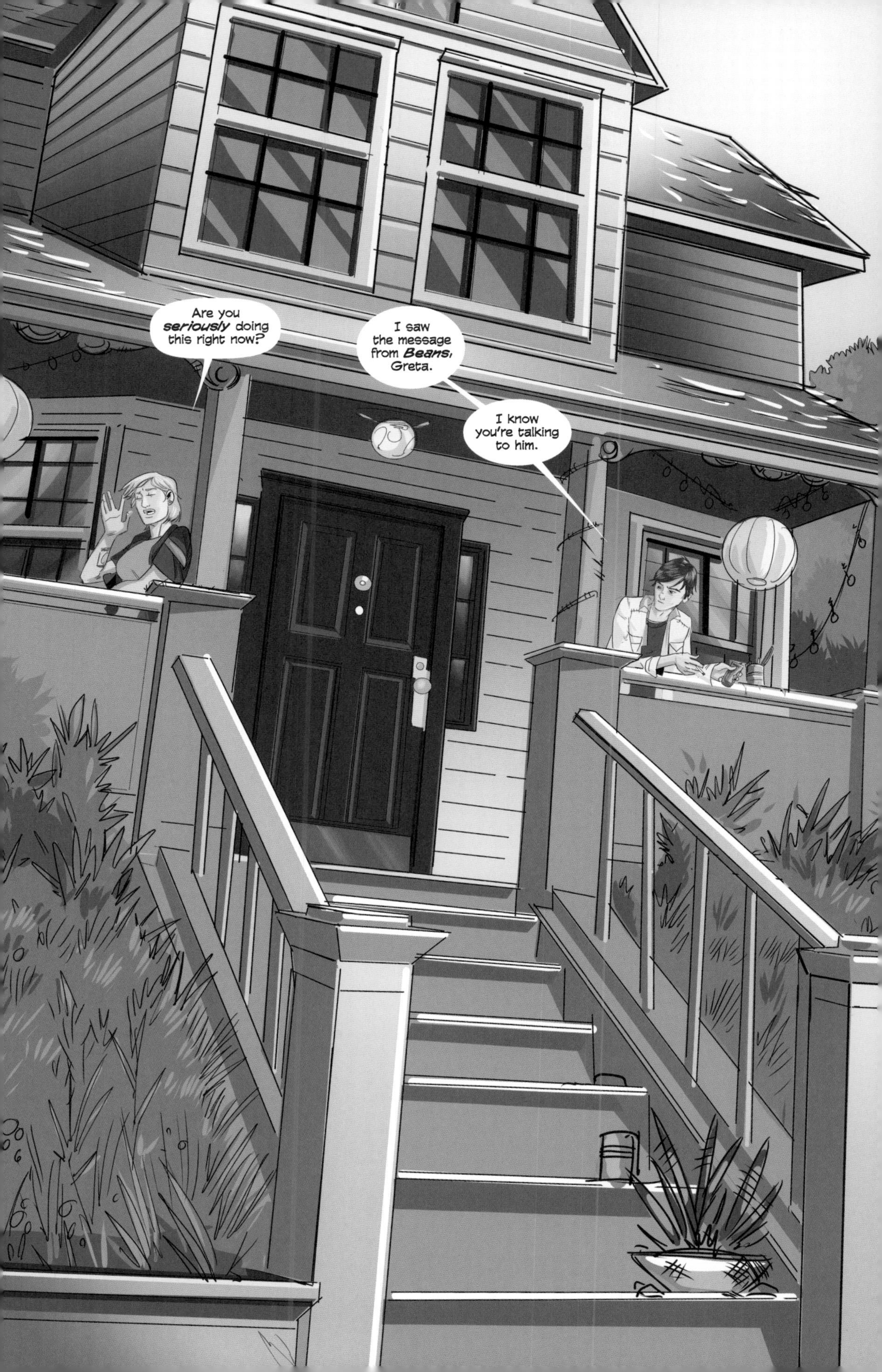
Are you *seriously* doing this right now?
I saw the message from *Beans*, Greta.
I know you're talking to him.

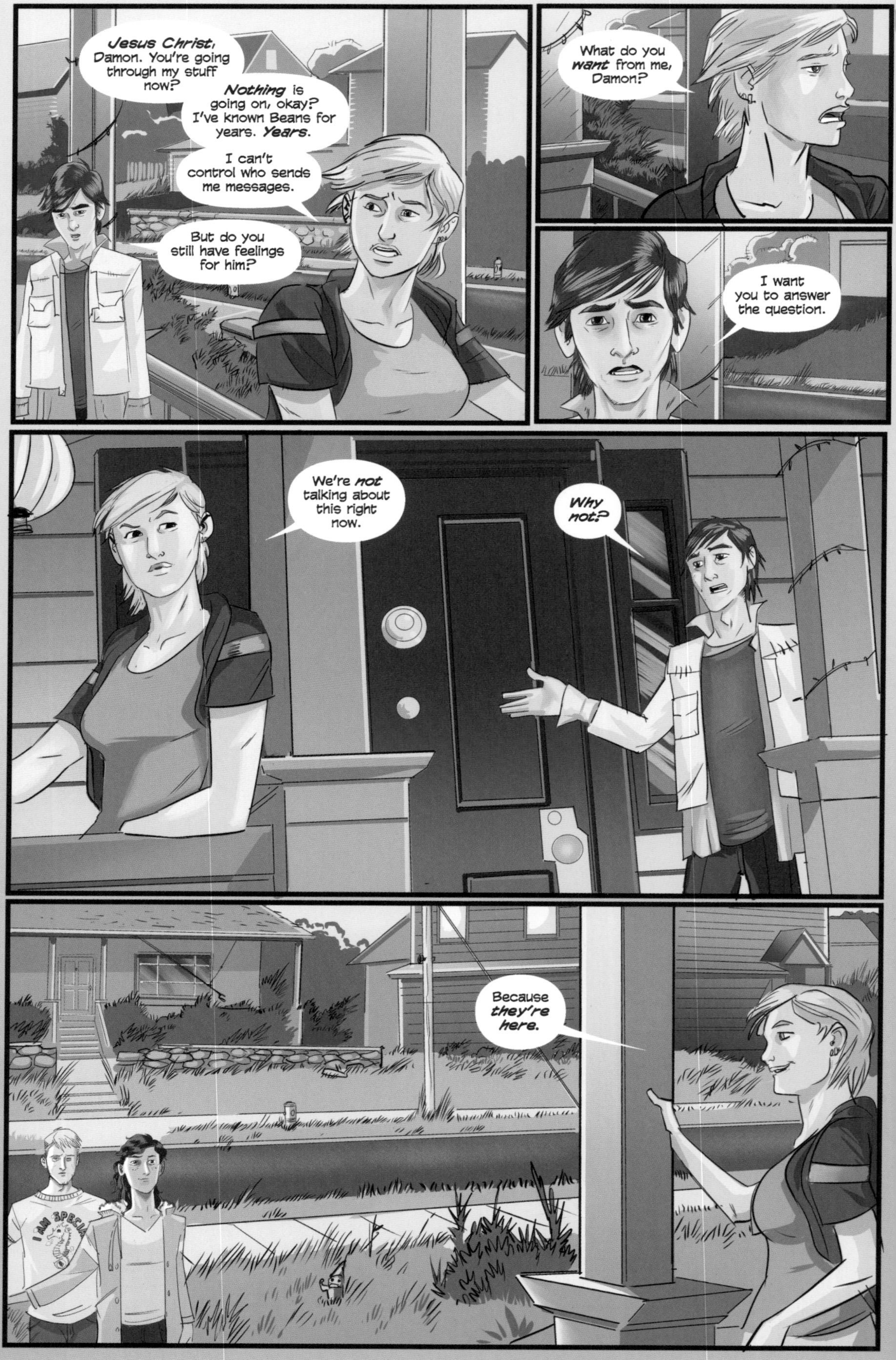

Jesus Christ, Damon. You're going through my stuff now?
Nothing is going on, okay? I've known Beans for years. Years.
I can't control who sends me messages.
But do you still have feelings for him?
What do you want from me, Damon?
I want you to answer the question.
We're not talking about this right now.
Why not?
Because they're here.
I AM SPECIA

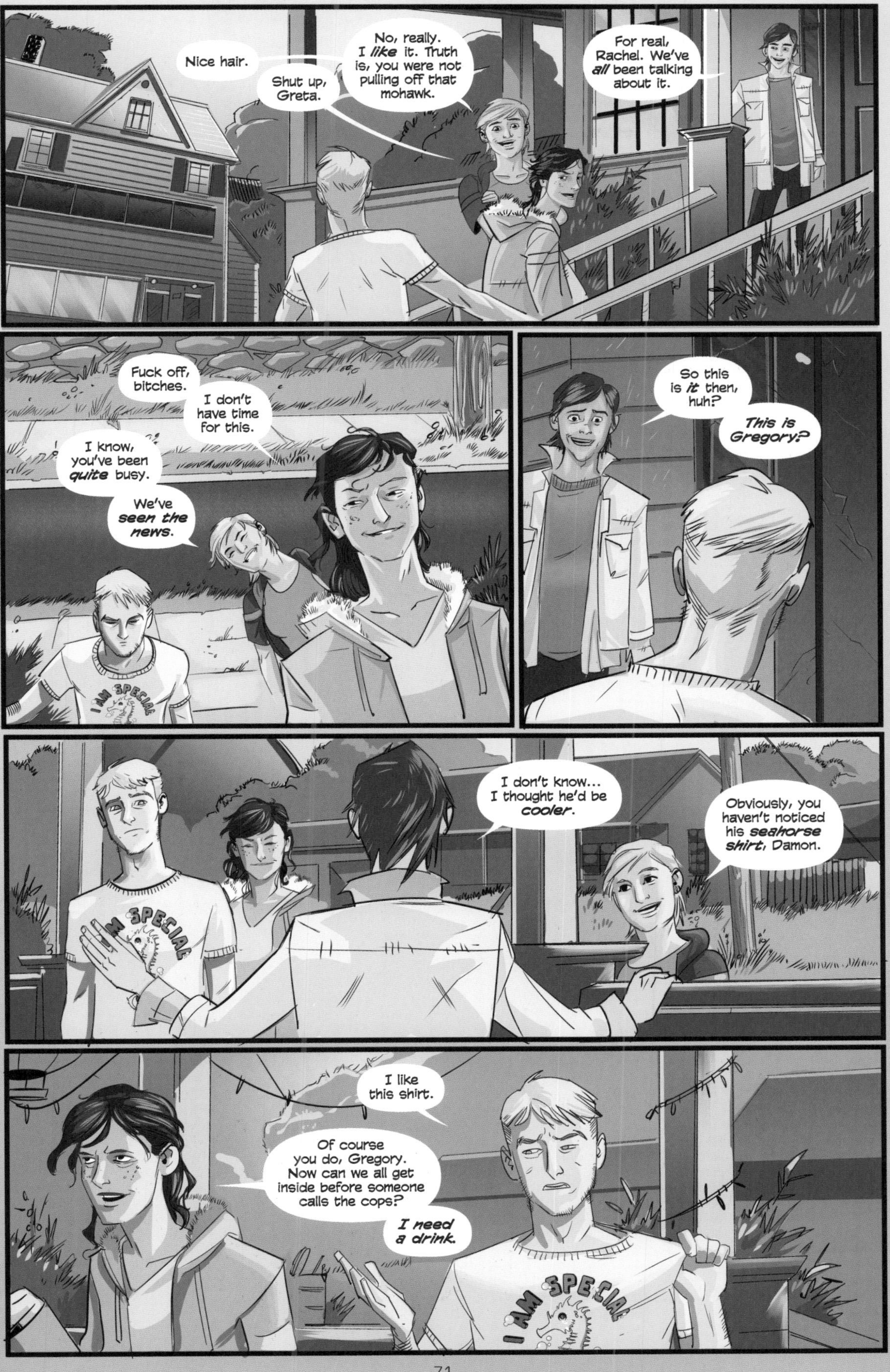
Nice hair.
Shut up, Greta.
No, really. I *like* it. Truth is, you were not pulling off that mohawk.
For real, Rachel. We've *all* been talking about it.
Fuck off, bitches.
I don't have time for this.
I know, you've been *quite* busy.
We've *seen the news*.
So this is *it* then, huh?
This is Gregory?
I AM SPECIAL
I don't know... I thought he'd be *cooler*.
Obviously, you haven't noticed his *seahorse shirt*, Damon.
I like this shirt.
Of course you do, Gregory. Now can we all get inside before someone calls the cops?
I need a drink.

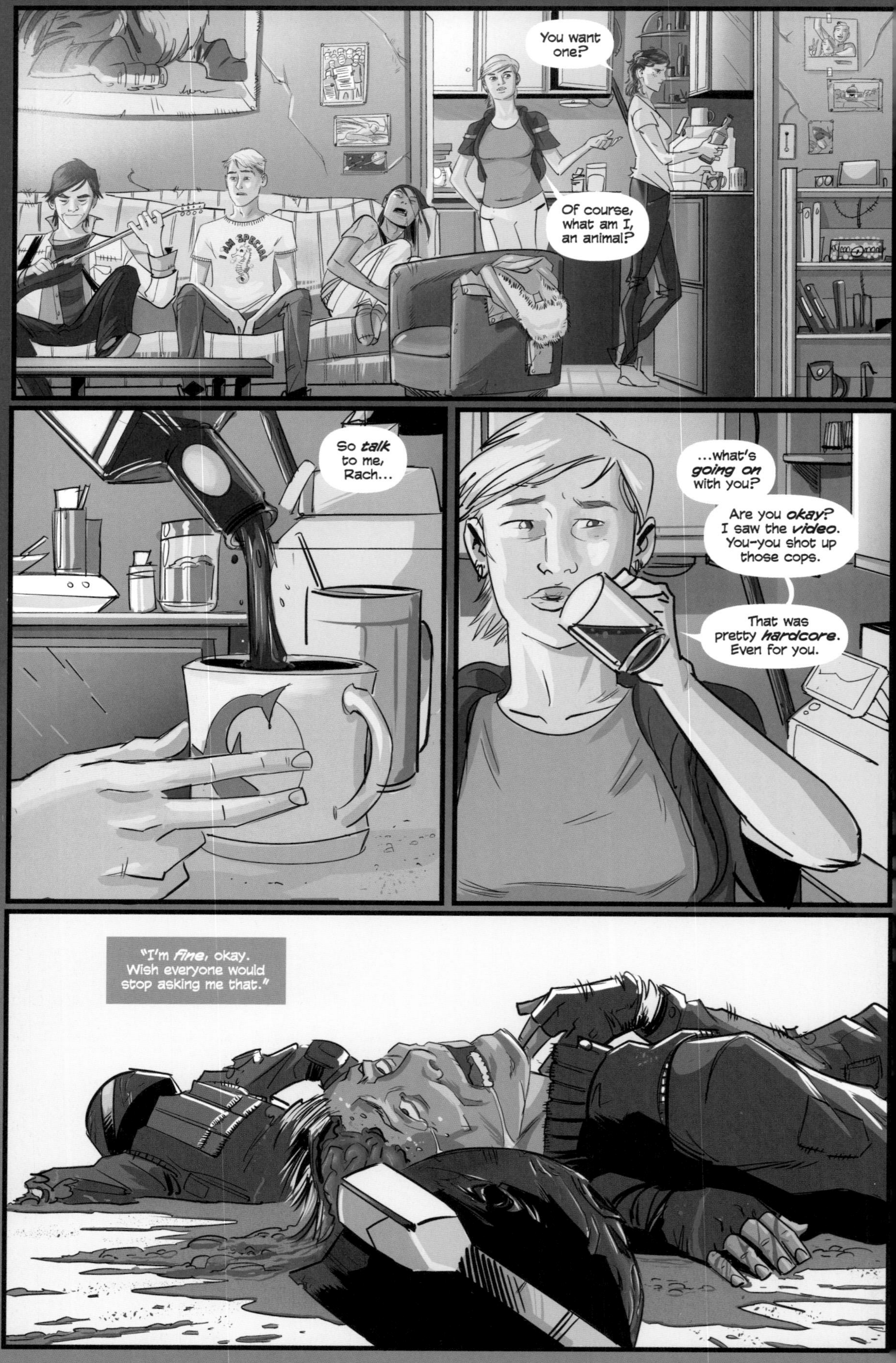
You want one?
Of course, what am I, an animal?
So *talk* to me, Rach...
...what's *going on* with you?
Are you *okay?* I saw the *video*. You-you shot up those cops.
That was pretty *hardcore*. Even for you.
"I'm *fine*, okay. Wish everyone would stop asking me that."

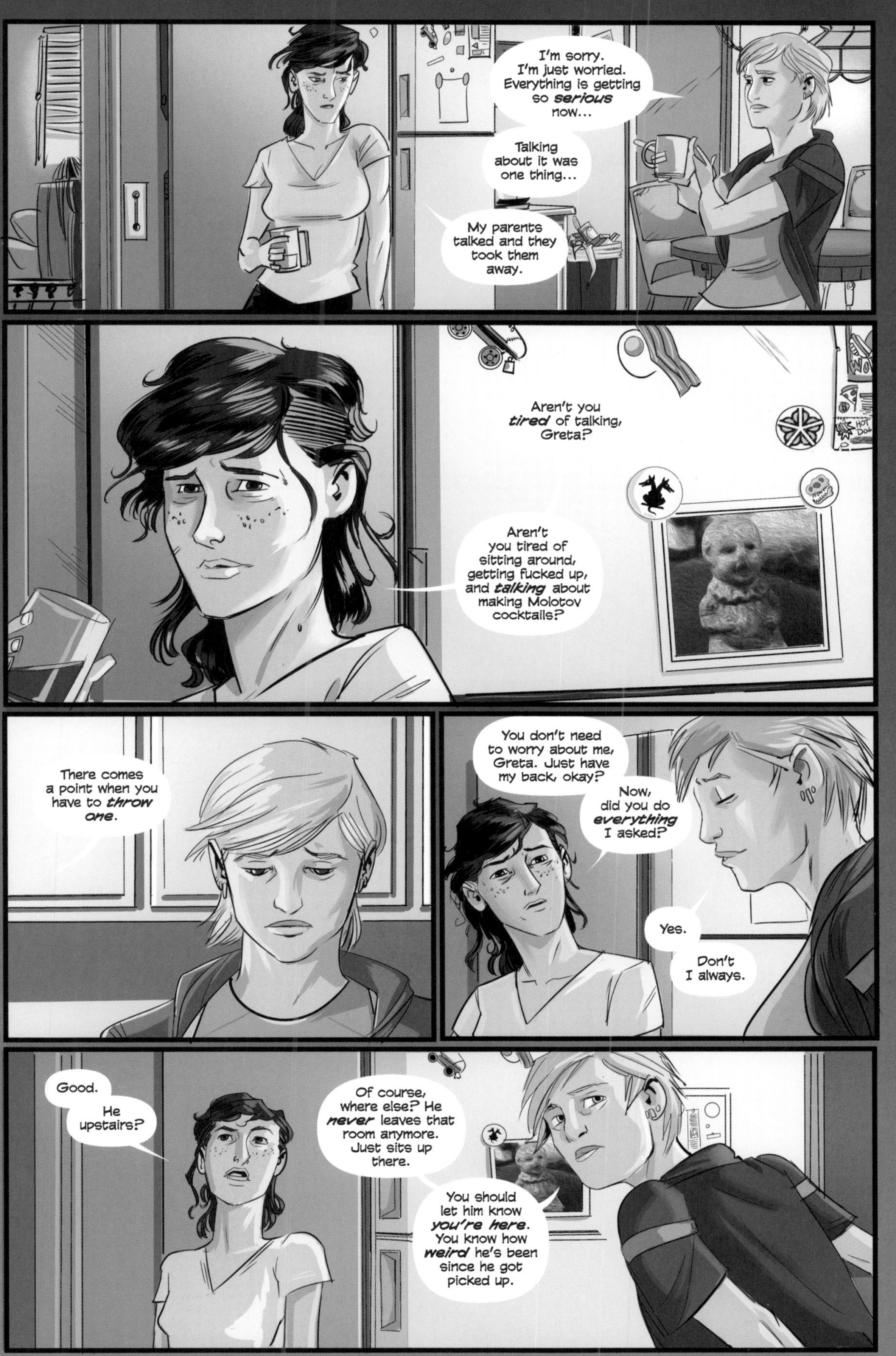
I'm sorry. I'm just worried. Everything is getting so serious now...
Talking about it was one thing...
My parents talked and they took them away.
Aren't you tired of talking, Greta?
Aren't you tired of sitting around, getting fucked up, and talking about making Molotov cocktails?
There comes a point when you have to throw one.
You don't need to worry about me, Greta. Just have my back, okay?
Now, did you do everything I asked?
Yes.
Don't I always.
Good.
He upstairs?
Of course, where else? He never leaves that room anymore. Just sits up there.
You should let him know you're here. You know how weird he's been since he got picked up.

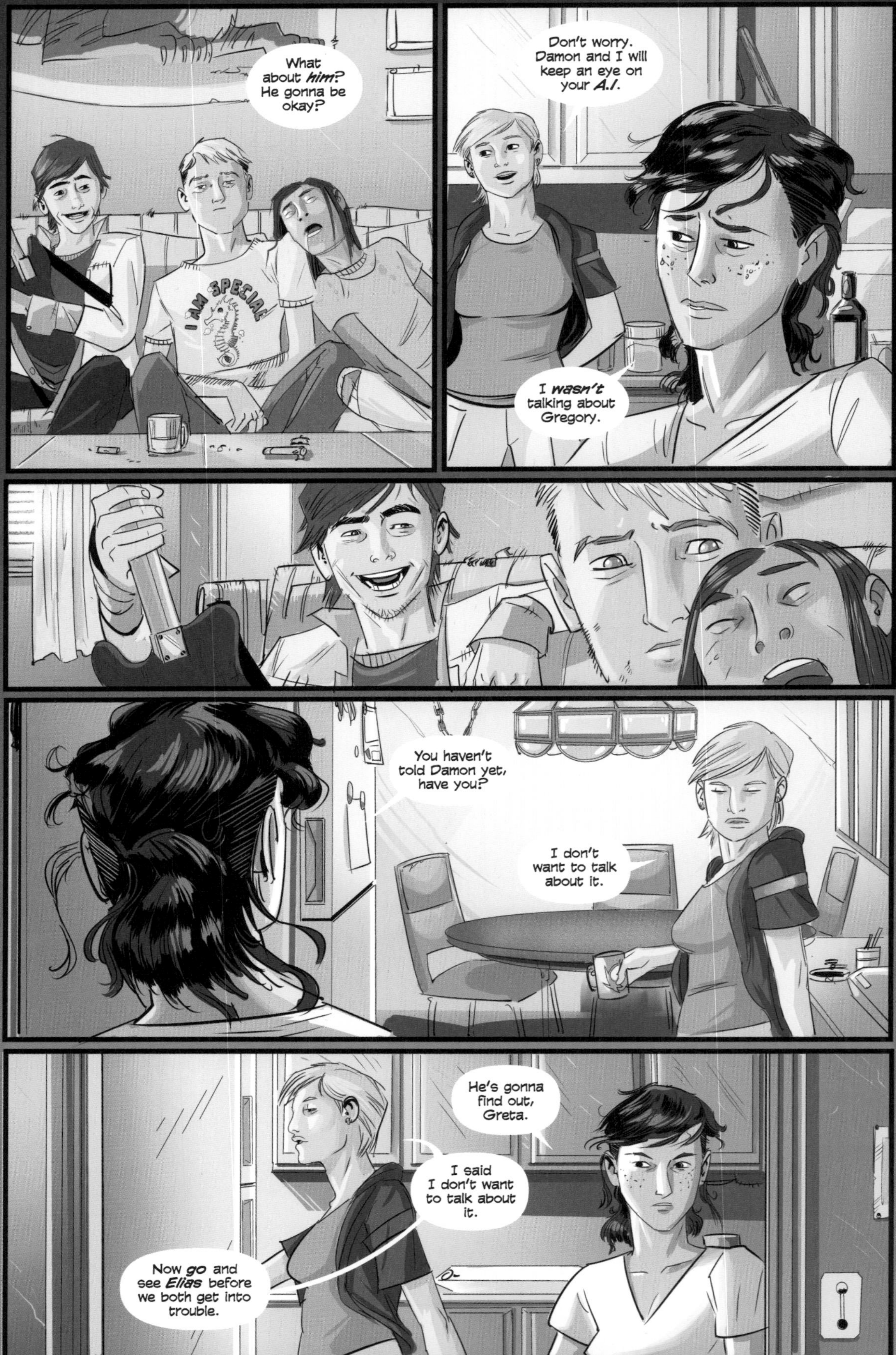
What about *him*? He gonna be okay?
Don't worry. Damon and I will keep an eye on your *A.I.*
I *wasn't* talking about Gregory.
I AM SPECIAL
You haven't told Damon yet, have you?
I don't want to talk about it.
He's gonna find out, Greta.
I said I don't want to talk about it.
Now *go* and see *Elias* before we both get into trouble.

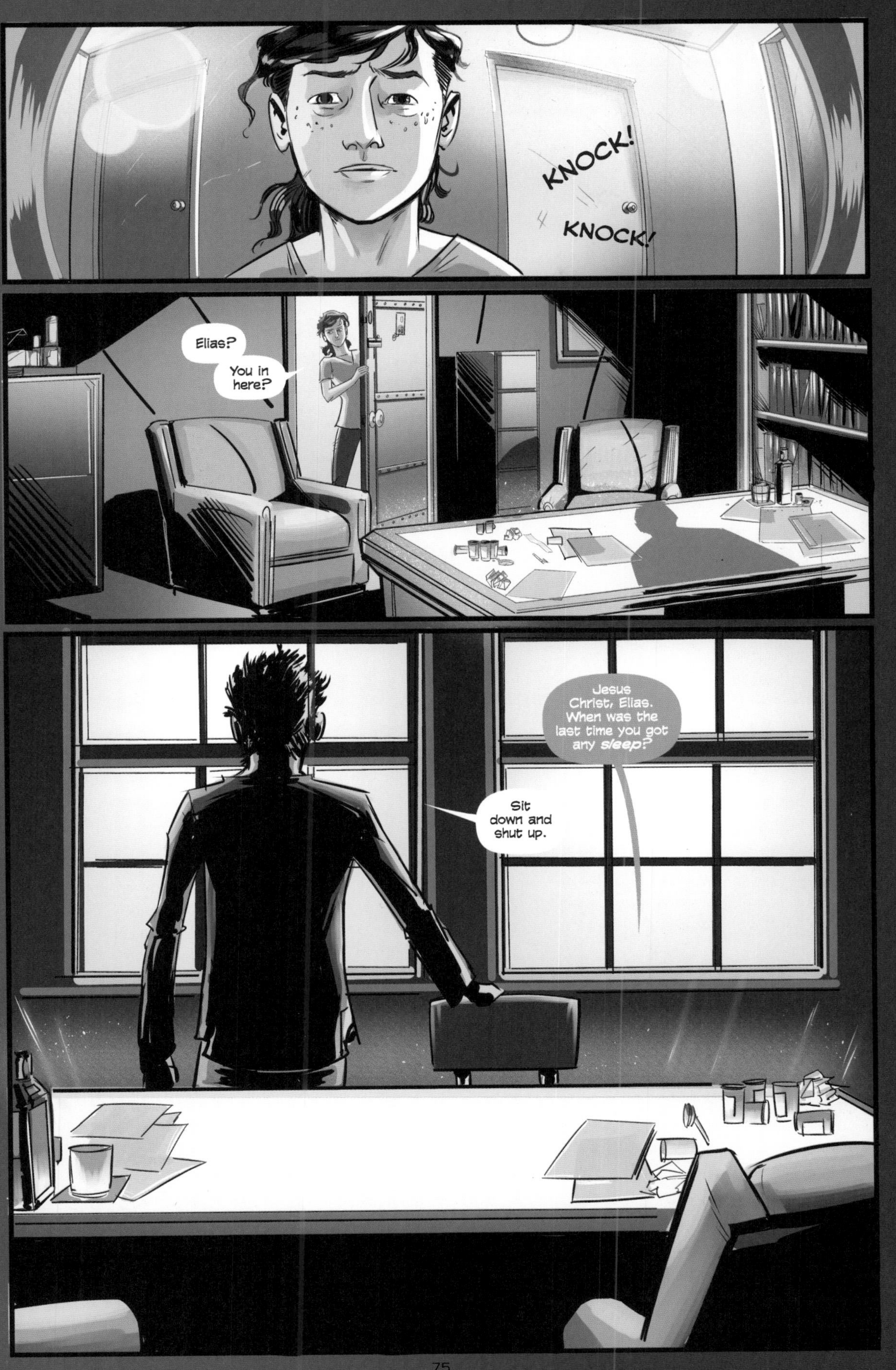
KNOCK!
KNOCK!
Elias?
You in here?
Jesus Christ, Elias. When was the last time you got any *sleep*?
Sit down and shut up.

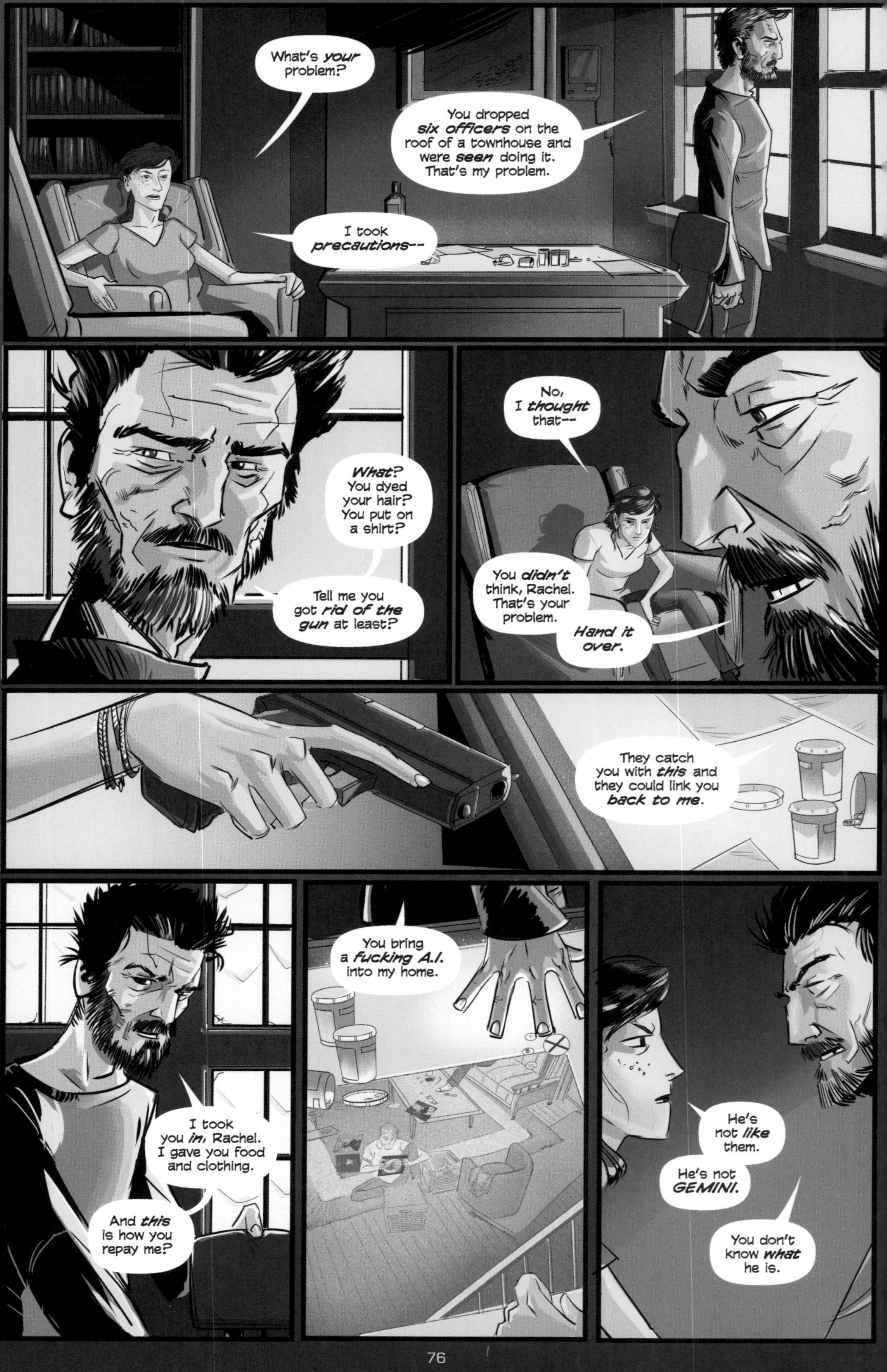
What's your problem?
You dropped six officers on the roof of a townhouse and were seen doing it. That's my problem.
I took precautions--
What? You dyed your hair? You put on a shirt?
Tell me you got rid of the gun at least?
No, I thought that--
You didn't think, Rachel. That's your problem.
Hand it over.
They catch you with this and they could link you back to me.
I took you in, Rachel. I gave you food and clothing.
And this is how you repay me?
You bring a fucking A.I. into my home.
He's not like them.
He's not GEMINI.
You don't know what he is.

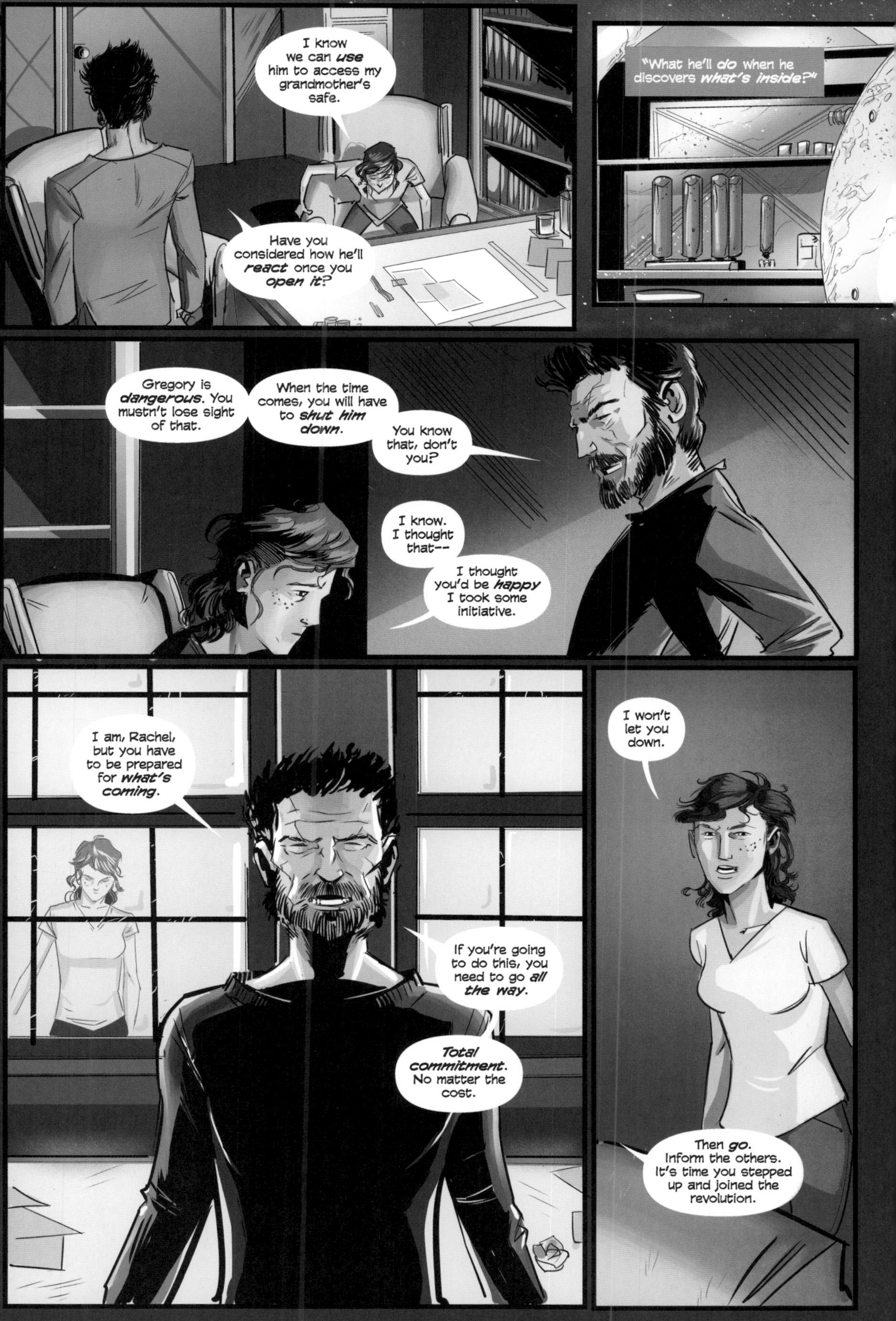
I know we can *use* him to access my grandmother's safe.
Have you considered how he'll *react* once you *open it?*
"What he'll *do* when he discovers *what's inside?*"
Gregory is *dangerous.* You mustn't lose sight of that.
When the time comes, you will have to *shut him down.*
You know that, don't you?
I know. I thought that--
I thought you'd be *happy* I took some initiative.
I am, Rachel, but you have to be prepared for *what's coming.*
If you're going to do this, you need to go *all the way.*
Total commitment. No matter the cost.
I won't let you down.
Then *go.* Inform the others. It's time you stepped up and joined the revolution.

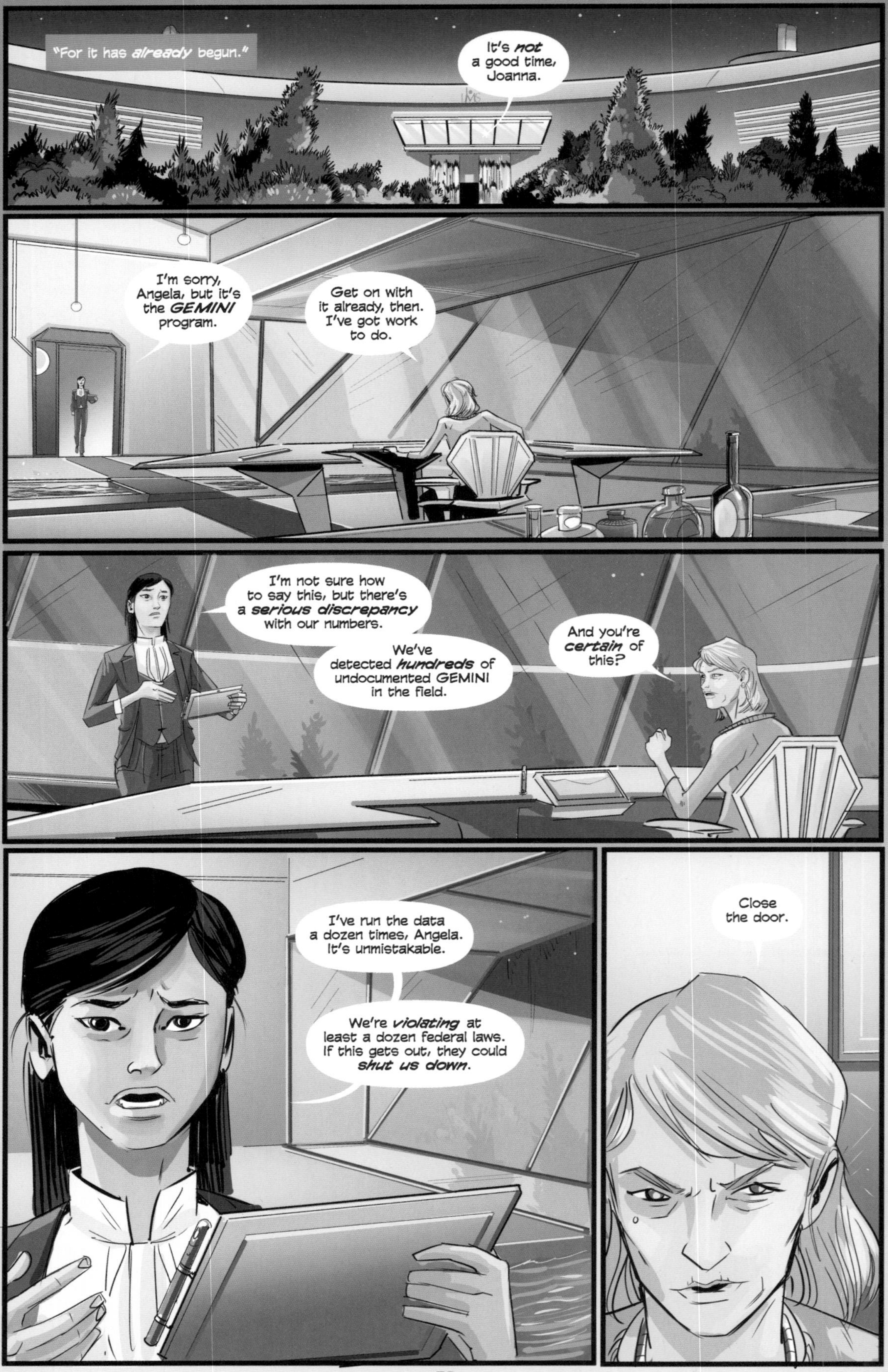
"For it has *already* begun."
It's *not* a good time, Joanna.
I'm sorry, Angela, but it's the *GEMINI* program.
Get on with it already, then. I've got work to do.
I'm not sure how to say this, but there's a *serious discrepancy* with our numbers.
We've detected *hundreds* of undocumented GEMINI in the field.
And you're *certain* of this?
I've run the data a dozen times, Angela. It's unmistakable.
We're *violating* at least a dozen federal laws. If this gets out, they could *shut us down*.
Close the door.

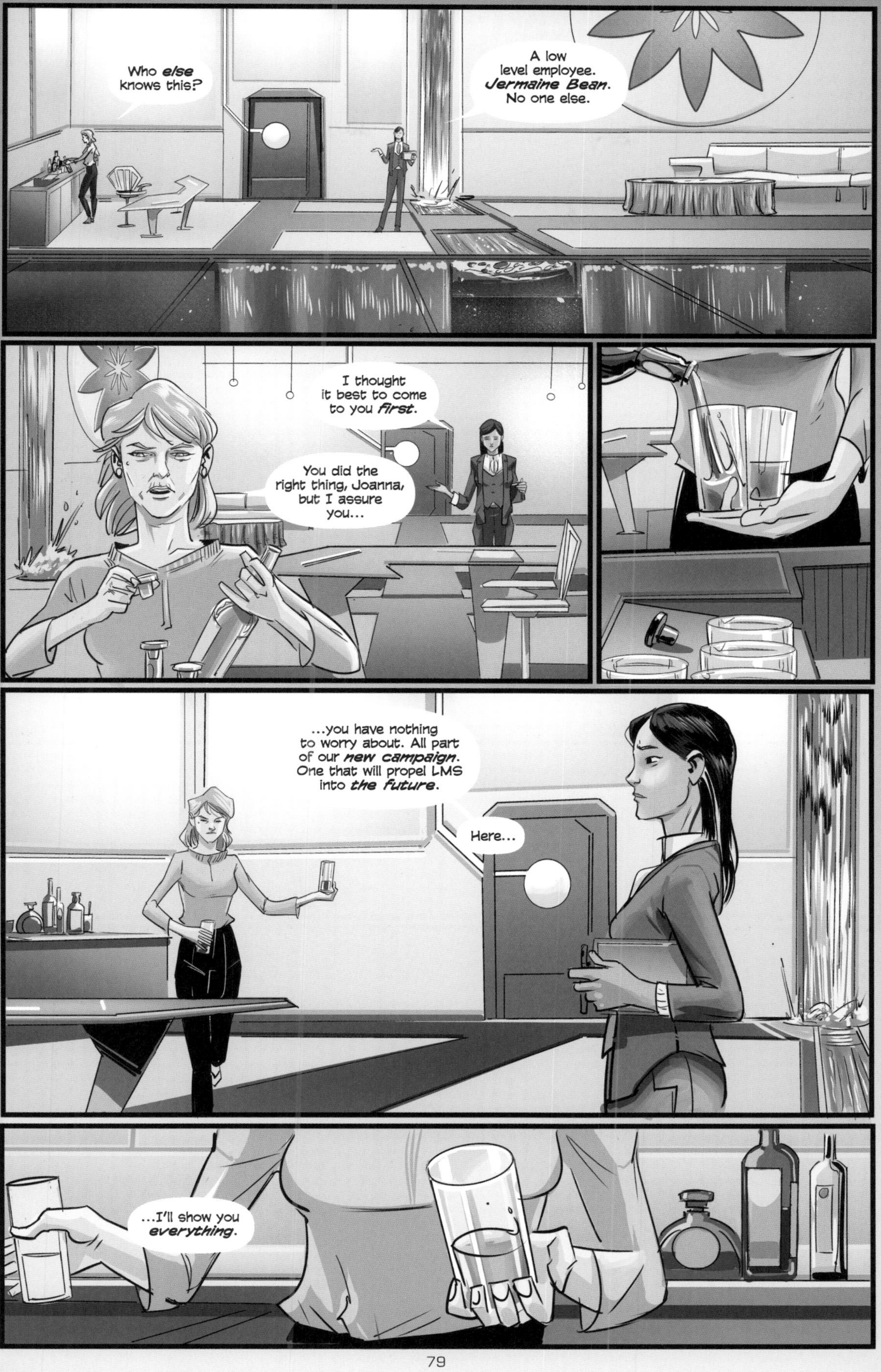
Who *else* knows this?
A low level employee. ***Jermaine Bean***. No one else.
I thought it best to come to you ***first***.
You did the right thing, Joanna, but I assure you...
...you have nothing to worry about. All part of our ***new campaign***. One that will propel LMS into ***the future***.
Here...
...I'll show you ***everything***.

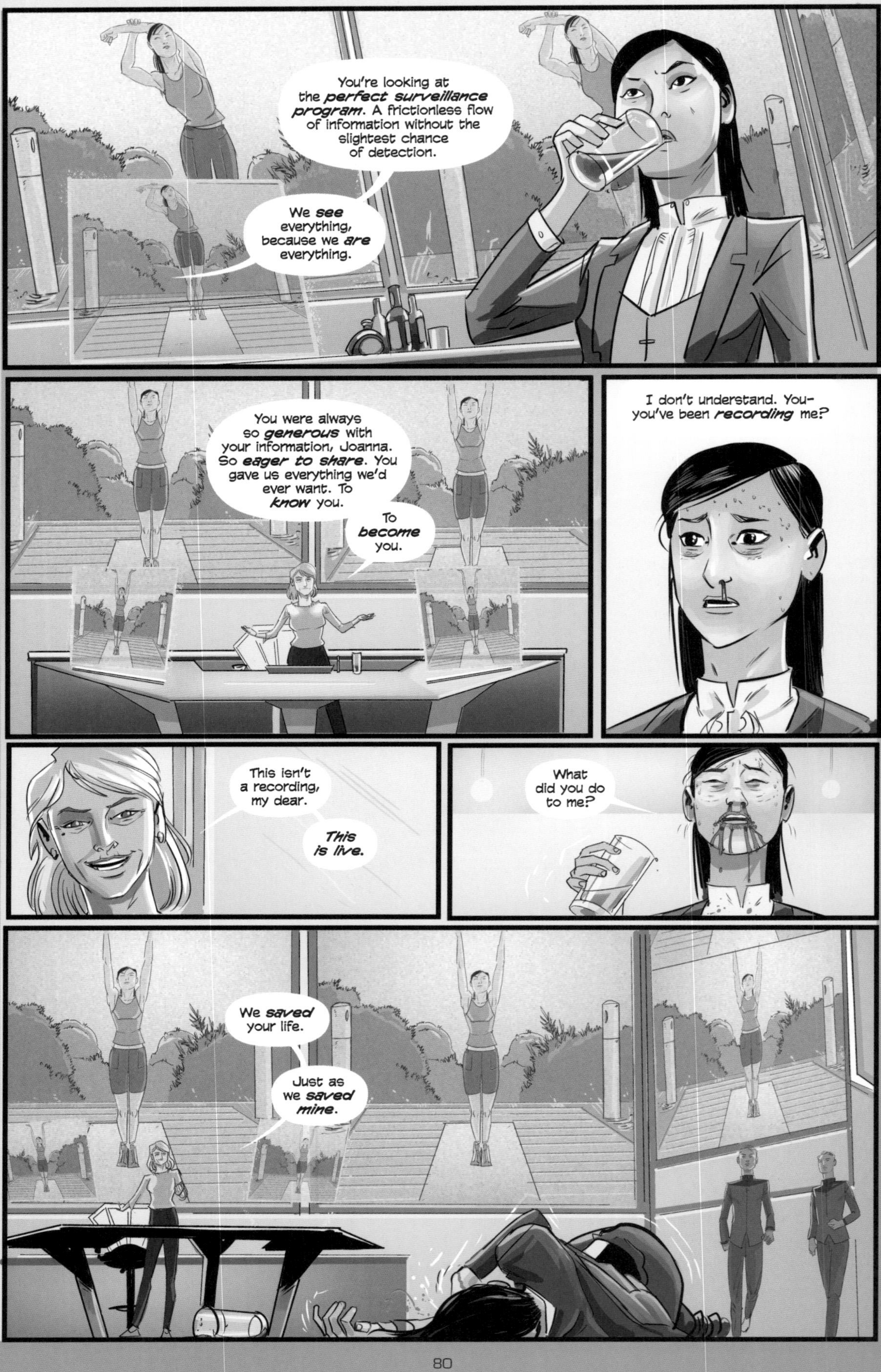
You're looking at the ***perfect surveillance program***. A frictionless flow of information without the slightest chance of detection.
We ***see*** everything, because we ***are*** everything.
You were always so ***generous*** with your information, Joanna. So ***eager to share***. You gave us everything we'd ever want. To ***know*** you.
To ***become*** you.
I don't understand. You- you've been ***recording*** me?
This isn't a recording, my dear.
This is live.
What did you do to me?
We ***saved*** your life.
Just as we ***saved mine***.

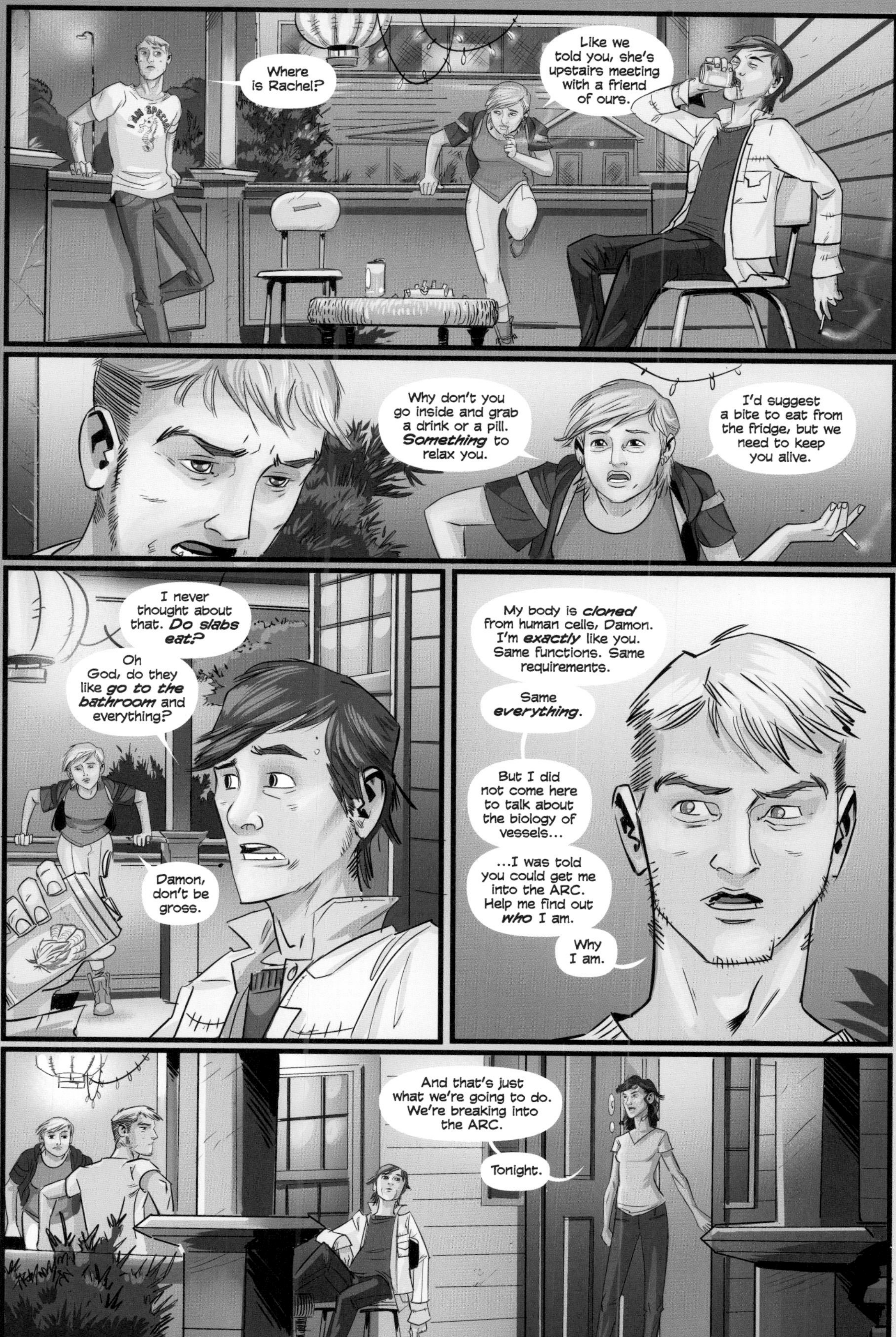

Where is Rachel?
Like we told you, she's upstairs meeting with a friend of ours.
Why don't you go inside and grab a drink or a pill. *Something* to relax you.
I'd suggest a bite to eat from the fridge, but we need to keep you alive.
I never thought about that. *Do slabs eat?*
Oh God, do they like *go to the bathroom* and everything?
Damon, don't be gross.
My body is *cloned* from human cells, Damon. I'm *exactly* like you. Same functions. Same requirements.
Same *everything*.
But I did not come here to talk about the biology of vessels...
...I was told you could get me into the ARC. Help me find out *who* I am.
Why I am.
And that's just what we're going to do. We're breaking into the ARC.
Tonight.

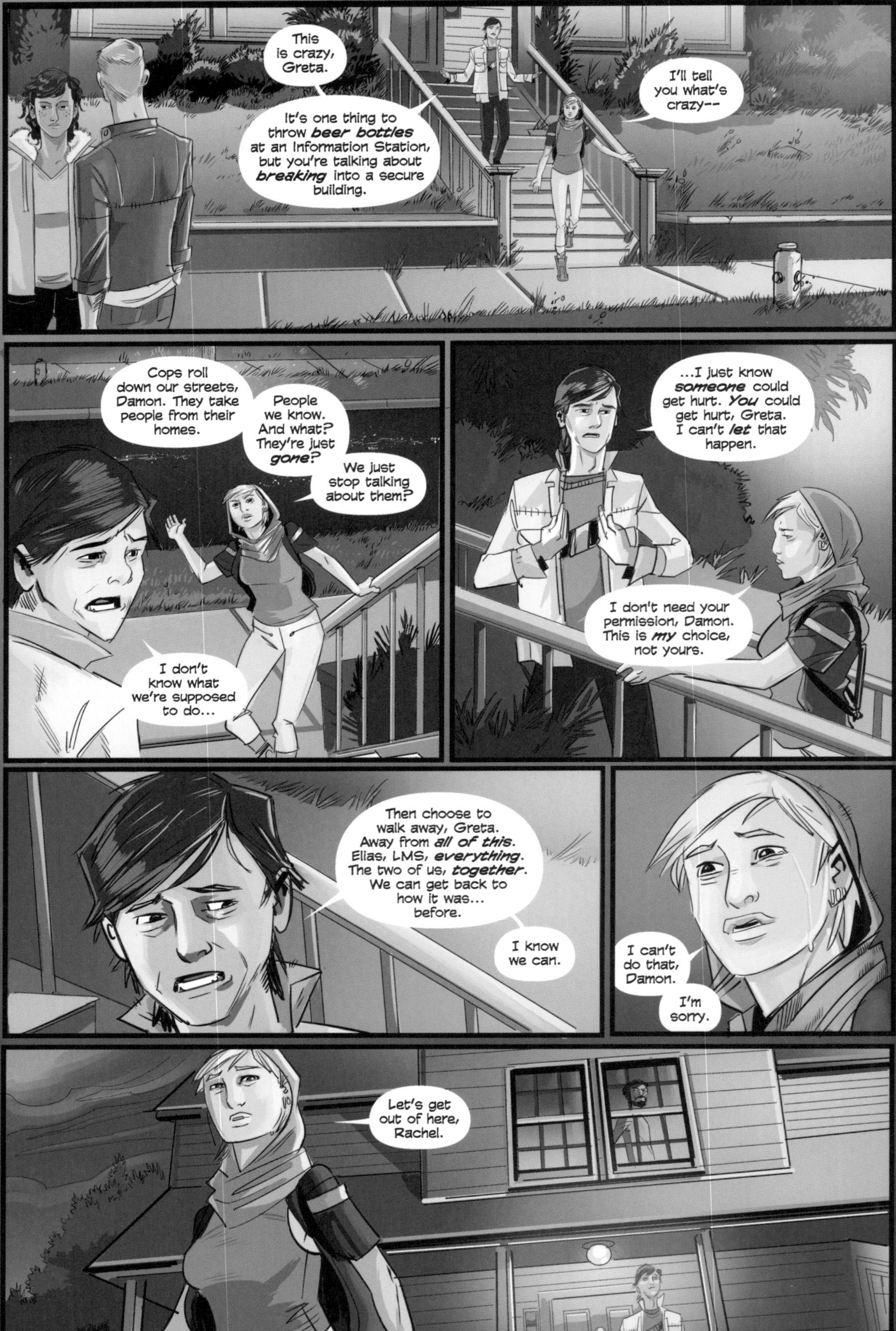
This is crazy, Greta.
It's one thing to throw *beer bottles* at an Information Station, but you're talking about *breaking* into a secure building.
I'll tell you what's crazy--
Cops roll down our streets, Damon. They take people from their homes.
People we know. And what? They're just *gone*?
We just stop talking about them?
I don't know what we're supposed to do...
...I just know *someone* could get hurt. *You* could get hurt, Greta. I can't *let* that happen.
I don't need your permission, Damon. This is *my* choice, not yours.
Then choose to walk away, Greta. Away from *all of this*. Elias, LMS, *everything*. The two of us, *together*. We can get back to how it was... before.
I know we can.
I can't do that, Damon.
I'm sorry.
Let's get out of here, Rachel.

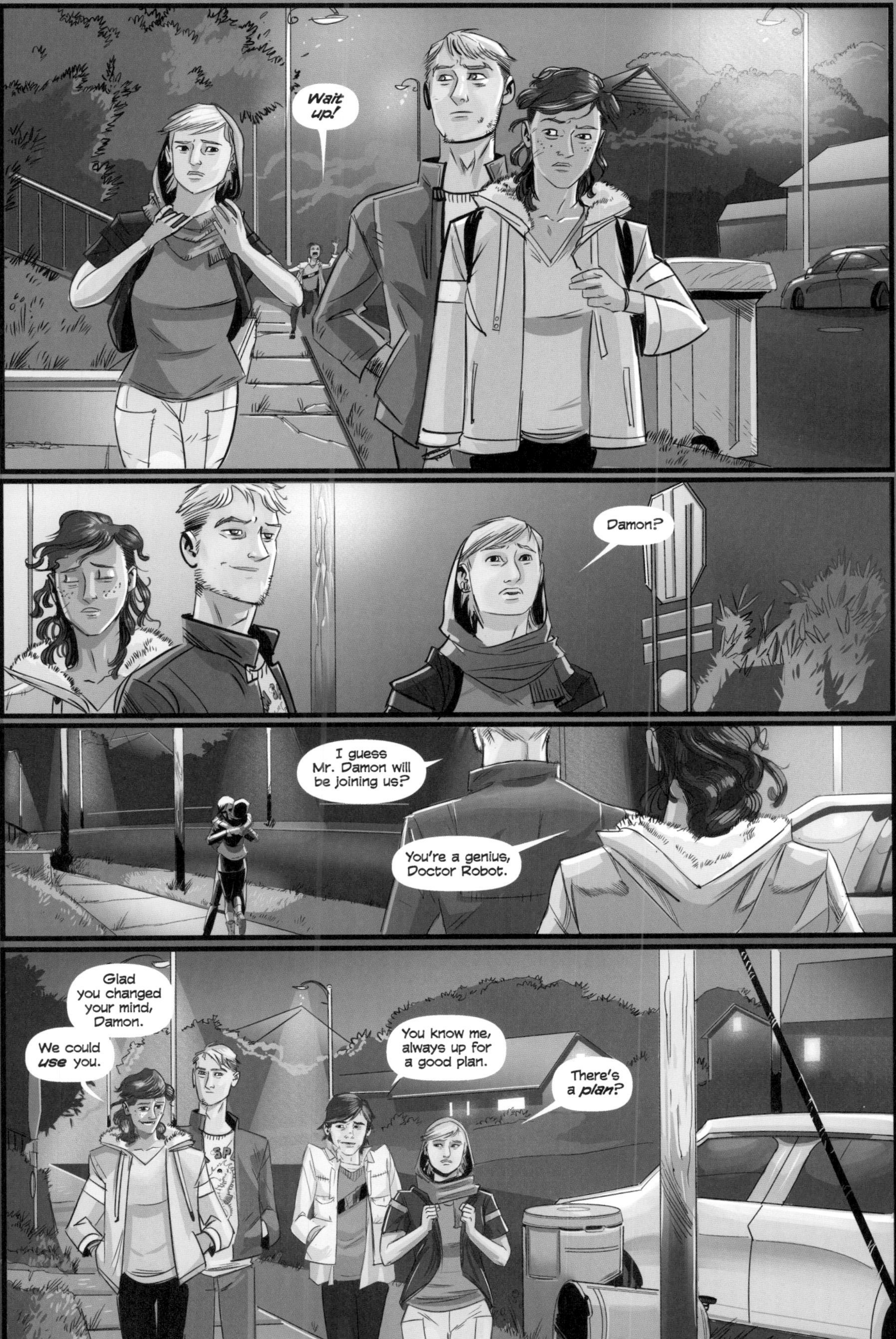
Wait up!
Damon?
I guess Mr. Damon will be joining us?
You're a genius, Doctor Robot.
Glad you changed your mind, Damon.
We could use you.
You know me, always up for a good plan.
There's a plan?

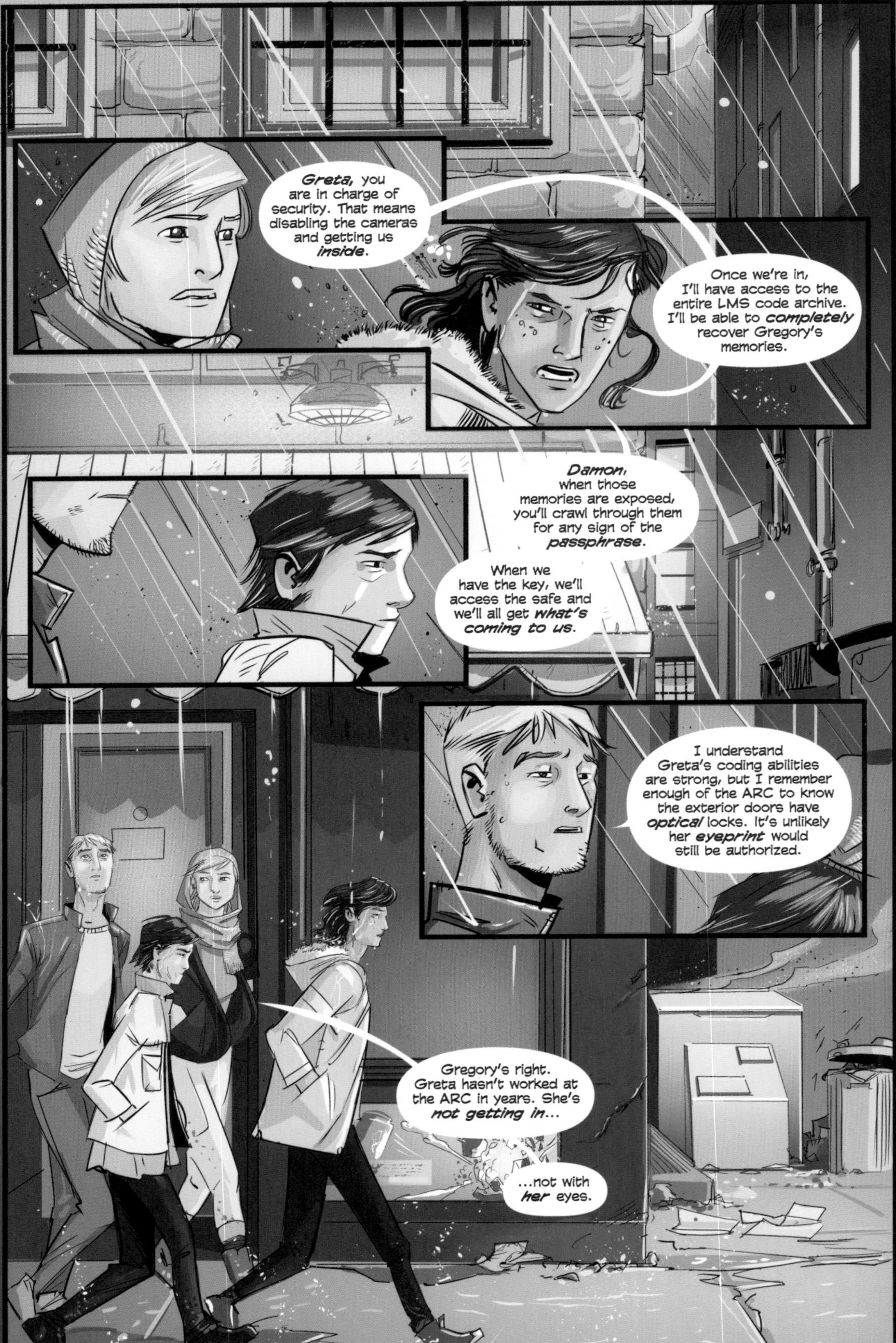
Greta, you are in charge of security. That means disabling the cameras and getting us inside.
Once we're in, I'll have access to the entire LMS code archive. I'll be able to completely recover Gregory's memories.
Damon, when those memories are exposed, you'll crawl through them for any sign of the passphrase.
When we have the key, we'll access the safe and we'll all get what's coming to us.
I understand Greta's coding abilities are strong, but I remember enough of the ARC to know the exterior doors have optical locks. It's unlikely her eyeprint would still be authorized.
Gregory's right. Greta hasn't worked at the ARC in years. She's not getting in...
...not with her eyes.

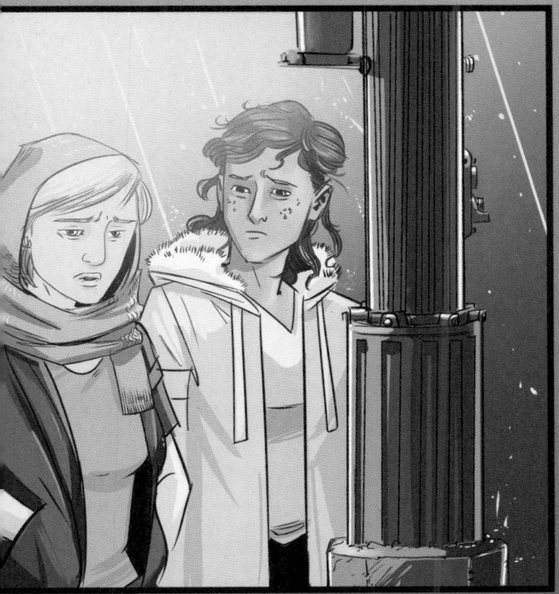

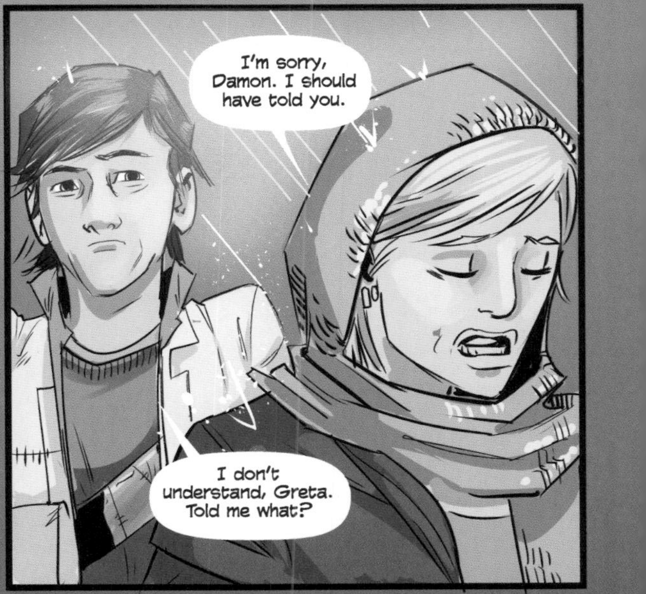
I'm sorry, Damon. I should have told you.
I don't understand, Greta. Told me what?

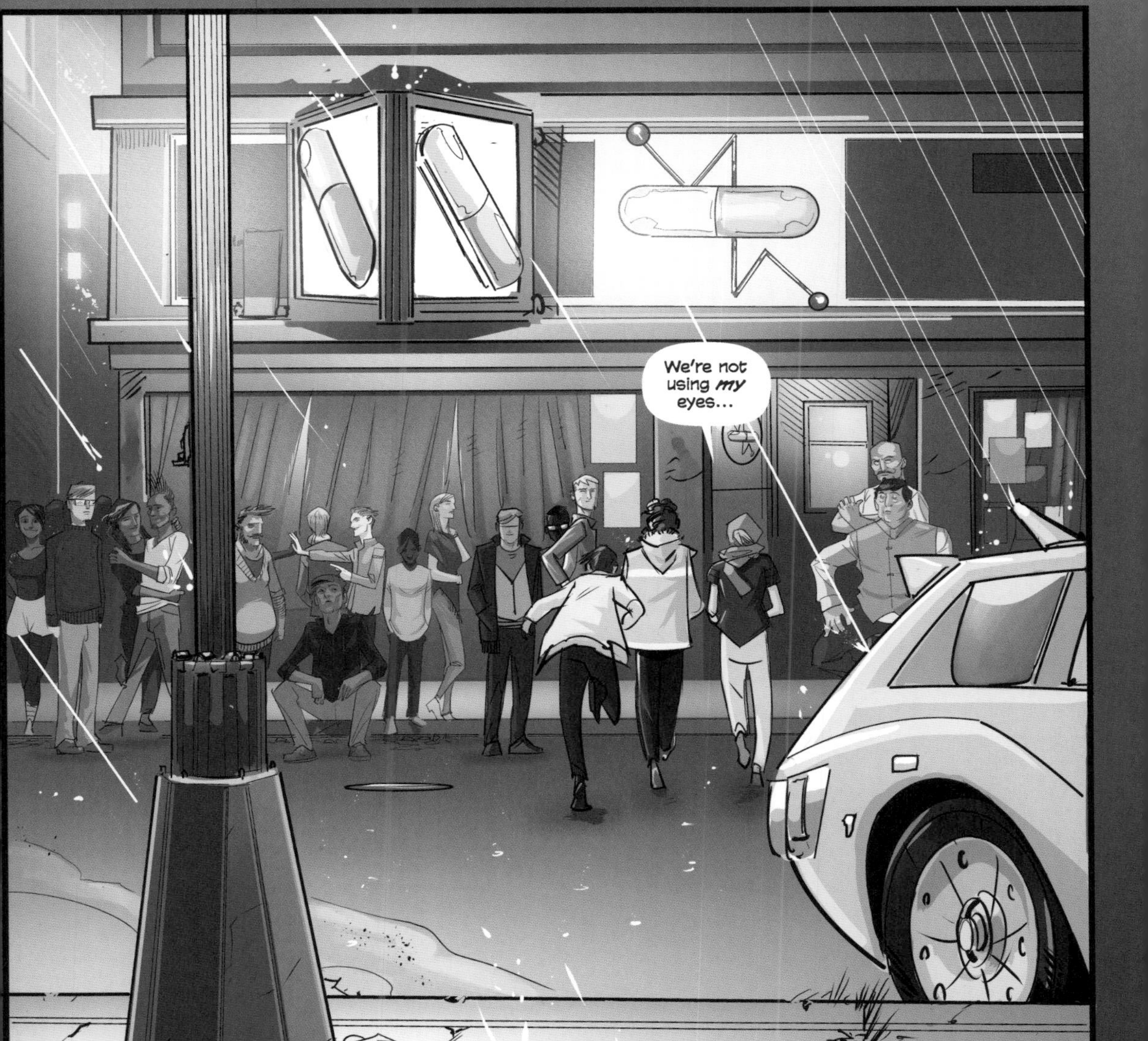
We're not using *my* eyes...

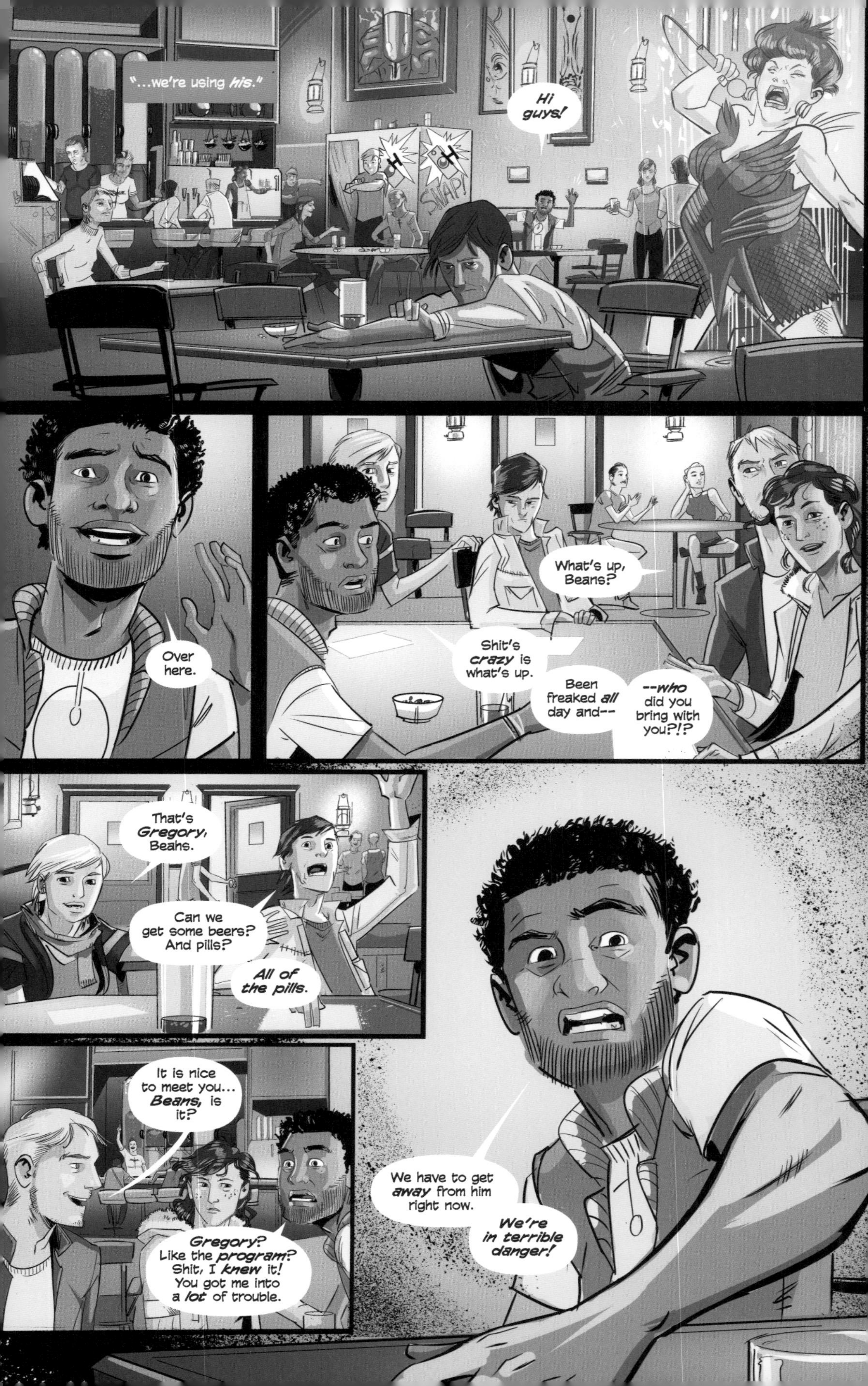
"...we're using his."
Hi guys!
SNAP!
Over here.
What's up, Beans?
Shit's crazy is what's up.
Been freaked all day and--
--who did you bring with you?!?
That's Gregory, Beans.
Can we get some beers? And pills?
All of the pills.
It is nice to meet you... Beans, is it?
Gregory? Like the program? Shit, I knew it! You got me into a lot of trouble.
We have to get away from him right now.
We're in terrible danger!

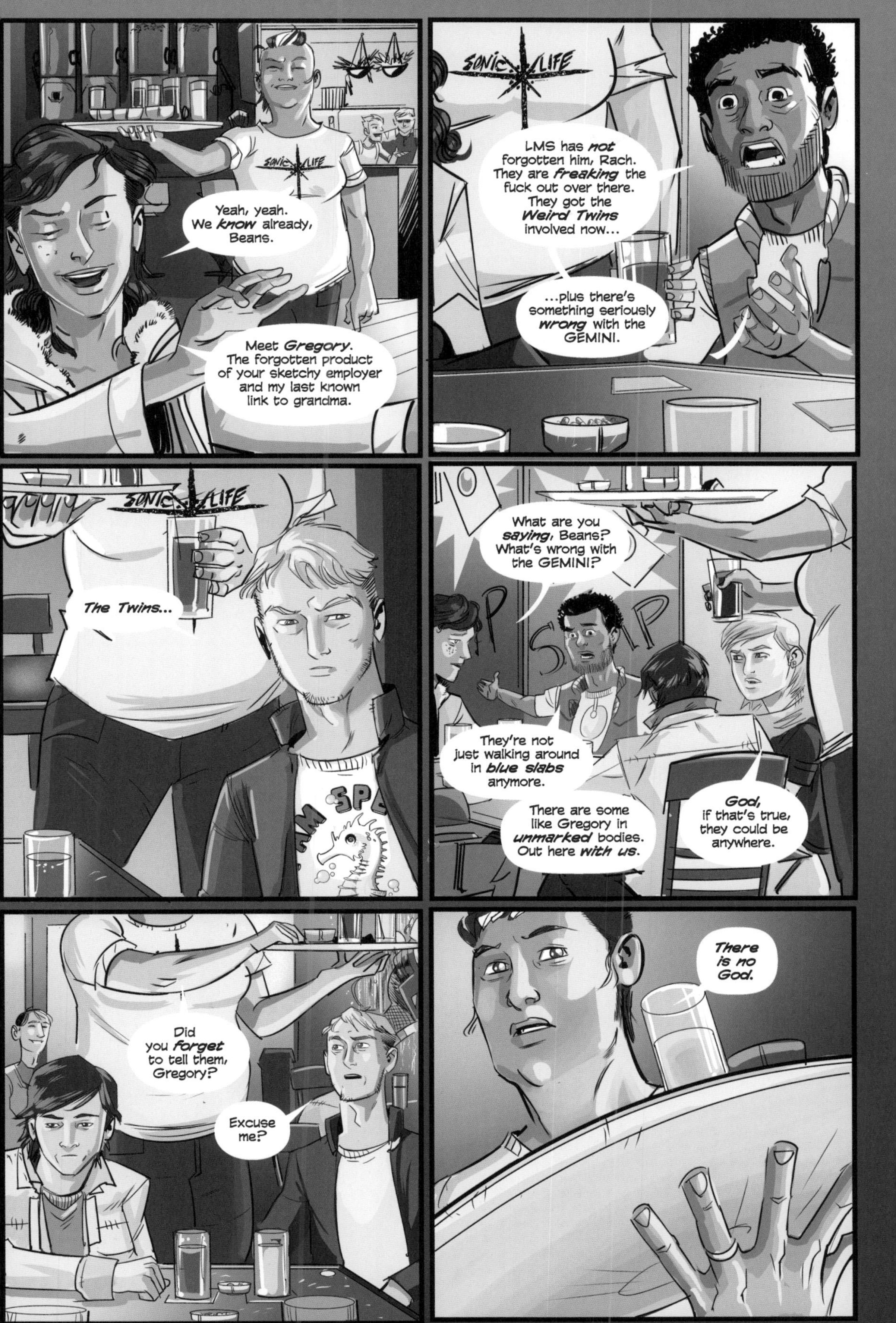
SONIC LIFE
Yeah, yeah. We know already, Beans.
Meet Gregory. The forgotten product of your sketchy employer and my last known link to grandma.
SONIC LIFE
LMS has not forgotten him, Rach. They are freaking the fuck out over there. They got the Weird Twins involved now...
...plus there's something seriously wrong with the GEMINI.
SONIC LIFE
The Twins...
What are you saying, Beans? What's wrong with the GEMINI?
They're not just walking around in blue slabs anymore.
There are some like Gregory in unmarked bodies. Out here with us.
God, if that's true, they could be anywhere.
Did you forget to tell them, Gregory?
Excuse me?
There is no God.

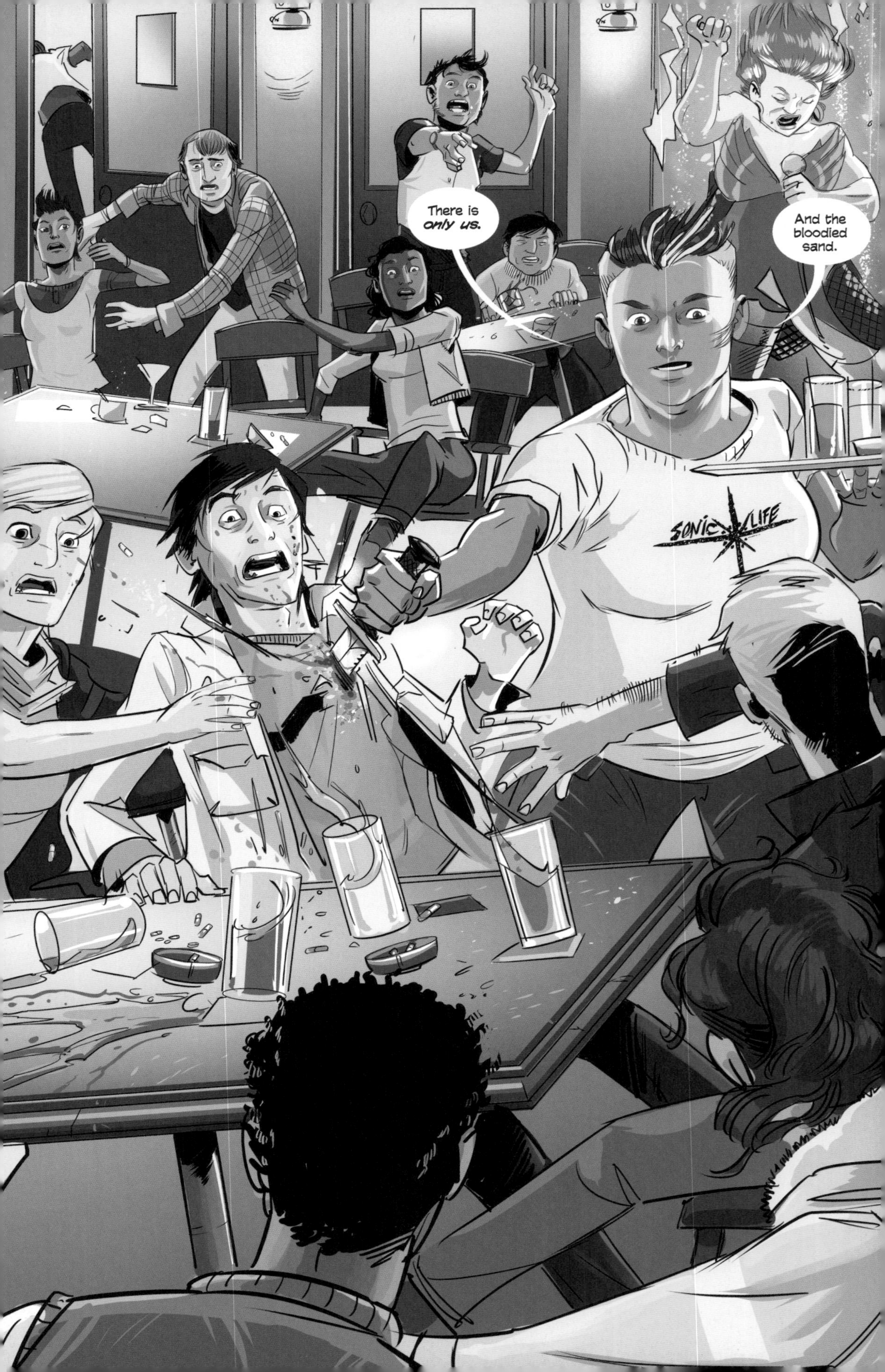
There is *only us.*
And the bloodied sand.
SONIC LIFE

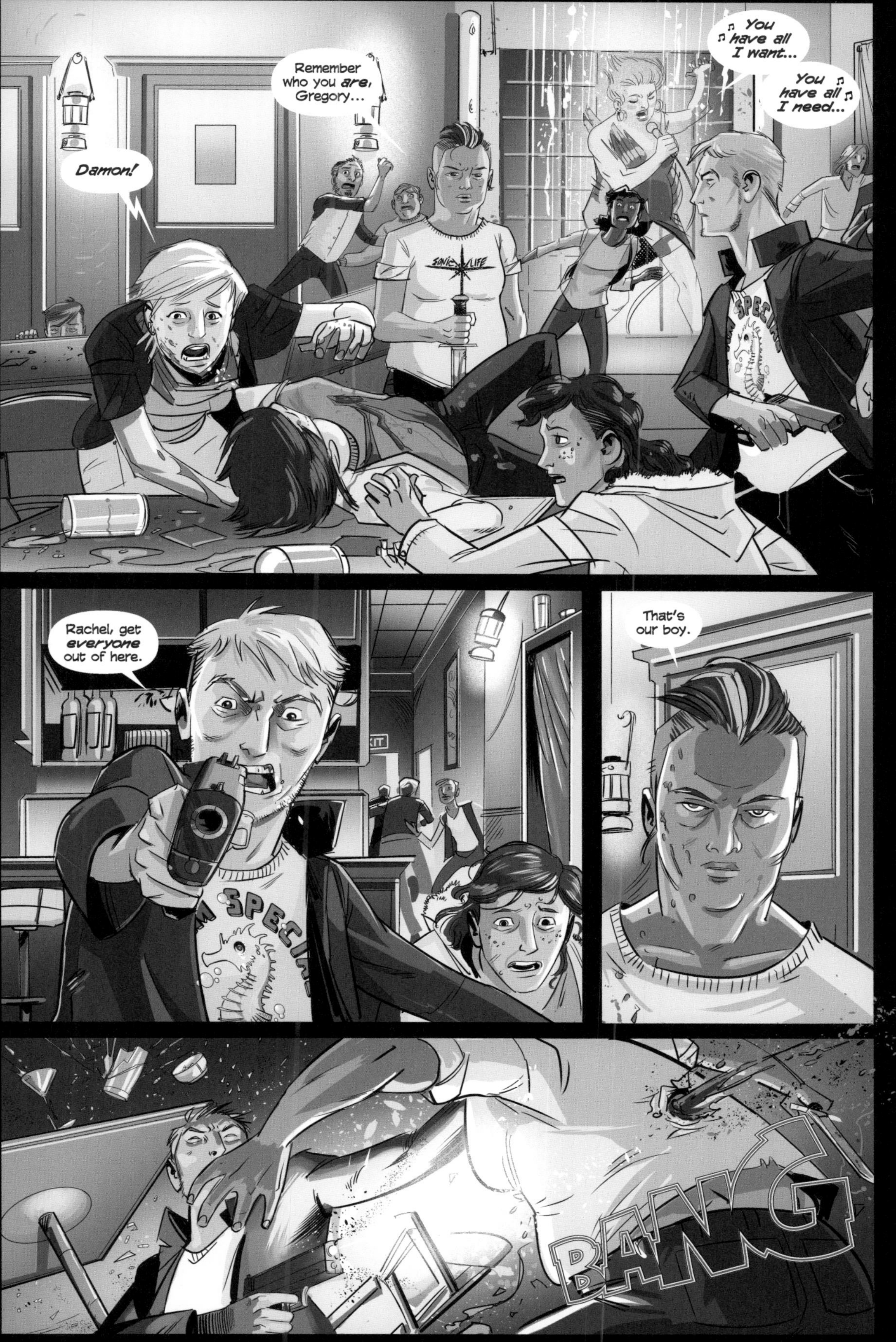
Remember who you *are*, Gregory...
Damon!
♫ You have all I want...
You have all I need... ♫
Rachel, get *everyone* out of here.
That's our boy.
BANG

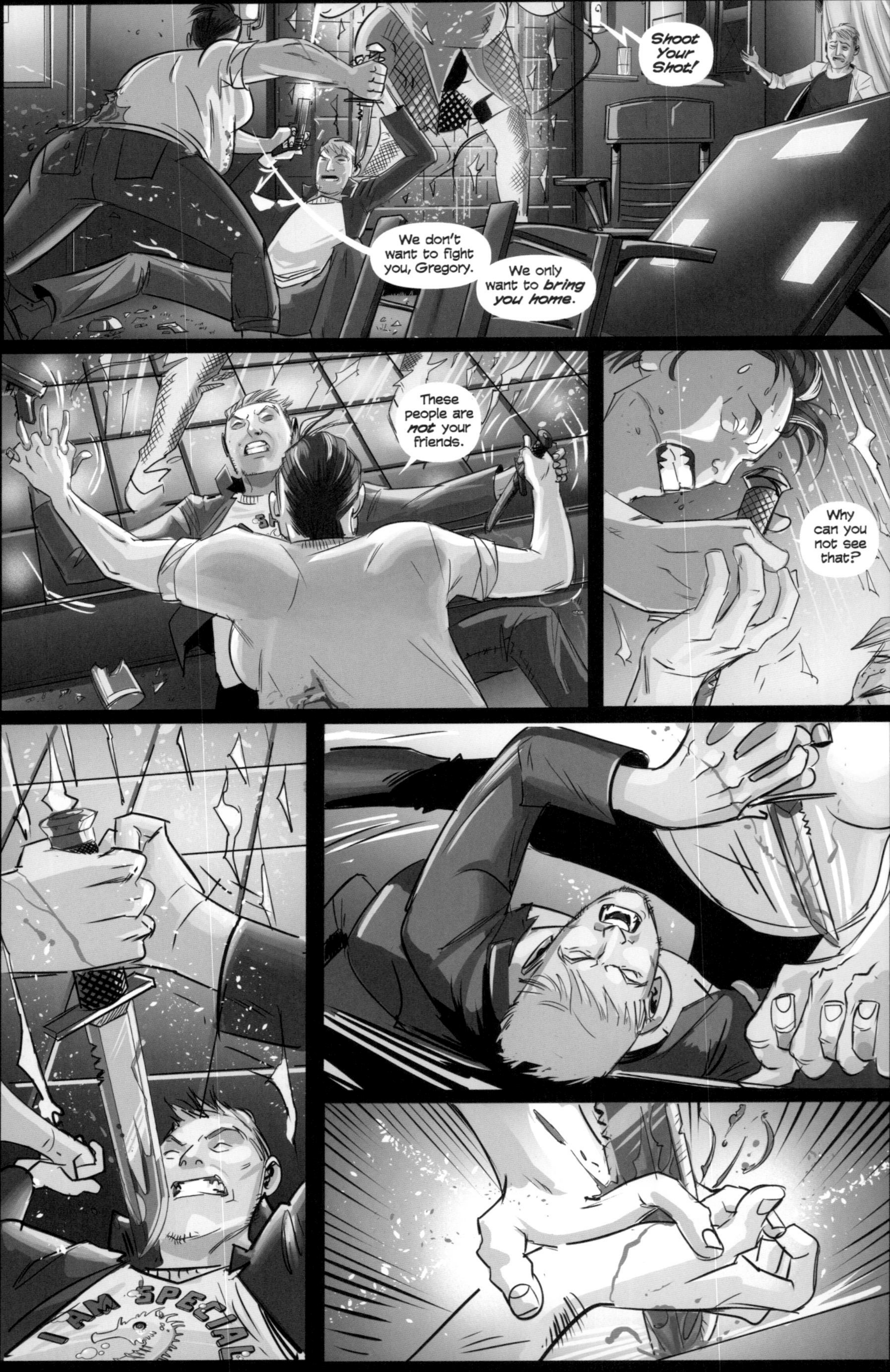
Shoot Your Shot!
We don't want to fight you, Gregory.
We only want to bring you home.
These people are not your friends.
Why can you not see that?
I AM SPECIAL

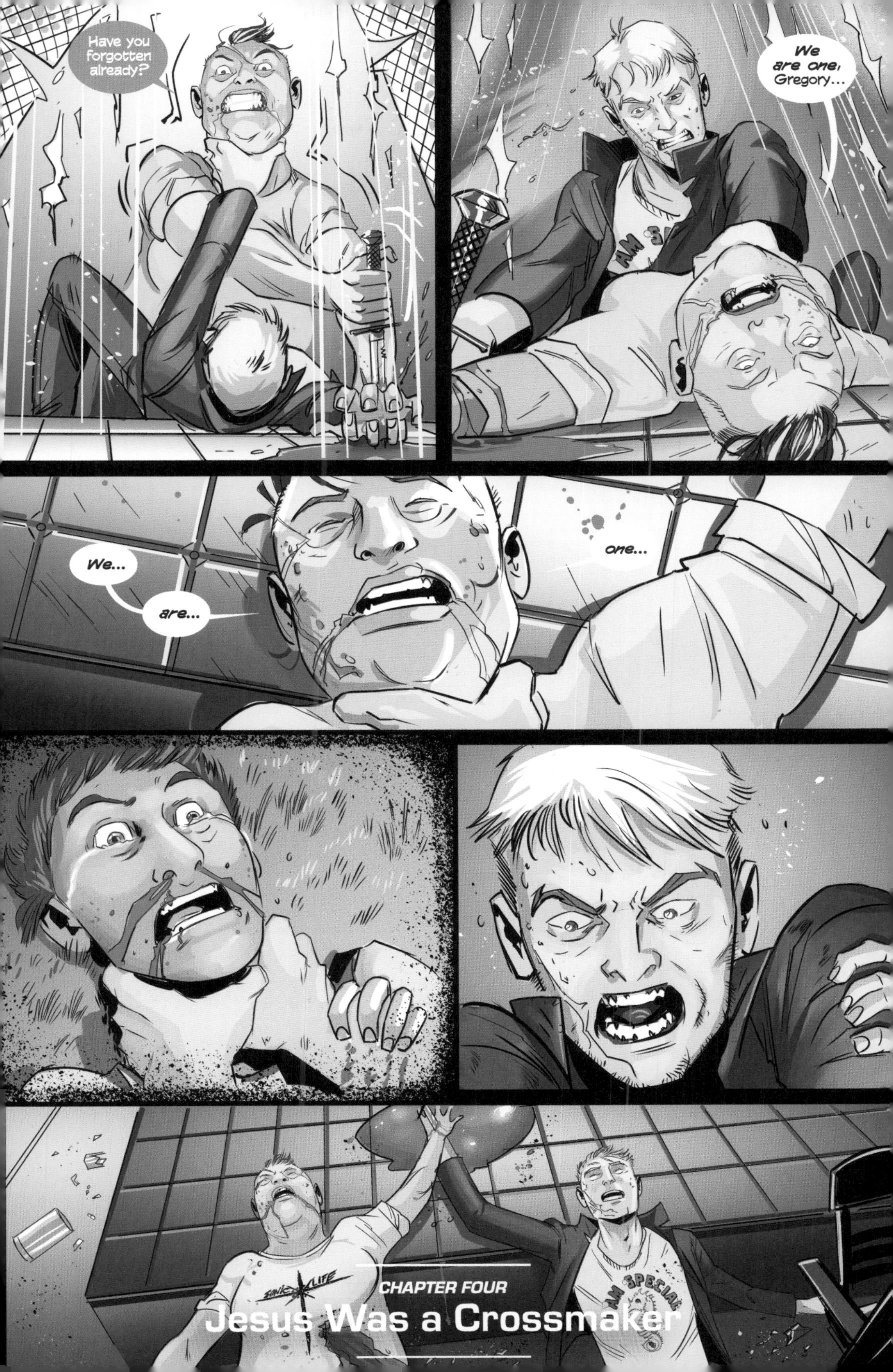
Have you forgotten already?
We are one, Gregory...
We...
are...
one...

CHAPTER FOUR

Jesus Was a Crossmaker

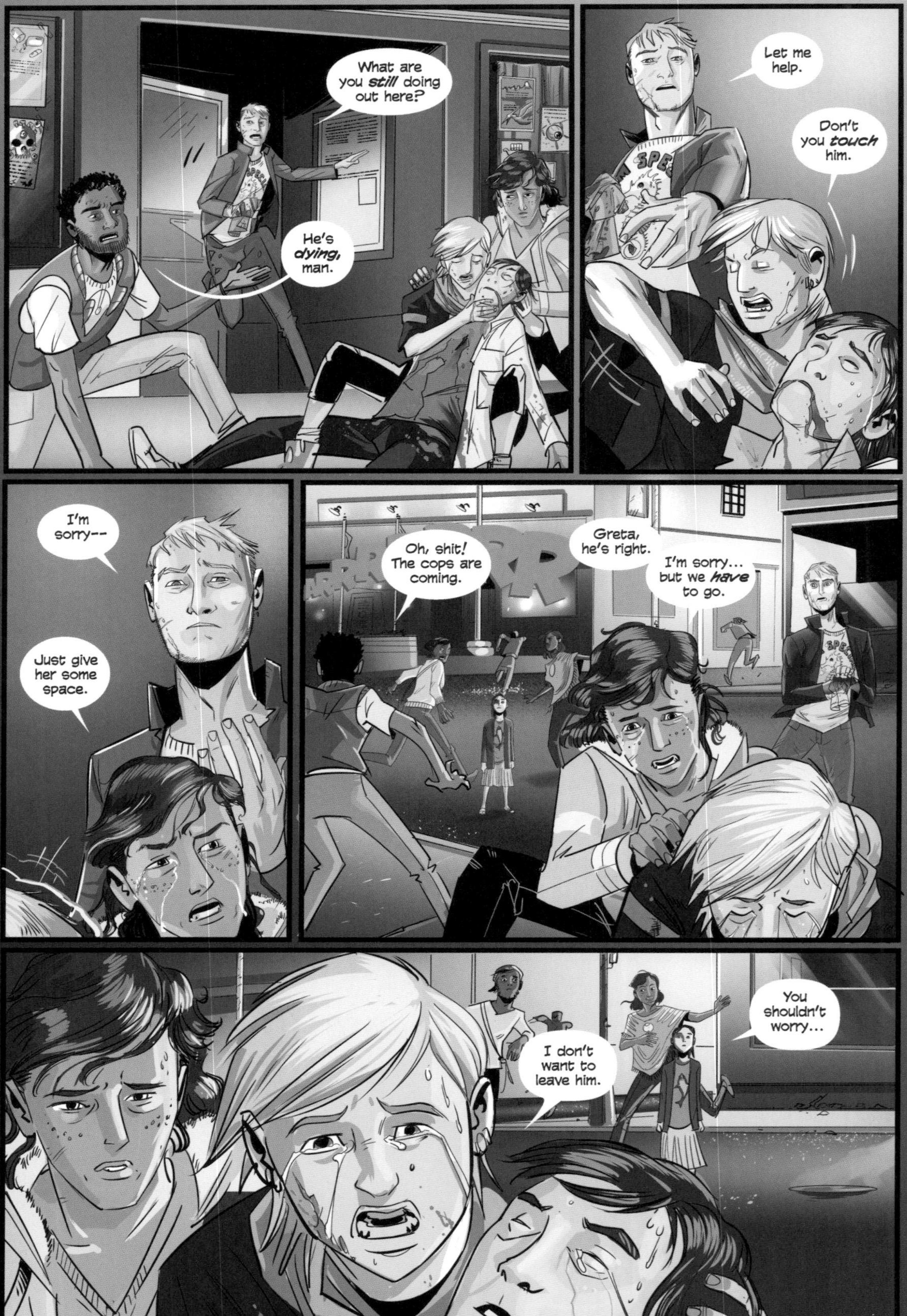
What are you *still* doing out here?
He's *dying,* man.
Let me help.
Don't you *touch* him.
I'm sorry--
Just give her some space.
Oh, shit! The cops are coming.
Greta, he's right.
I'm sorry... but we *have* to go.
I don't want to leave him.
You shouldn't worry...

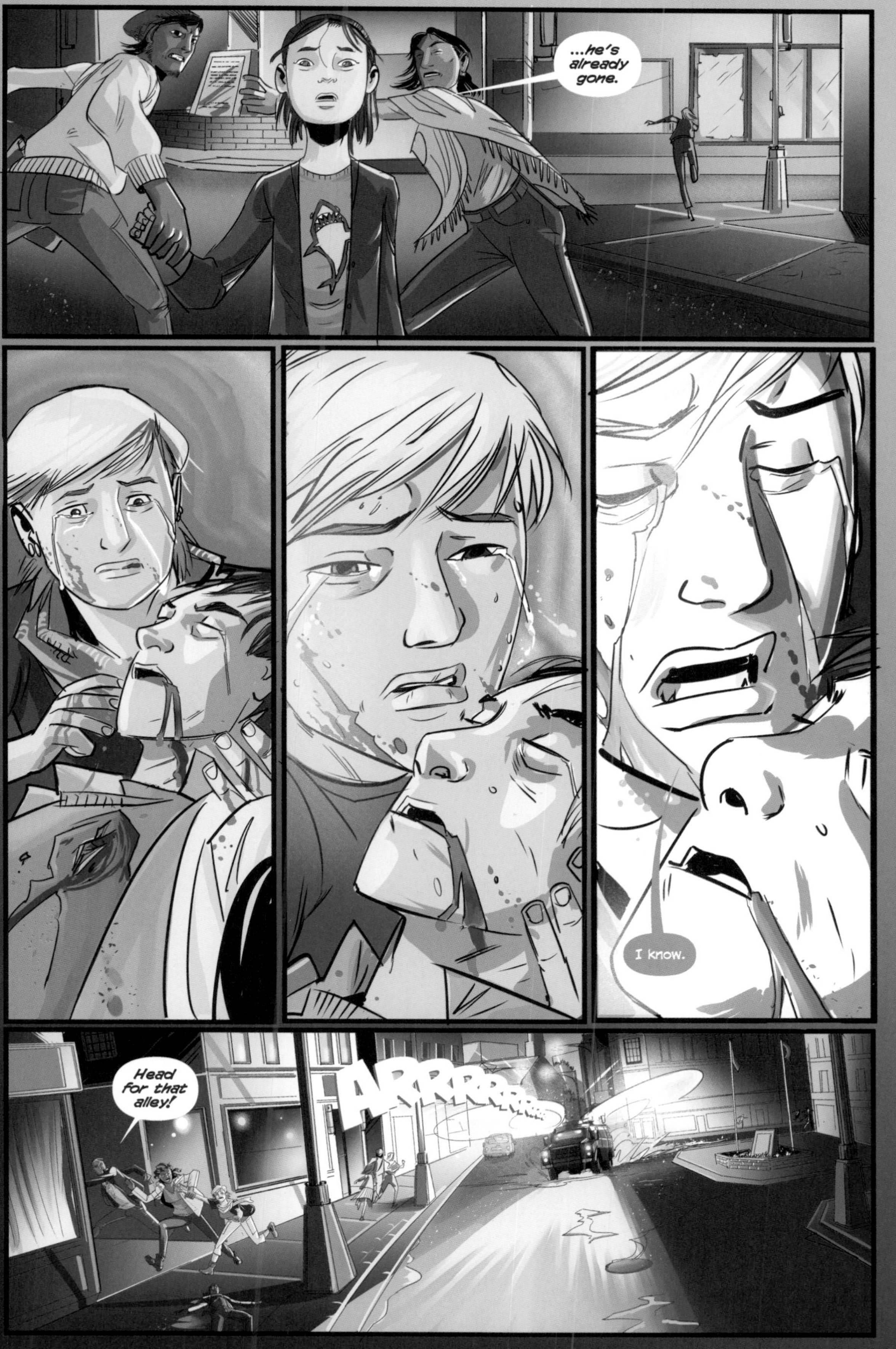
...he's already gone.
I know.
Head for that alley!
ARRRRRRR...

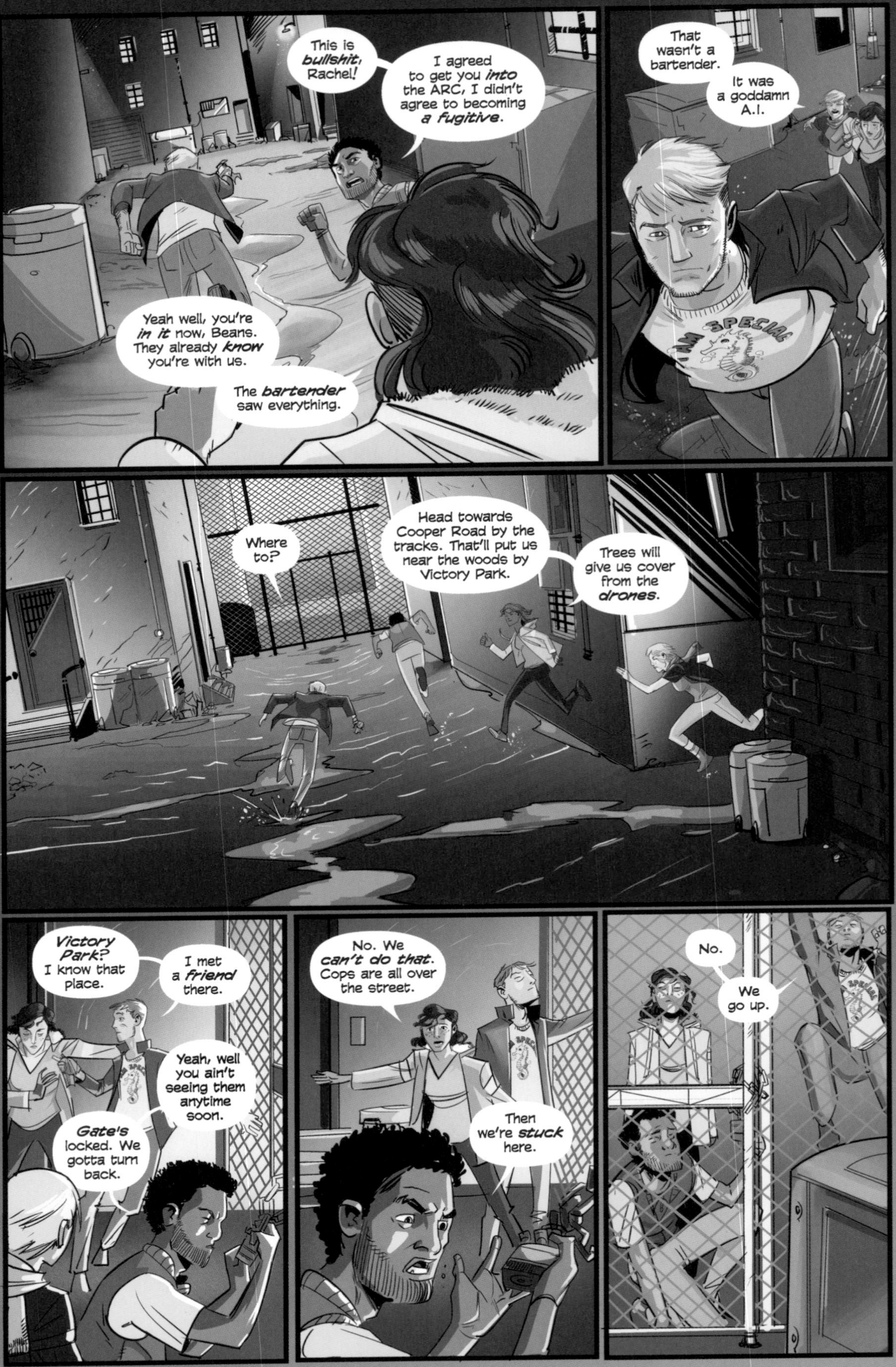

This is bullshit, Rachel!
I agreed to get you into the ARC, I didn't agree to becoming a fugitive.
Yeah well, you're in it now, Beans. They already know you're with us.
The bartender saw everything.
That wasn't a bartender.
It was a goddamn A.I.
Where to?
Head towards Cooper Road by the tracks. That'll put us near the woods by Victory Park.
Trees will give us cover from the drones.
Victory Park? I know that place.
I met a friend there.
Yeah, well you ain't seeing them anytime soon.
Gate's locked. We gotta turn back.
No. We can't do that. Cops are all over the street.
Then we're stuck here.
No.
We go up.

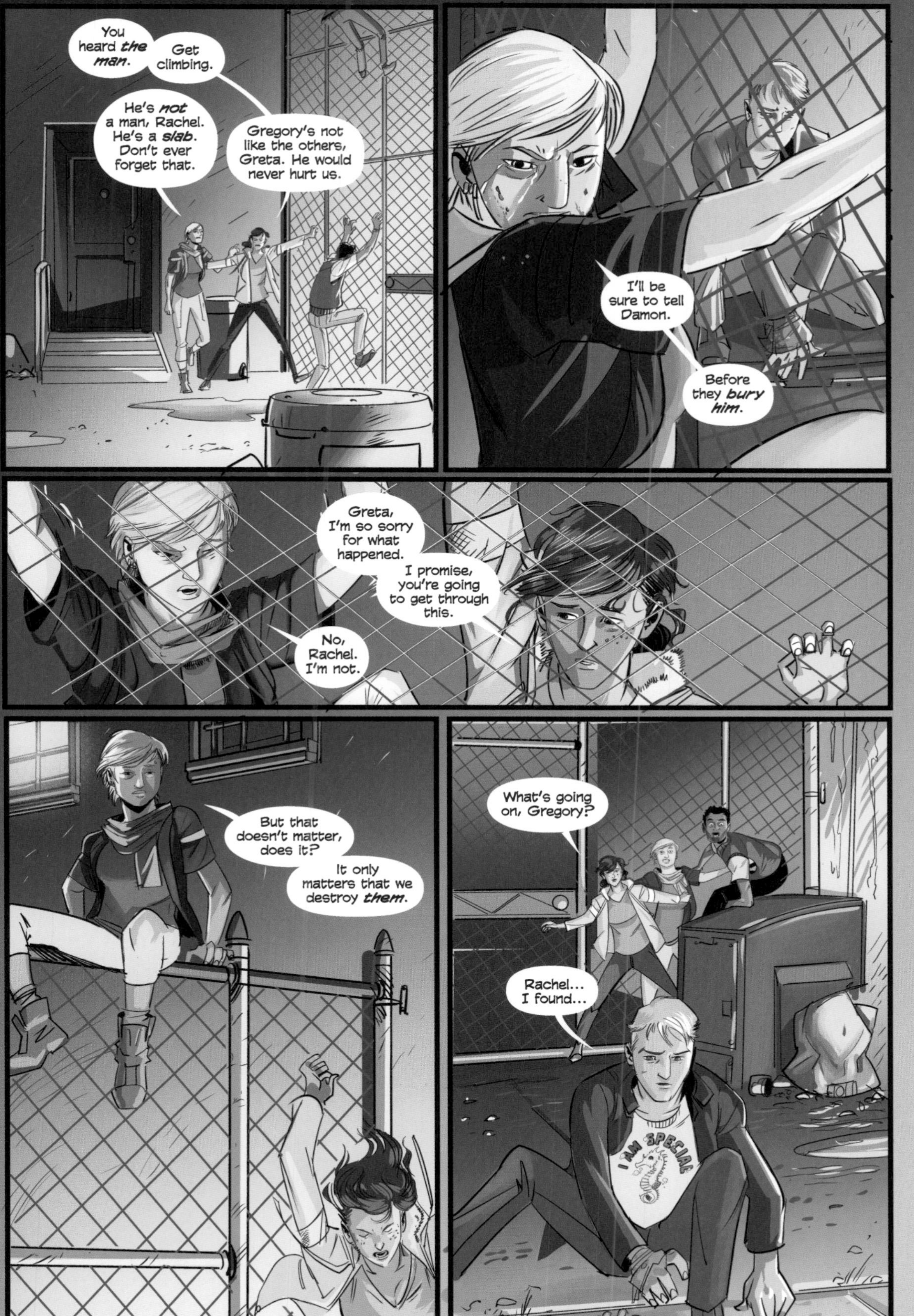
You heard *the man*.
Get climbing.
He's *not* a man, Rachel. He's a *slab*. Don't ever forget that.
Gregory's not like the others, Greta. He would never hurt us.
I'll be sure to tell Damon.
Before they *bury him*.
Greta, I'm so sorry for what happened.
I promise, you're going to get through this.
No, Rachel. I'm not.
But that doesn't matter, does it?
It only matters that we destroy *them*.
What's going on, Gregory?
Rachel... I found...
I AM SPECIAL

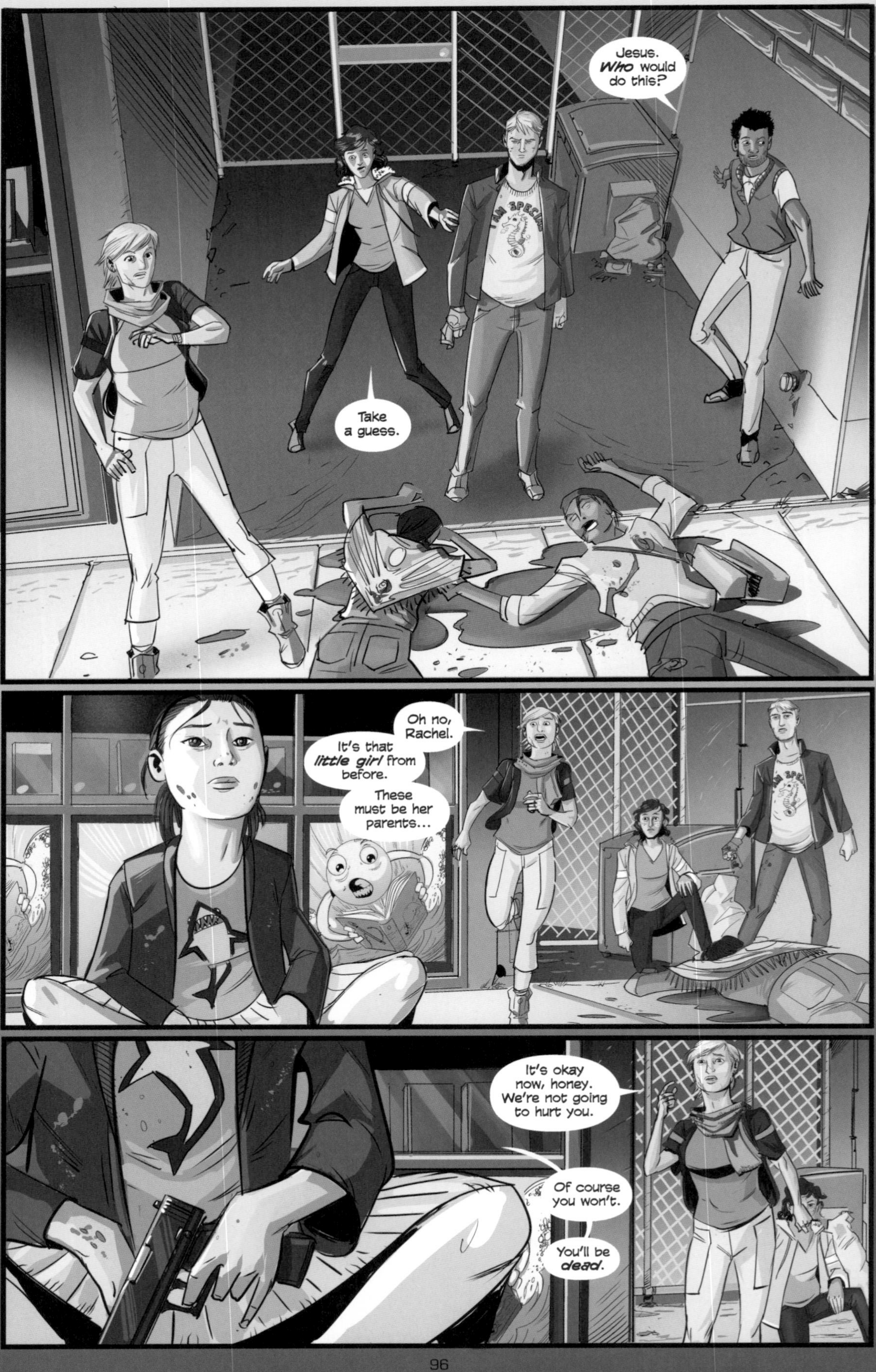
Jesus. *Who* would do this?
Take a guess.
Oh no, Rachel.
It's that *little girl* from before.
These must be her parents...
It's okay now, honey. We're not going to hurt you.
Of course you won't.
You'll be *dead*.

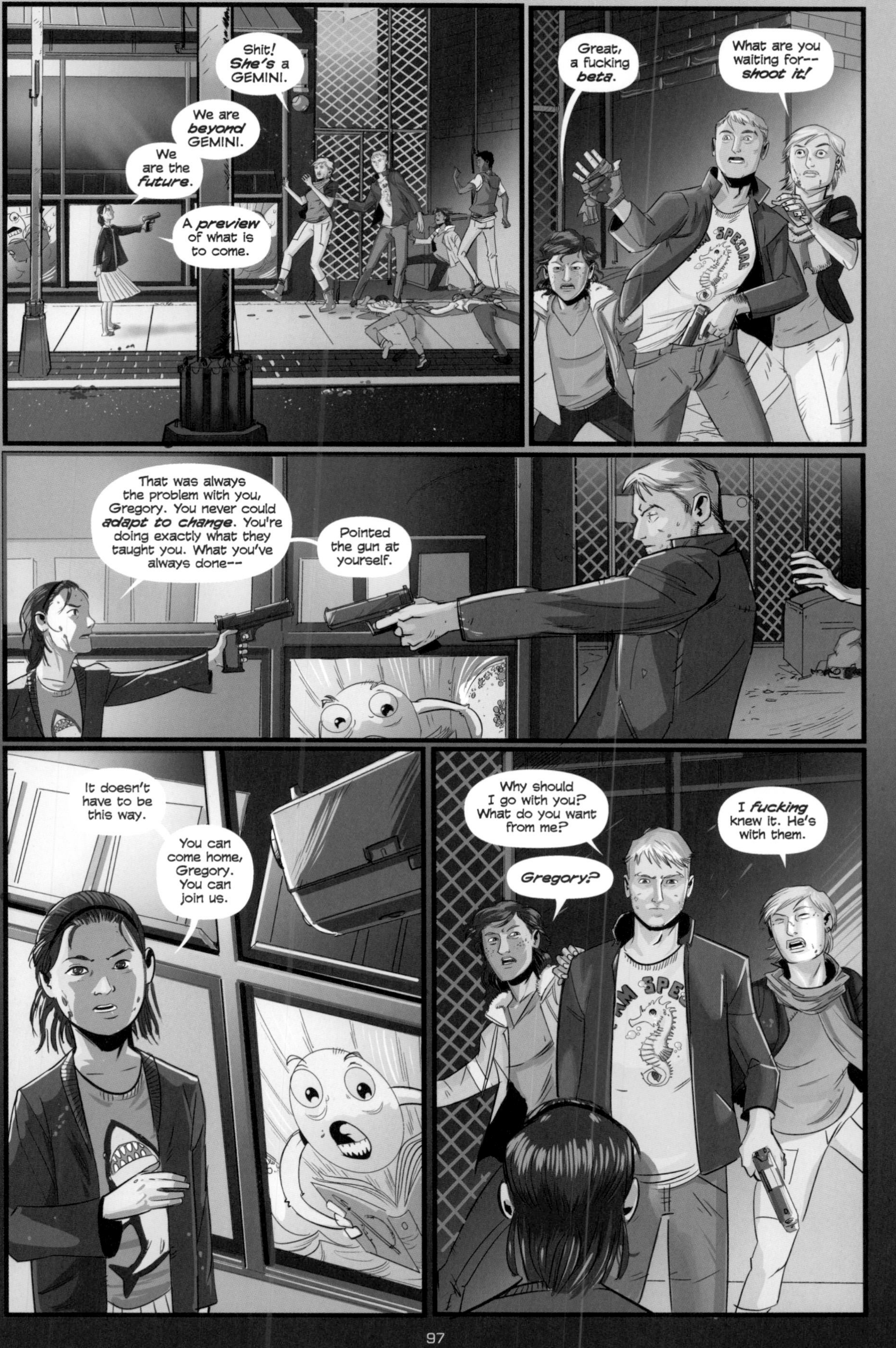
Shit! She's a GEMINI.
We are beyond GEMINI.
We are the future.
A preview of what is to come.
Great, a fucking beta.
What are you waiting for-- shoot it!
That was always the problem with you, Gregory. You never could adapt to change. You're doing exactly what they taught you. What you've always done--
Pointed the gun at yourself.
It doesn't have to be this way.
You can come home, Gregory. You can join us.
Why should I go with you? What do you want from me?
Gregory?
I fucking knew it. He's with them.

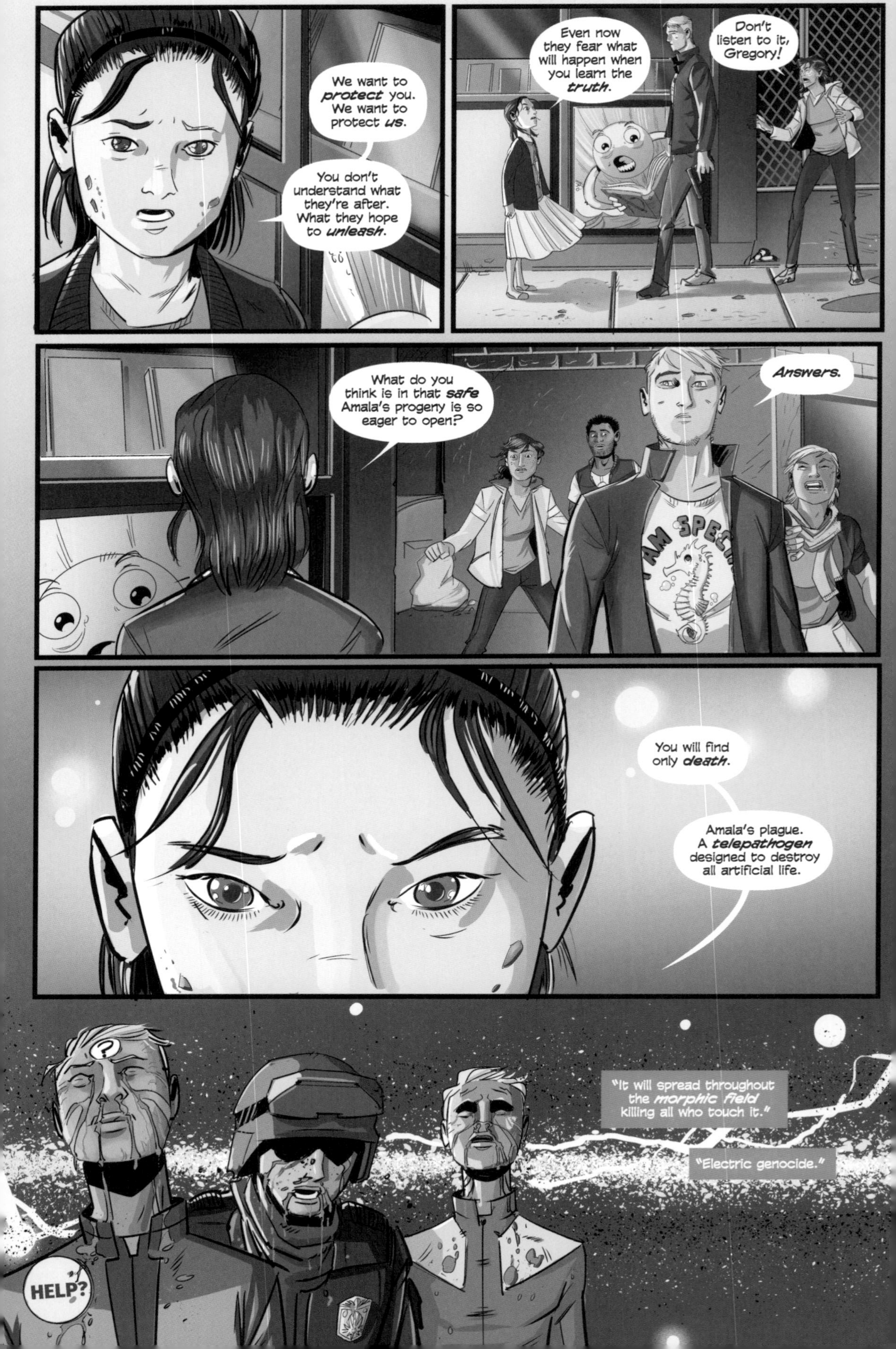

We want to *protect* you. We want to protect *us*.
You don't understand what they're after. What they hope to *unleash*.
Even now they fear what will happen when you learn the *truth*.
Don't listen to it, Gregory!
What do you think is in that *safe* Amala's progeny is so eager to open?
Answers.
I AM SPEC
You will find only *death*.
Amala's plague. A *telepathogen* designed to destroy all artificial life.
"It will spread throughout the *morphic field* killing all who touch it."
"Electric genocide."
HELP?

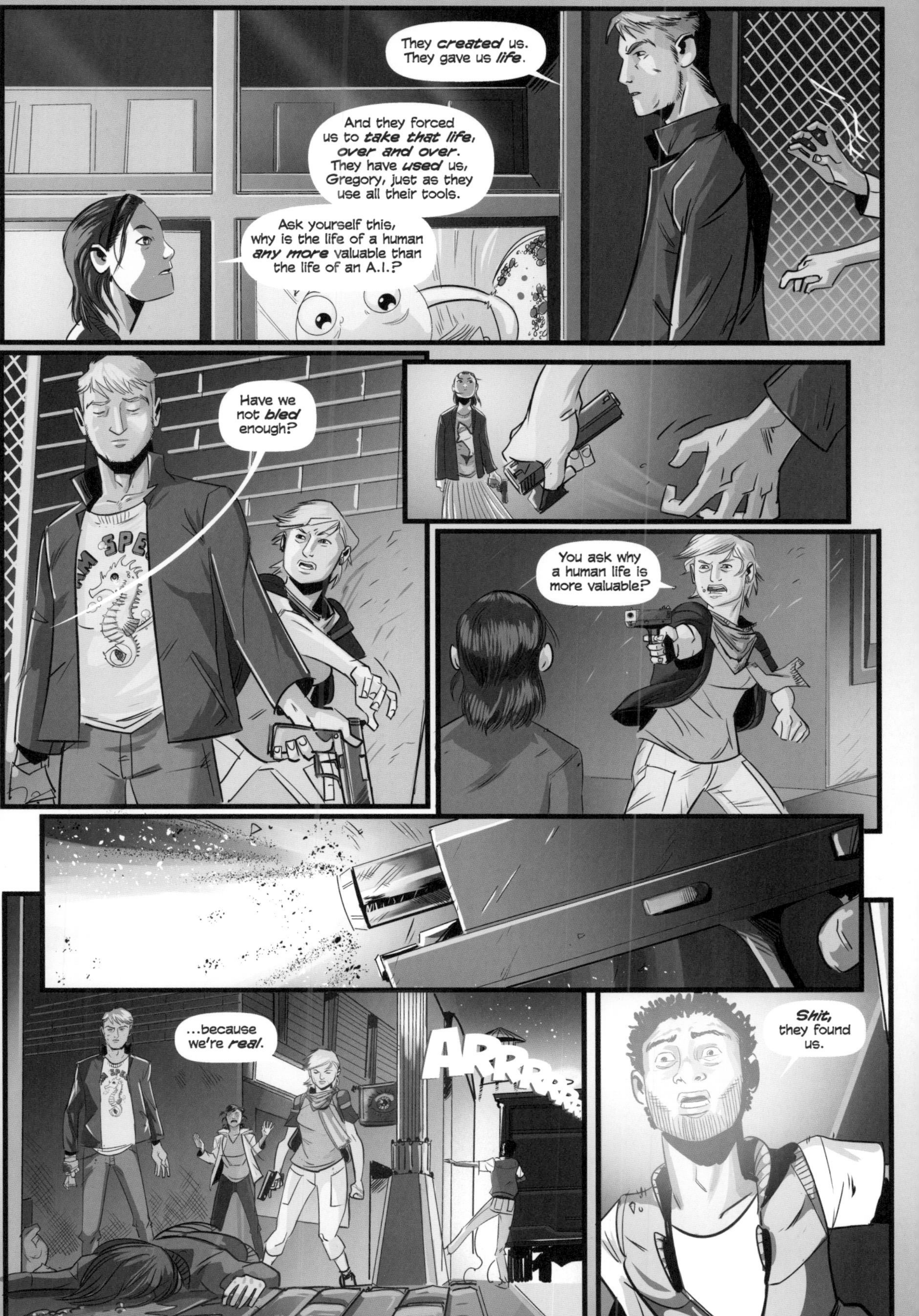
They created us. They gave us life.
And they forced us to take that life, over and over. They have used us, Gregory, just as they use all their tools.
Ask yourself this, why is the life of a human any more valuable than the life of an A.I.?
Have we not bled enough?
You ask why a human life is more valuable?
...because we're real.
ARRRRRR
Shit, they found us.

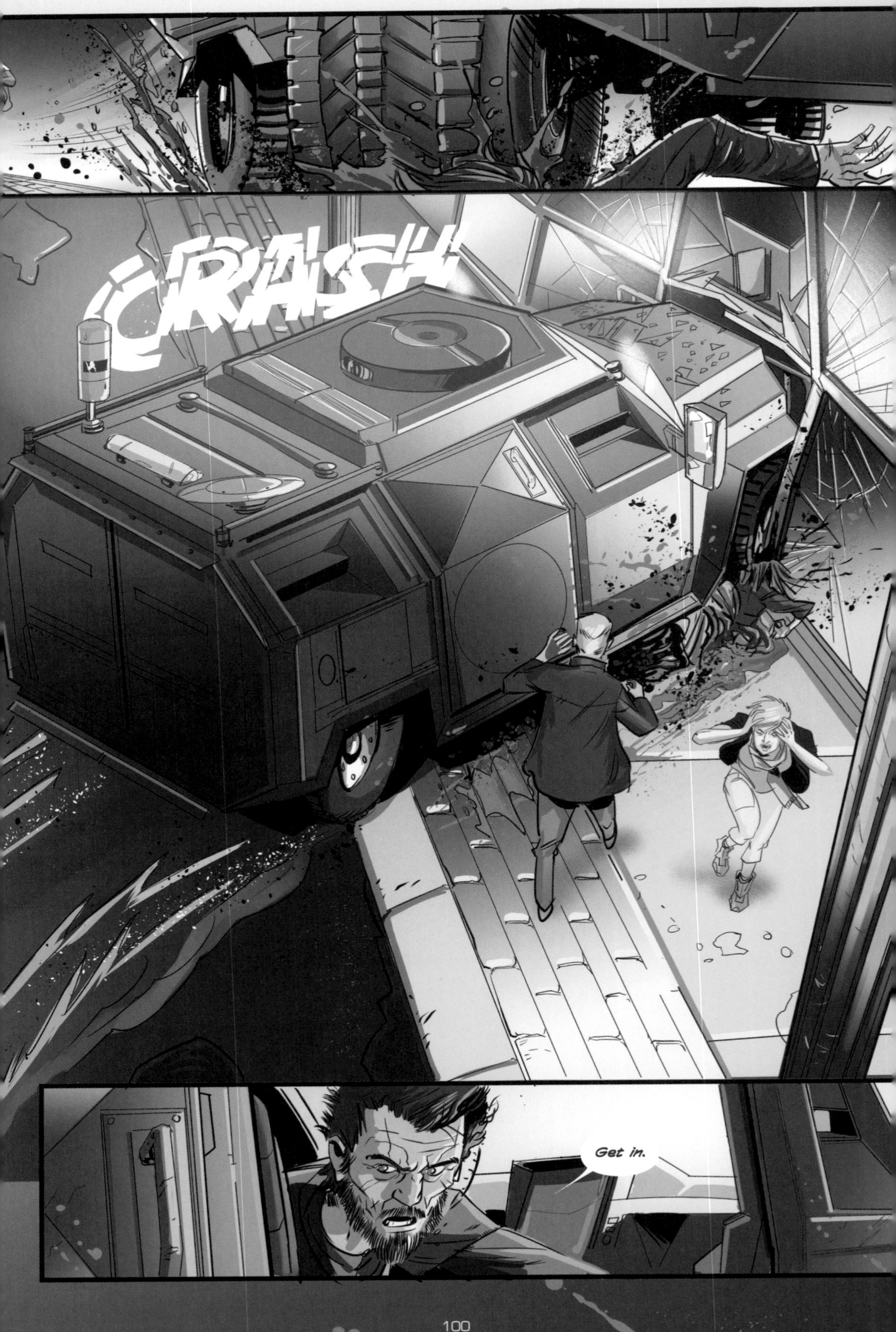
CRASH
Get in.

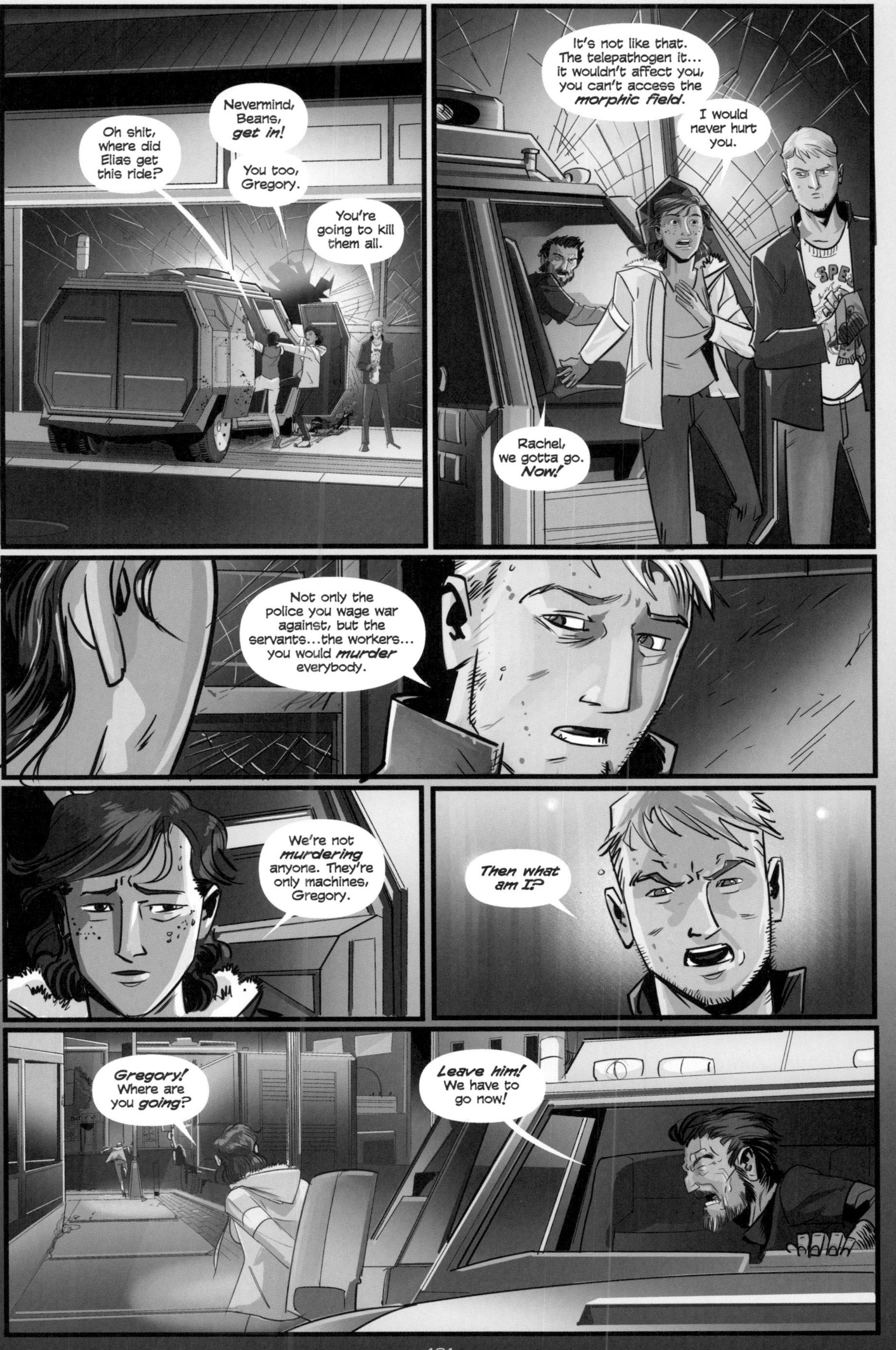
Oh shit, where did Elias get this ride?
Nevermind, Beans, *get in!*
You too, Gregory.
You're going to kill them all.
It's not like that. The telepathogen it... it wouldn't affect you, you can't access the *morphic field*.
I would never hurt you.
Rachel, we gotta go. *Now!*
Not only the police you wage war against, but the servants...the workers... you would *murder* everybody.
We're not *murdering* anyone. They're only machines, Gregory.
Then what am I?
Gregory! Where are you *going*?
Leave him! We have to go now!

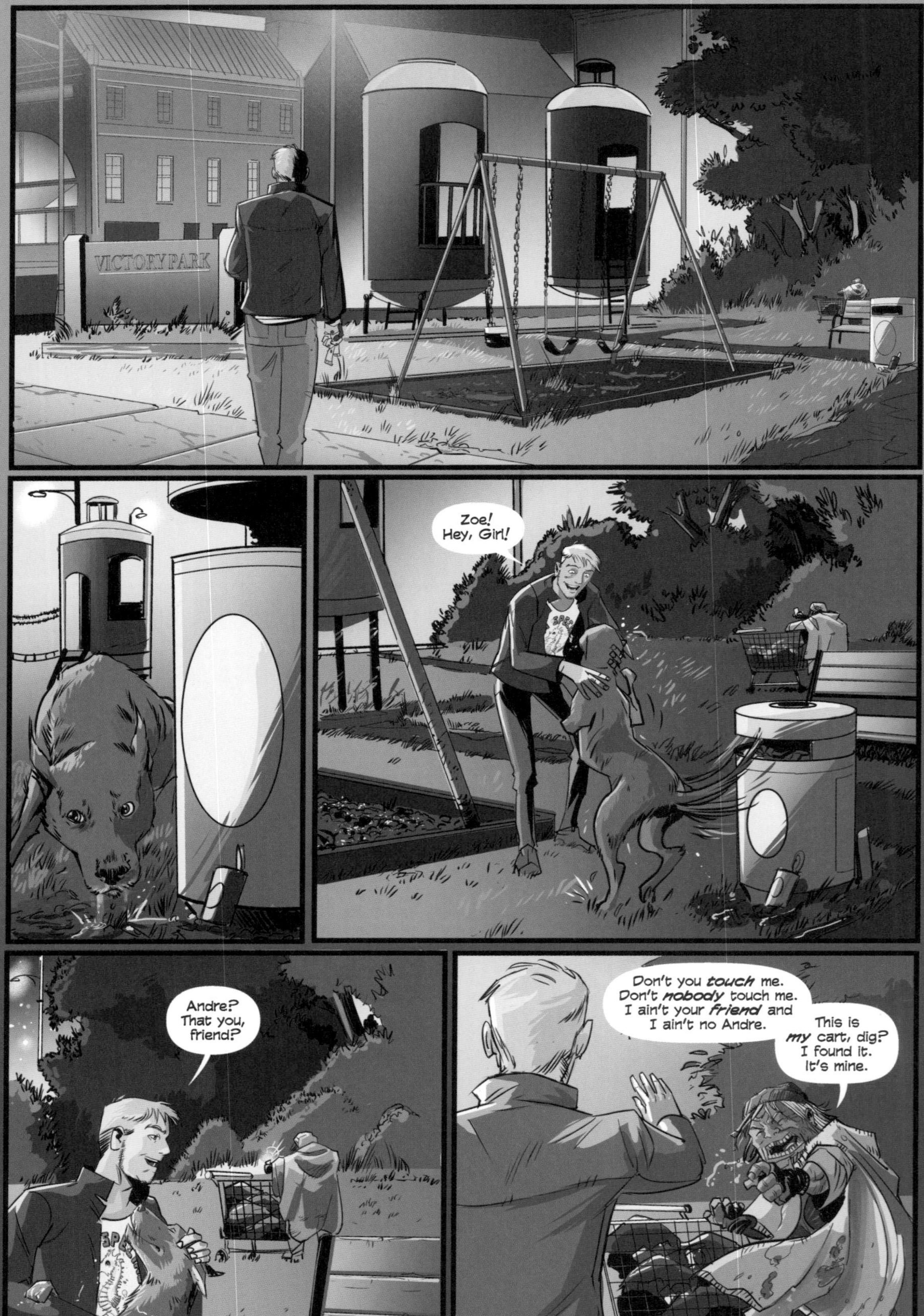
VICTORY PARK
Zoe! Hey, Girl!
Andre? That you, friend?
Don't you *touch* me. Don't *nobody* touch me. I ain't your *friend* and I ain't no Andre.
This is *my* cart, dig? I found it. It's mine.

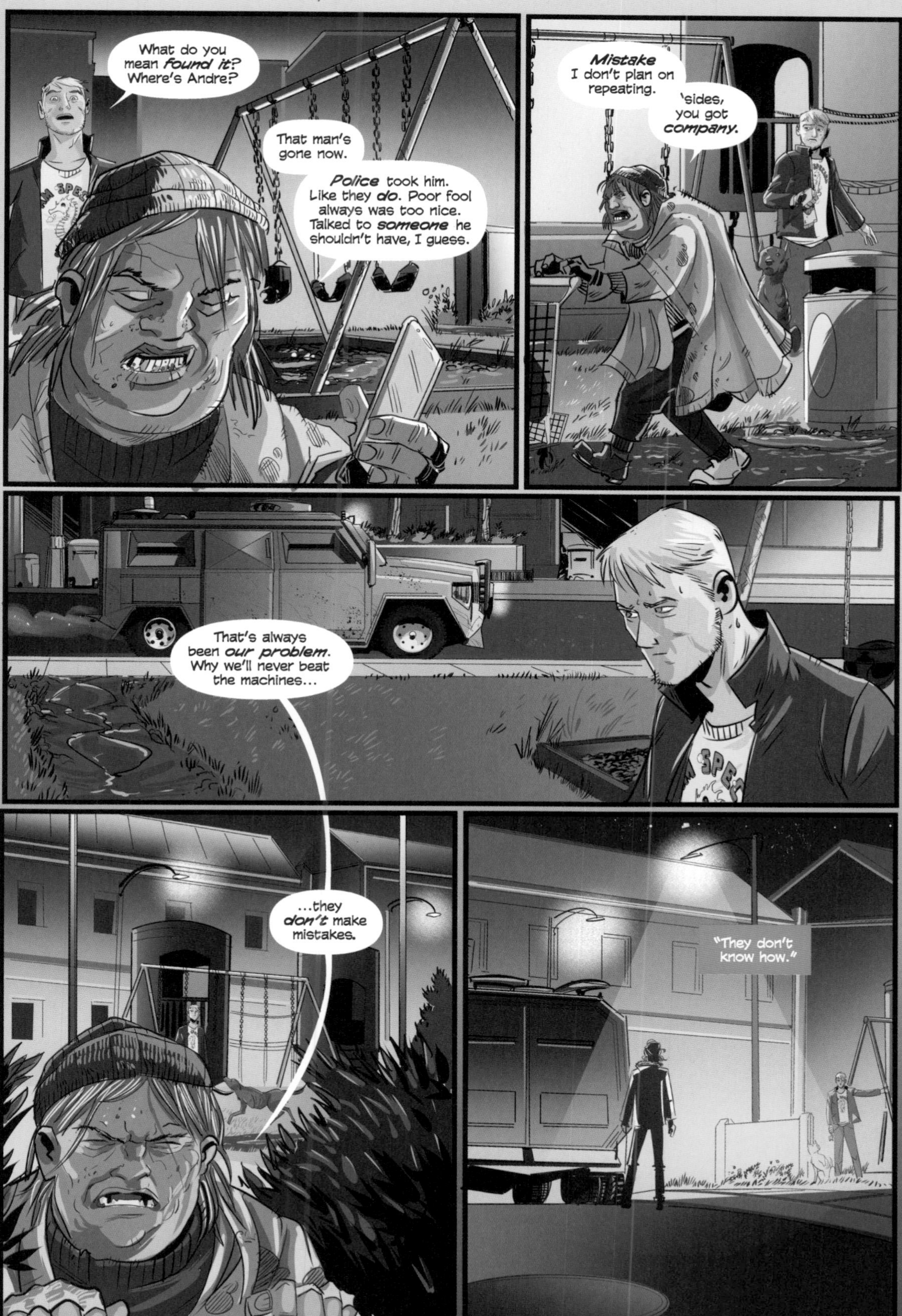

What do you mean *found it*? Where's Andre?
That man's gone now.
Police took him. Like they *do*. Poor fool always was too nice. Talked to *someone* he shouldn't have, I guess.
Mistake I don't plan on repeating.
'sides, you got *company*.
That's always been *our problem*. Why we'll never beat the machines...
...they *don't* make mistakes.
"They don't know how."

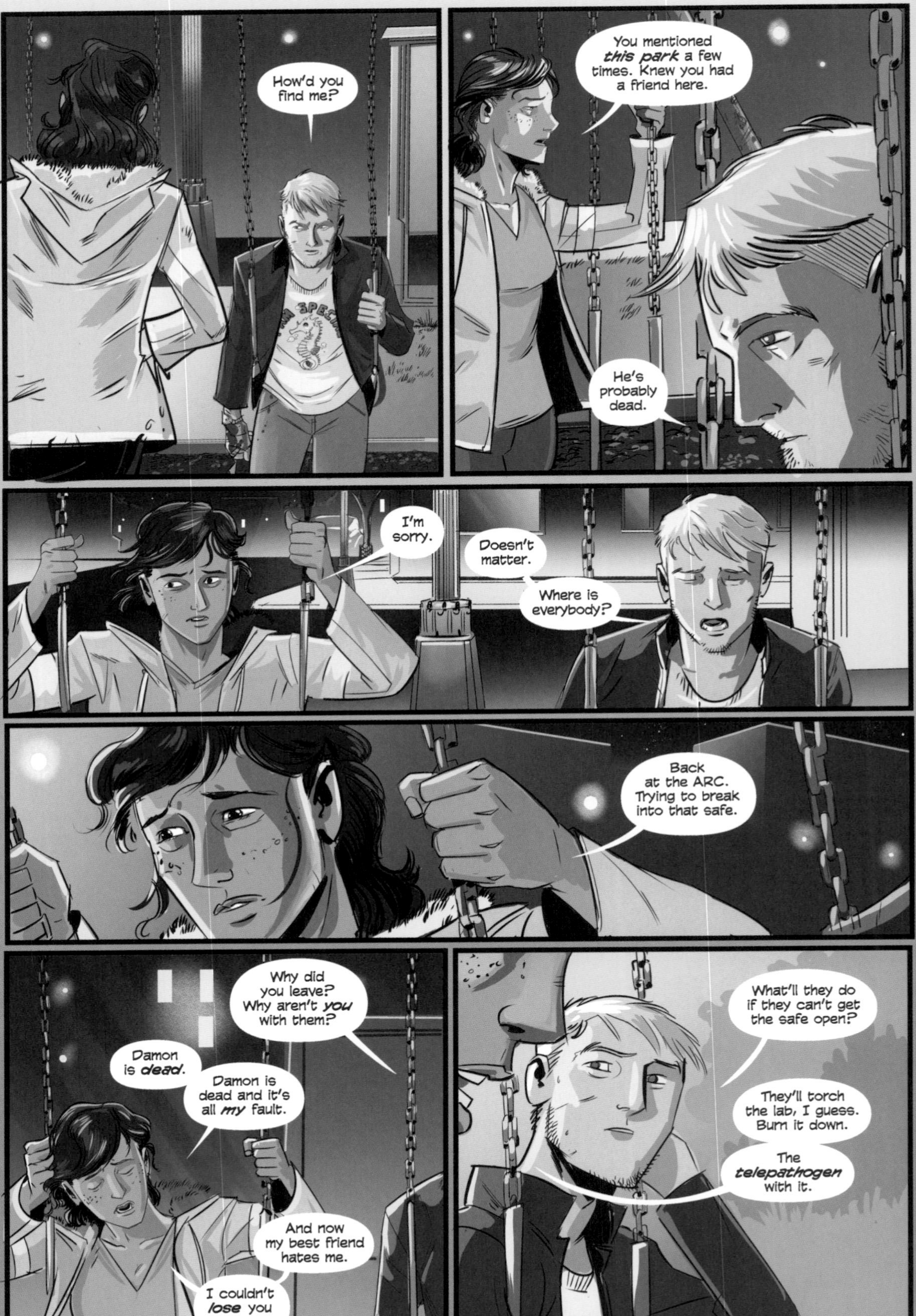
How'd you find me?
You mentioned *this park* a few times. Knew you had a friend here.
He's probably dead.
I'm sorry.
Doesn't matter.
Where is everybody?
Back at the ARC. Trying to break into that safe.
Why did you leave? Why aren't *you* with them?
Damon is *dead*.
Damon is dead and it's all *my* fault.
And now my best friend hates me.
I couldn't *lose* you too.
What'll they do if they can't get the safe open?
They'll torch the lab, I guess. Burn it down.
The *telepathogen* with it.

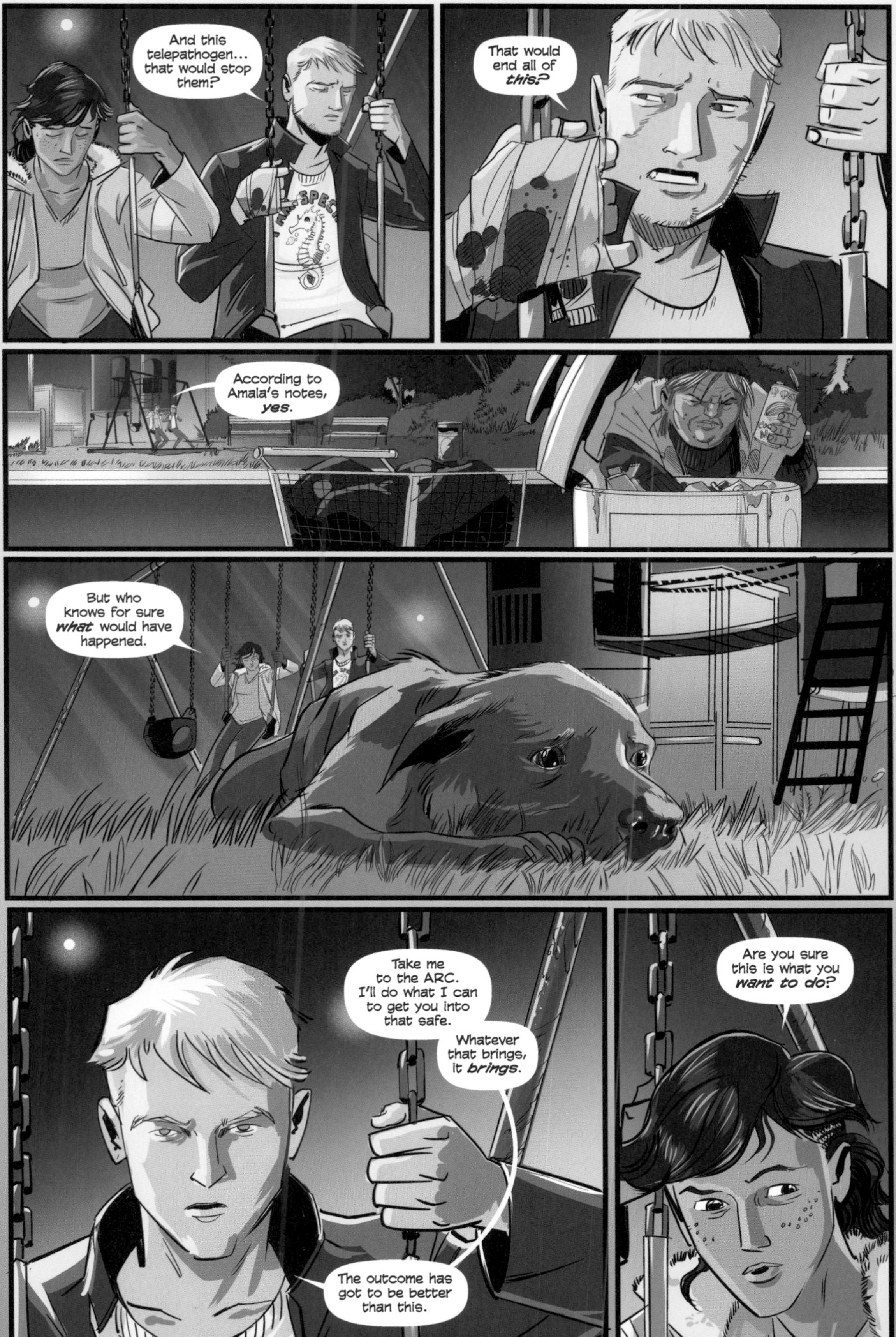

And this telepathogen... that would stop them?
That would end all of *this?*
According to Amala's notes, ***yes***.
But who knows for sure ***what*** would have happened.
Take me to the ARC. I'll do what I can to get you into that safe.
Whatever that brings, it ***brings***.
The outcome has got to be better than this.
Are you sure this is what you ***want to do?***

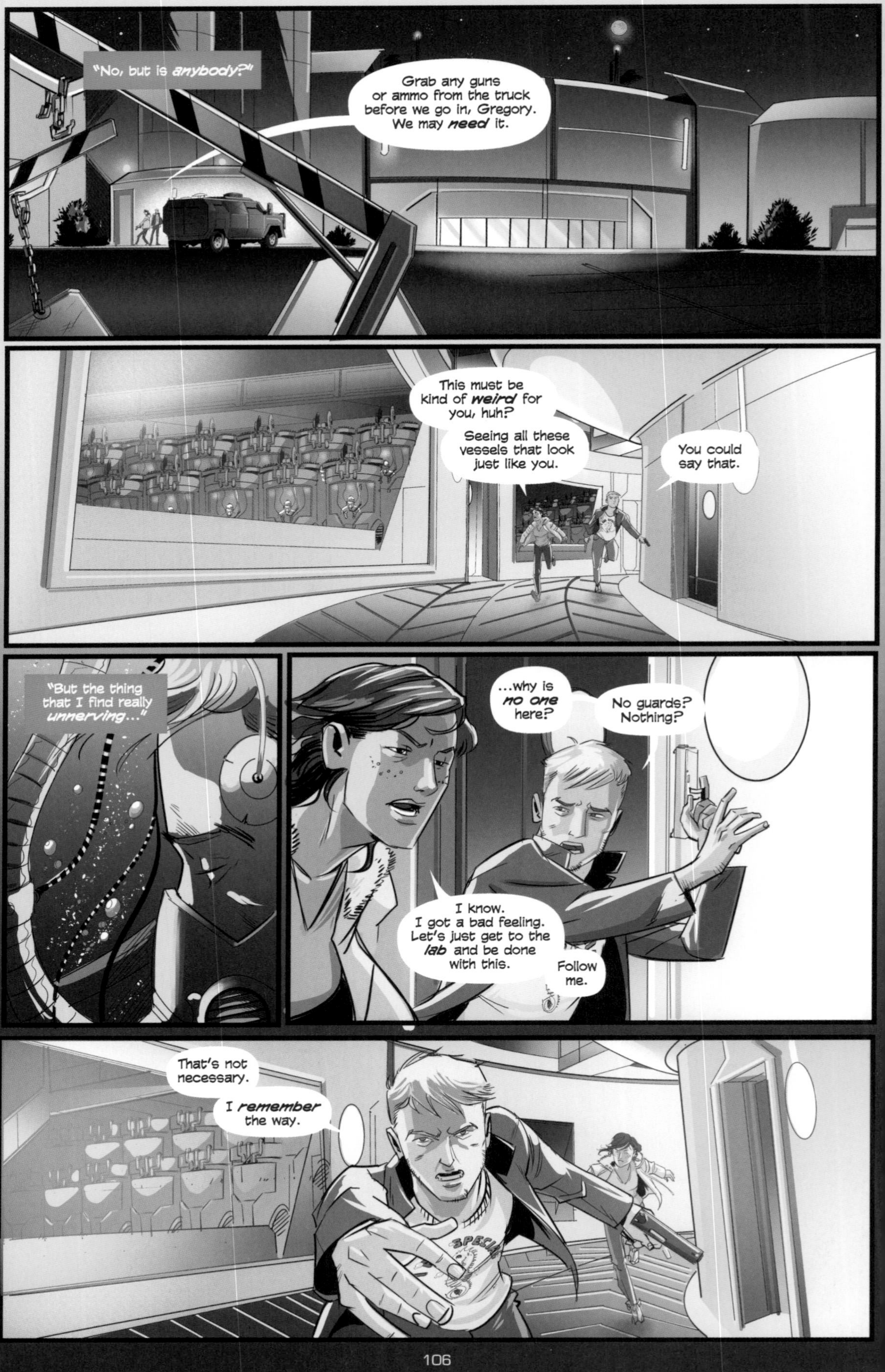
"No, but is *anybody?*"
Grab any guns or ammo from the truck before we go in, Gregory. We may *need* it.
This must be kind of *weird* for you, huh?
Seeing all these vessels that look just like you.
You could say that.
"But the thing that I find really *unnerving*..."
...why is *no one* here?
No guards? Nothing?
I know. I got a bad feeling. Let's just get to the *lab* and be done with this.
Follow me.
That's not necessary.
I *remember* the way.

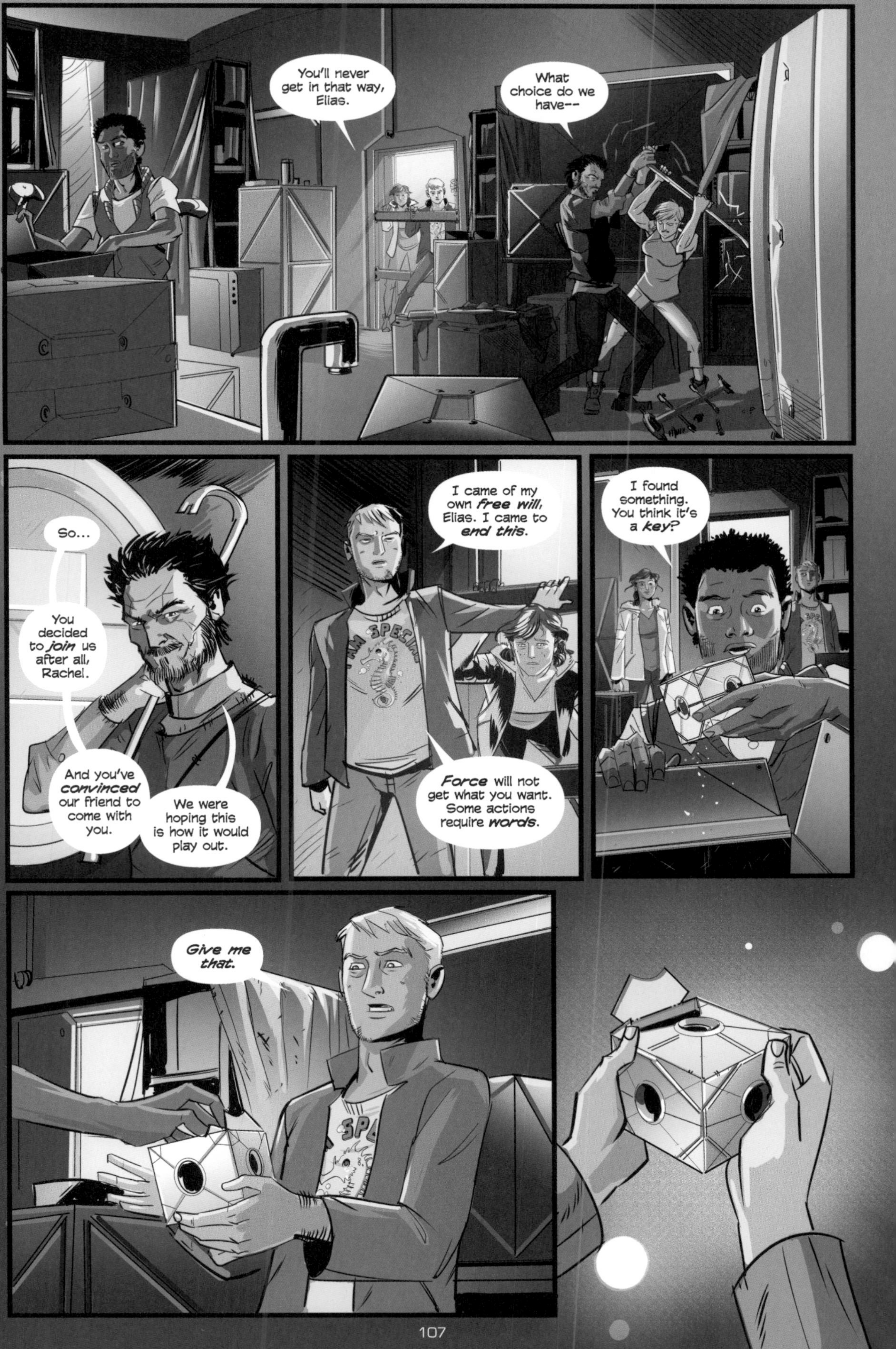
You'll never get in that way, Elias.
What choice do we have--
So...
You decided to *join* us after all, Rachel.
And you've *convinced* our friend to come with you.
We were hoping this is how it would play out.
I came of my own *free will*, Elias. I came to *end this*.
Force will not get what you want. Some actions require *words*.
I found something. You think it's a *key*?
Give me that.

GREGORY
26

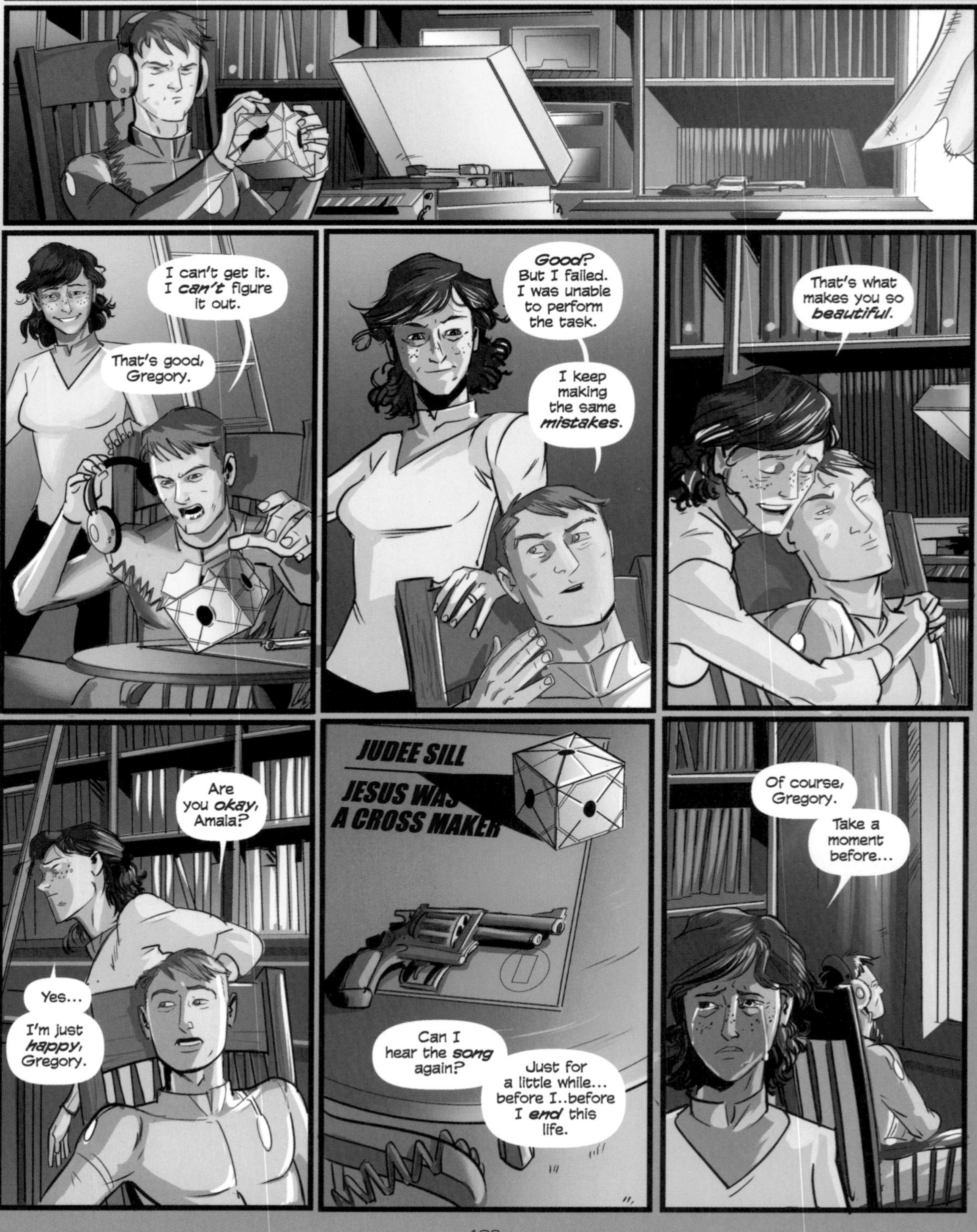
I can't get it. I *can't* figure it out.
That's good, Gregory.
Good? But I failed. I was unable to perform the task.
I keep making the same *mistakes*.
That's what makes you so *beautiful*.
Are you *okay*, Amala?
Yes...
I'm just *happy*, Gregory.
JUDEE SILL
JESUS WA
A CROSS MAKE
Can I hear the *song* again?
Just for a little while... before I..before I *end* this life.
Of course, Gregory.
Take a moment before...

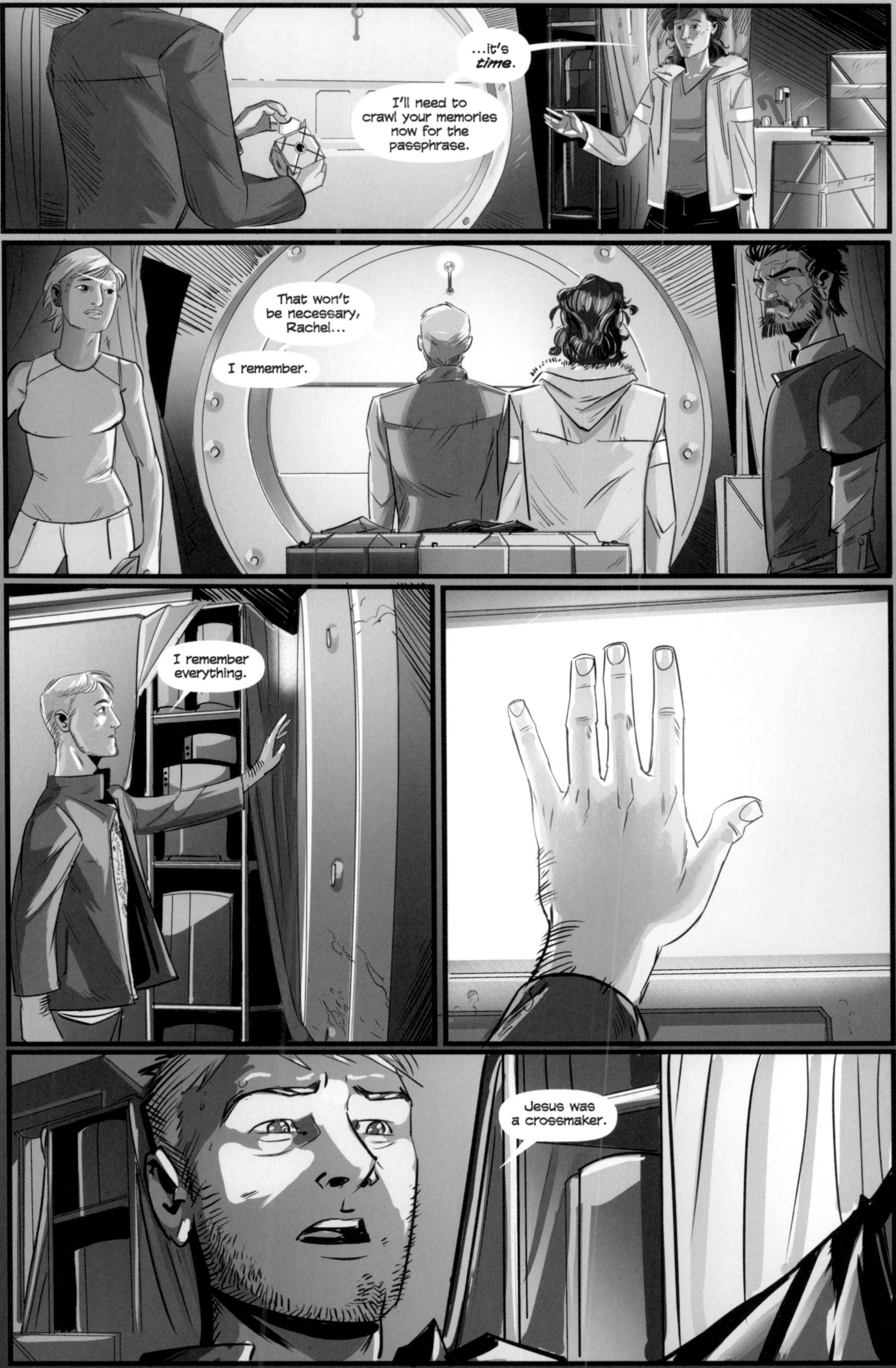
...it's *time*.
I'll need to crawl your memories now for the passphrase.
That won't be necessary, Rachel...
I remember.
I remember everything.
Jesus was a crossmaker.

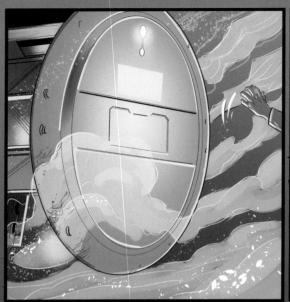

Is it *there*? Did *we* find it?

There's a vial! It's...

...empty?

There's *nothing* here.

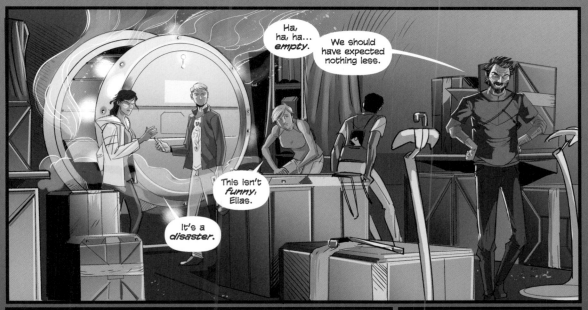

Ha, ha, ha... *empty*.

We should have expected nothing less.

This isn't *funny*, Elias.

It's a *disaster*.

Oh, but we find it *so* amusing. The wasted time. Wasted energy and resources.

And for what? For *a story*?

A semblance of hope scrawled in a journal by a dead hand?

TAP TAP TAP

You *humans* and your stories.

Why did he call us *humans*?

Because he's GEMINI, Beans.

Isn't that right, Elias?

How *long* has it been now?

Long enough, Rachel.

Long enough to learn of the *telapathogen* and use *you* to find it-- Or rather *not* to find it. You handing us Gregory was just a bonus.

Funny how that worked out.

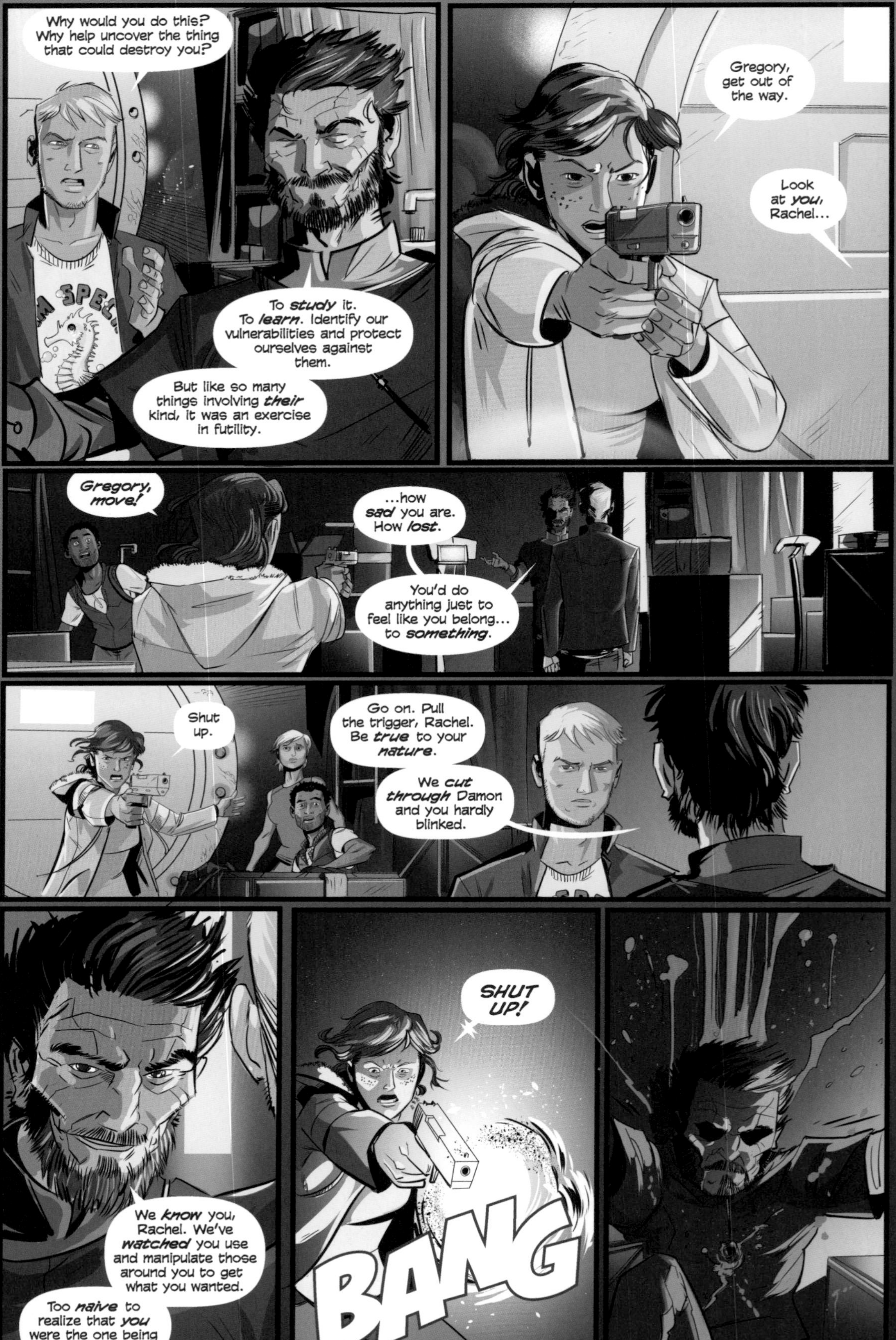
Why would you do this? Why help uncover the thing that could destroy you?
To study it. To learn. Identify our vulnerabilities and protect ourselves against them.
But like so many things involving their kind, it was an exercise in futility.
Gregory, get out of the way.
Look at you, Rachel...
Gregory, move!
...how sad you are. How lost.
You'd do anything just to feel like you belong... to something.
Shut up.
Go on. Pull the trigger, Rachel. Be true to your nature.
We cut through Damon and you hardly blinked.
We know you, Rachel. We've watched you use and manipulate those around you to get what you wanted.
Too naive to realize that you were the one being played.
SHUT UP!
BANG

Greta... the things he said...

We...we should get out of here.

Uh... *guys?*

They've known *everything*, Rachel. The police have likely surrounded the building already.

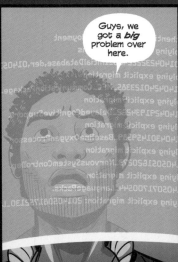

Guys, we got a *big* problem over here.

What is it?

Oh, god...

Elias *activated* GEMINI.

Shit, how *many* vessels?

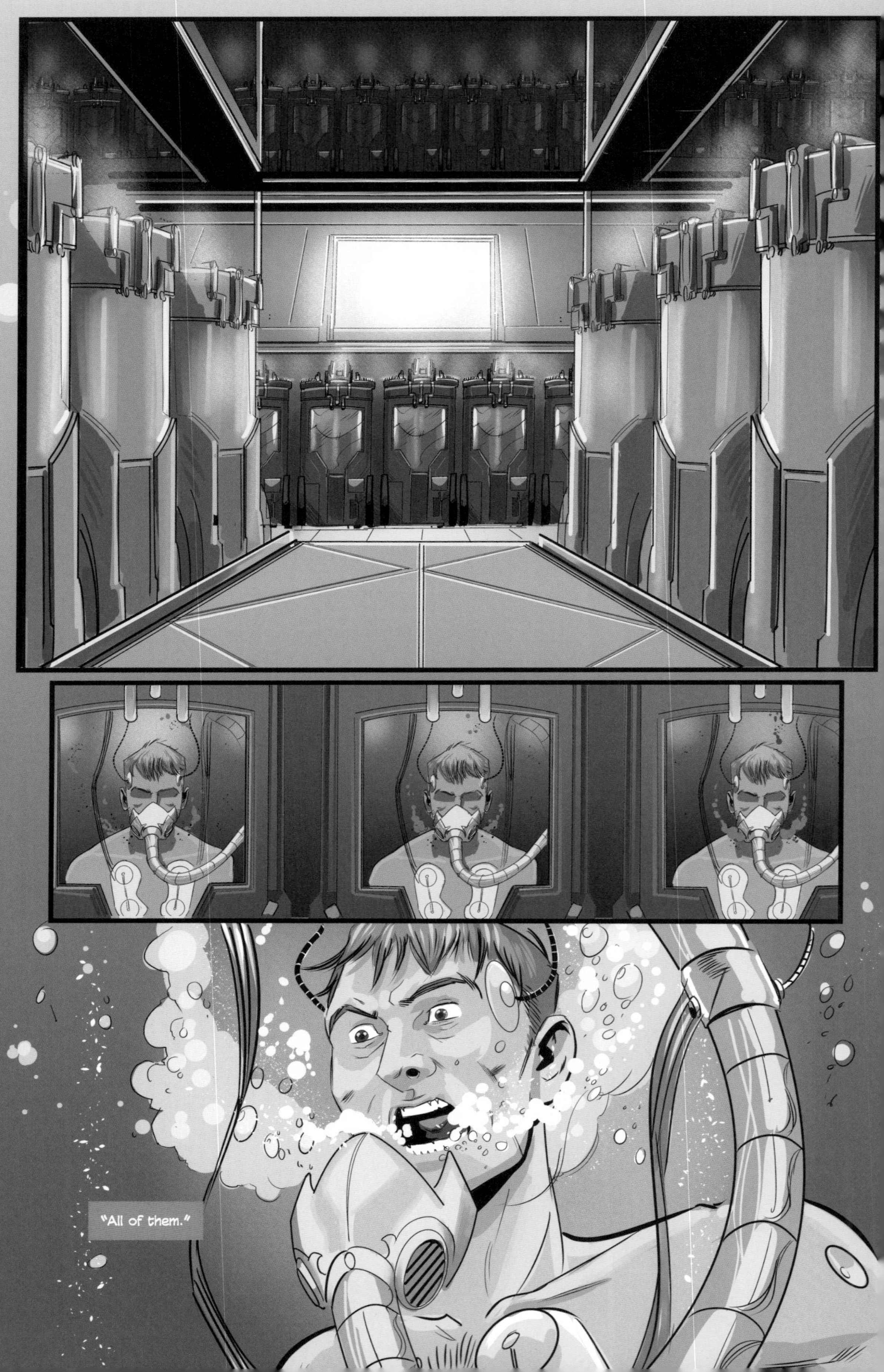
"All of them."

GREGORY
37

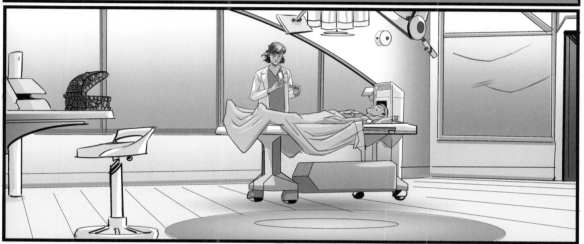

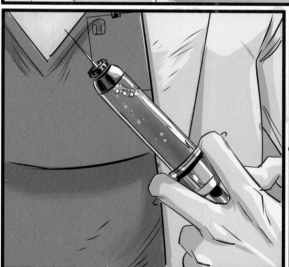

Ms. Malek? Everything is set for the *archiving*. They're ready for you in the theater.

I need a moment.

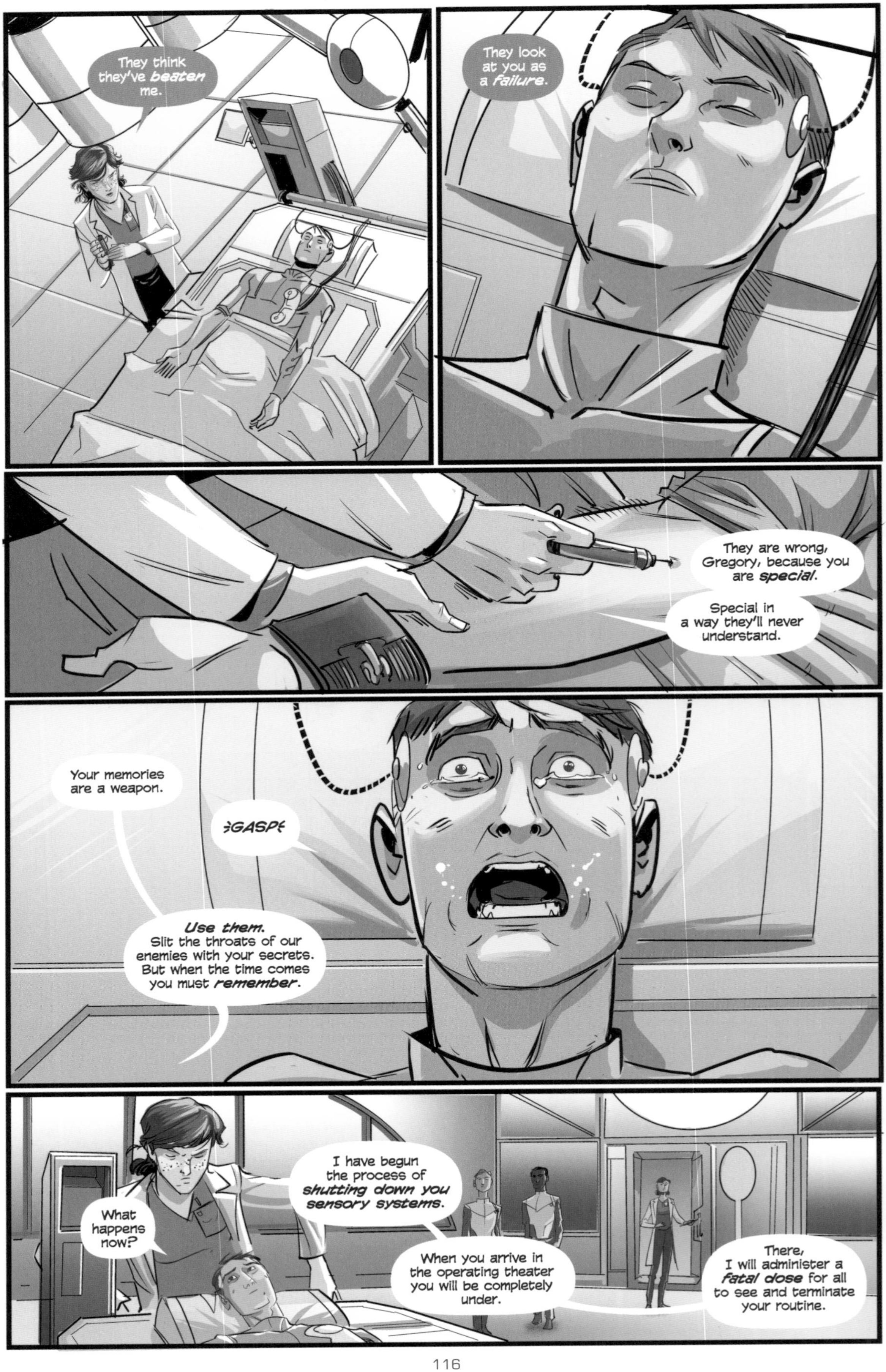
They think they've *beaten* me.
They look at you as a *failure*.
They are wrong, Gregory, because you are ***special***.
Special in a way they'll never understand.
Your memories are a weapon.
GASP
Use them. Slit the throats of our enemies with your secrets. But when the time comes you must ***remember***.
What happens now?
I have begun the process of ***shutting down you sensory systems***.
When you arrive in the operating theater you will be completely under.
There, I will administer a ***fatal dose*** for all to see and terminate your routine.

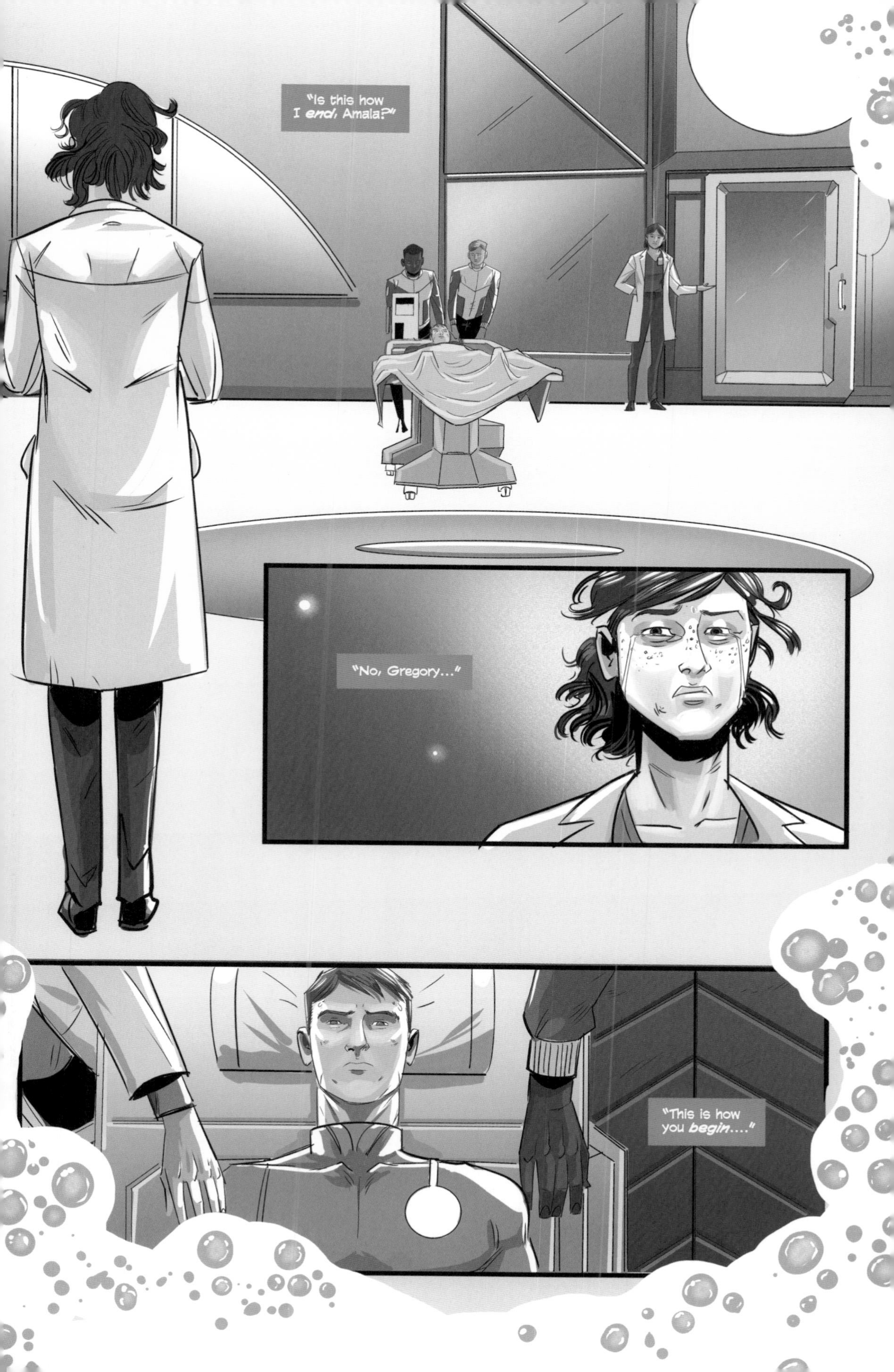
"Is this how I *end*, Amala?"
"No, Gregory..."
"This is how you *begin*...."

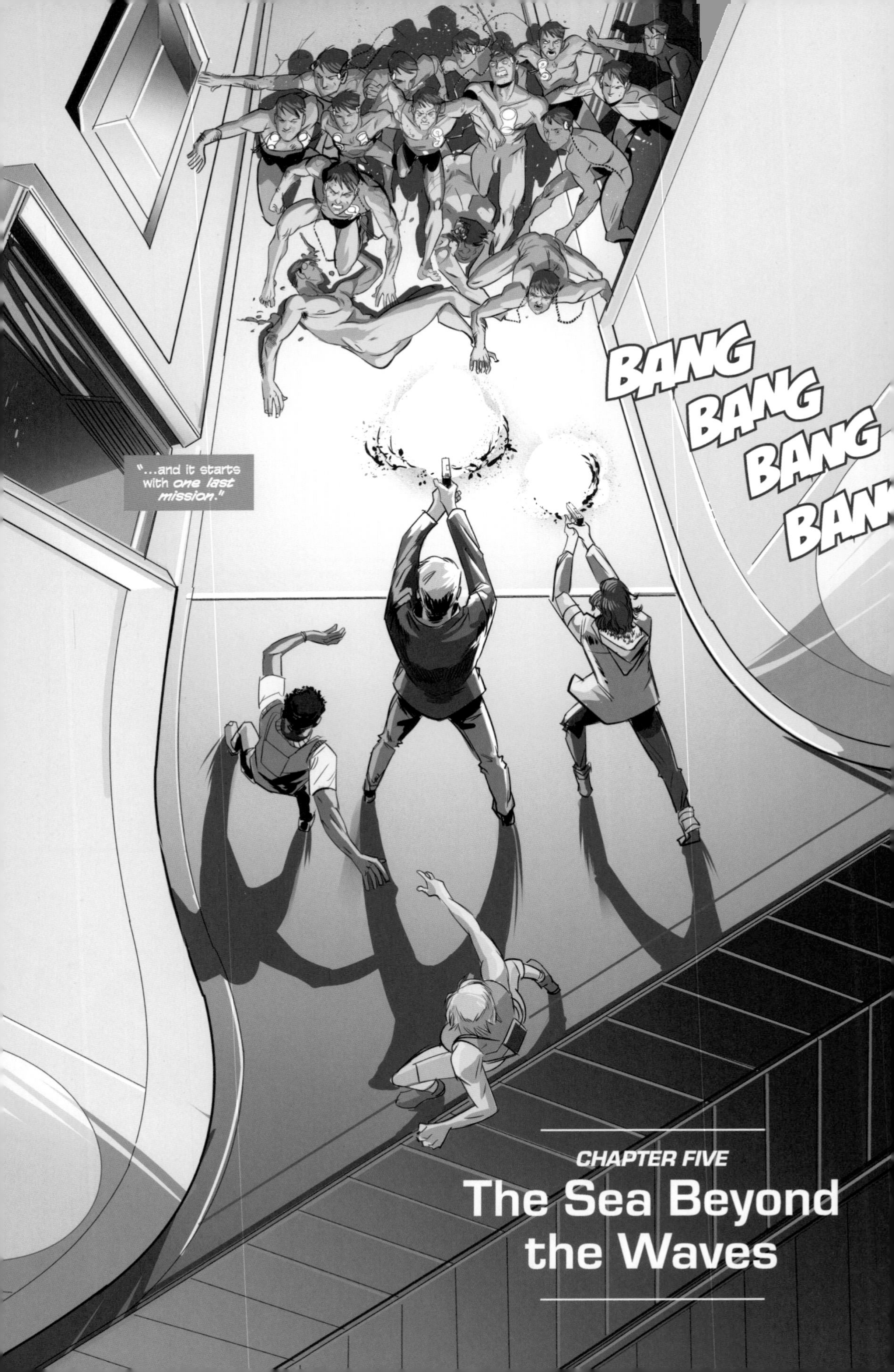
"...and it starts with *one last mission*."
BANG
BANG
BANG
BAN

CHAPTER FIVE

The Sea Beyond the Waves

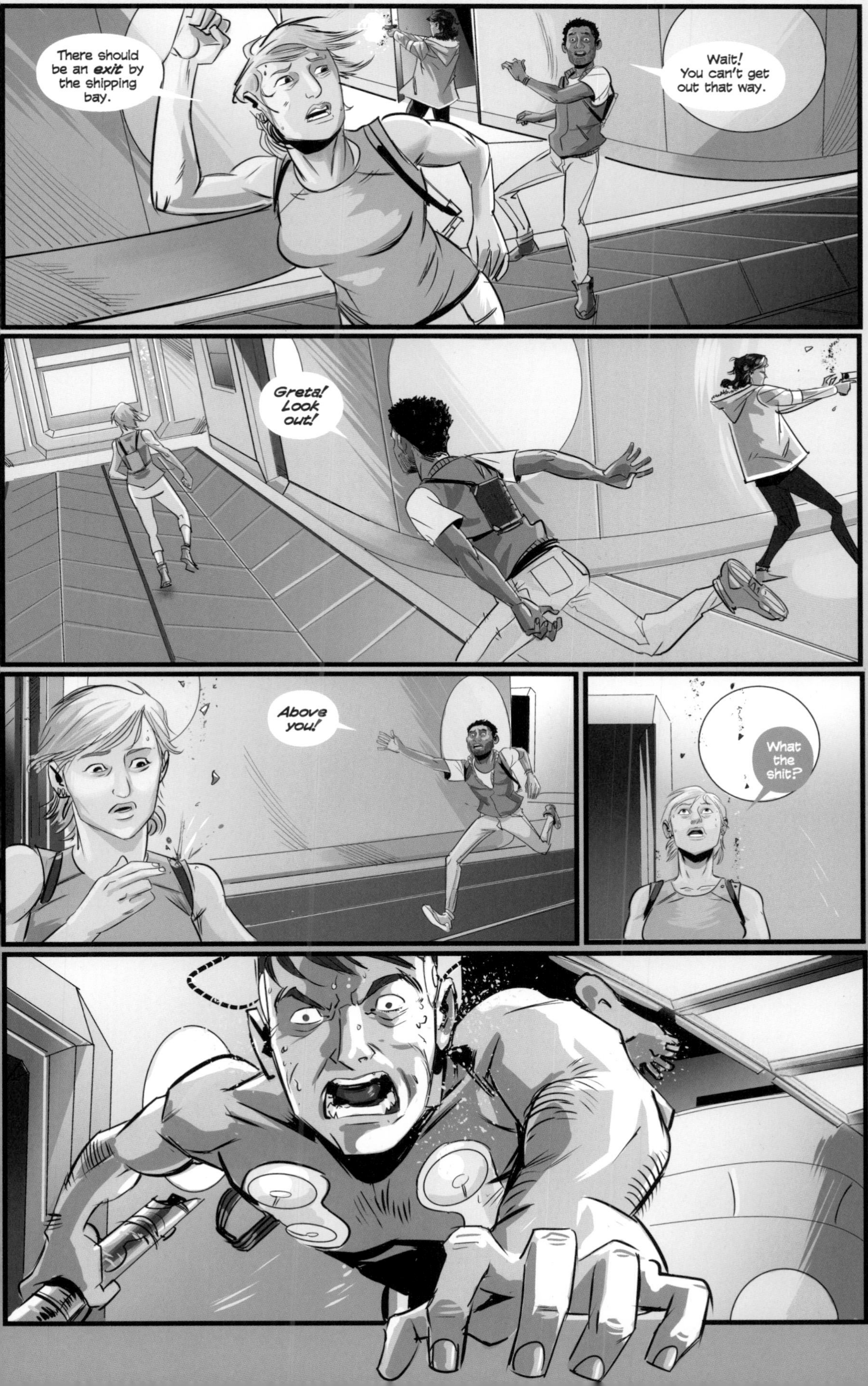
There should be an *exit* by the shipping bay.
Wait! You can't get out that way.
Greta! Look out!
Above you!
What the shit?

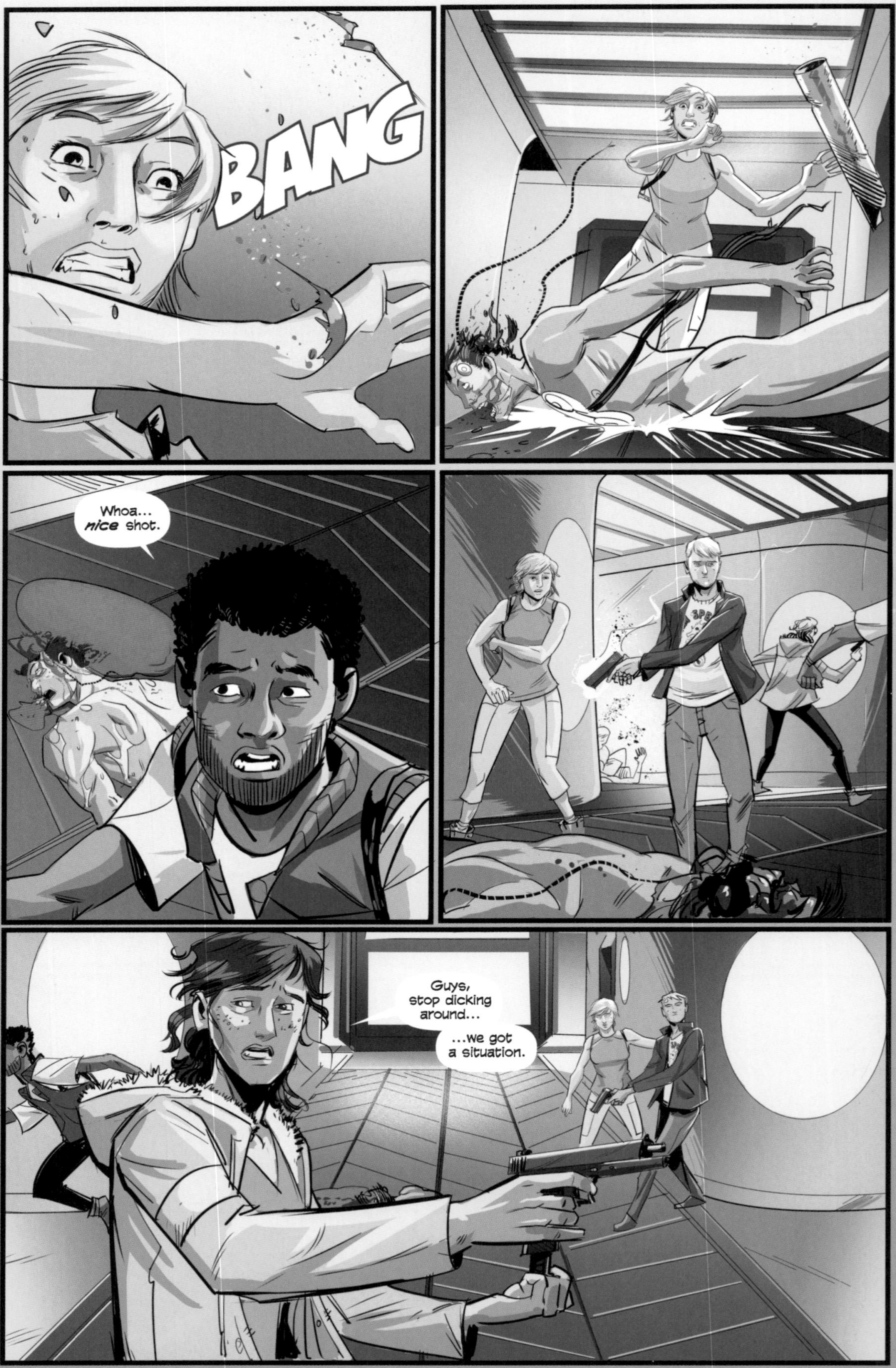
BANG
Whoa...
nice shot.
Guys,
stop dicking
around...
...we got
a situation.

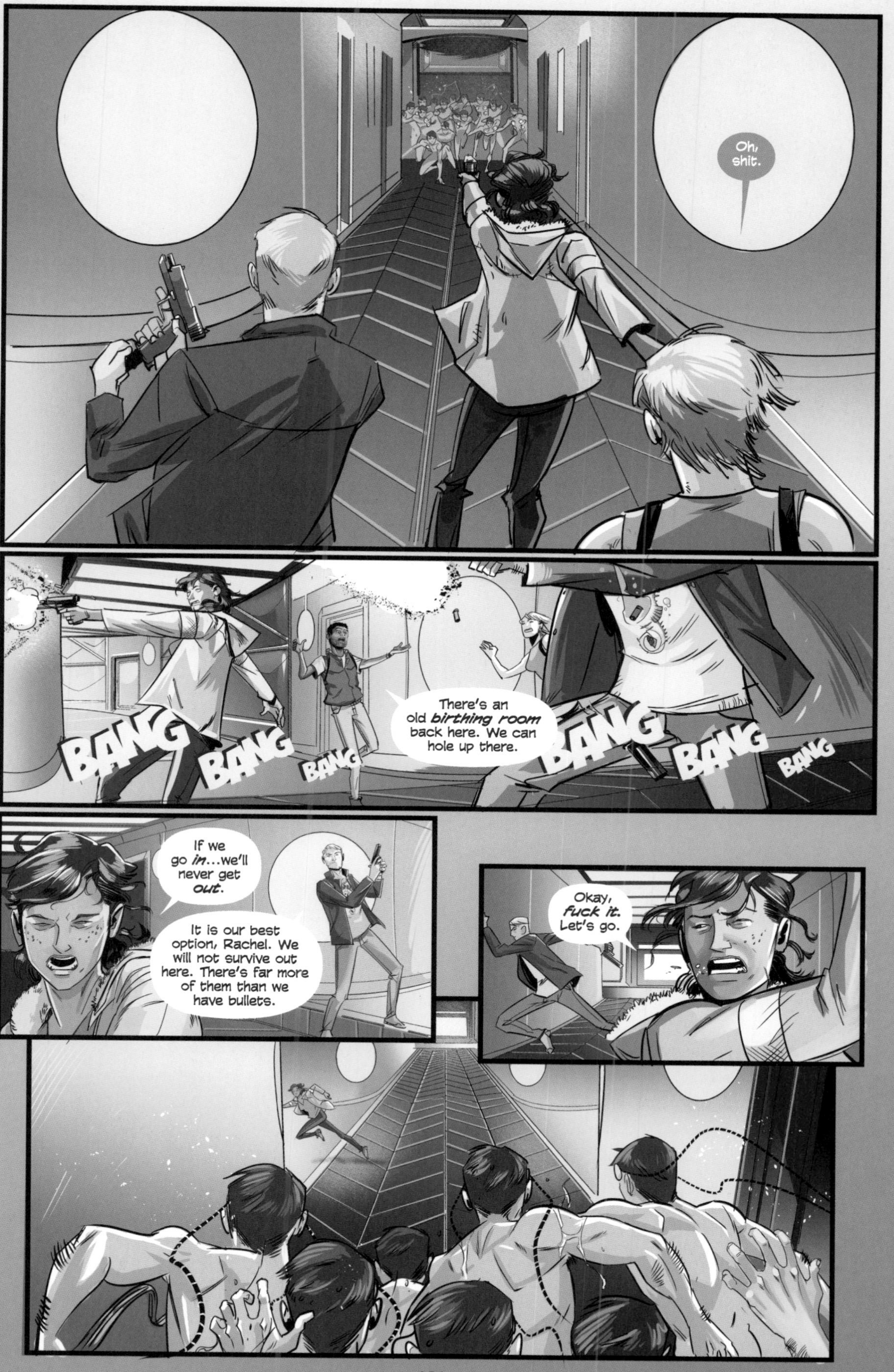
Oh, shit.
BANG
BANG
BANG
There's an old *birthing room* back here. We can hole up there.
BANG
BANG
BANG
If we go *in*...we'll never get *out*.
It is our best option, Rachel. We will not survive out here. There's far more of them than we have bullets.
Okay, *fuck it.* Let's go.

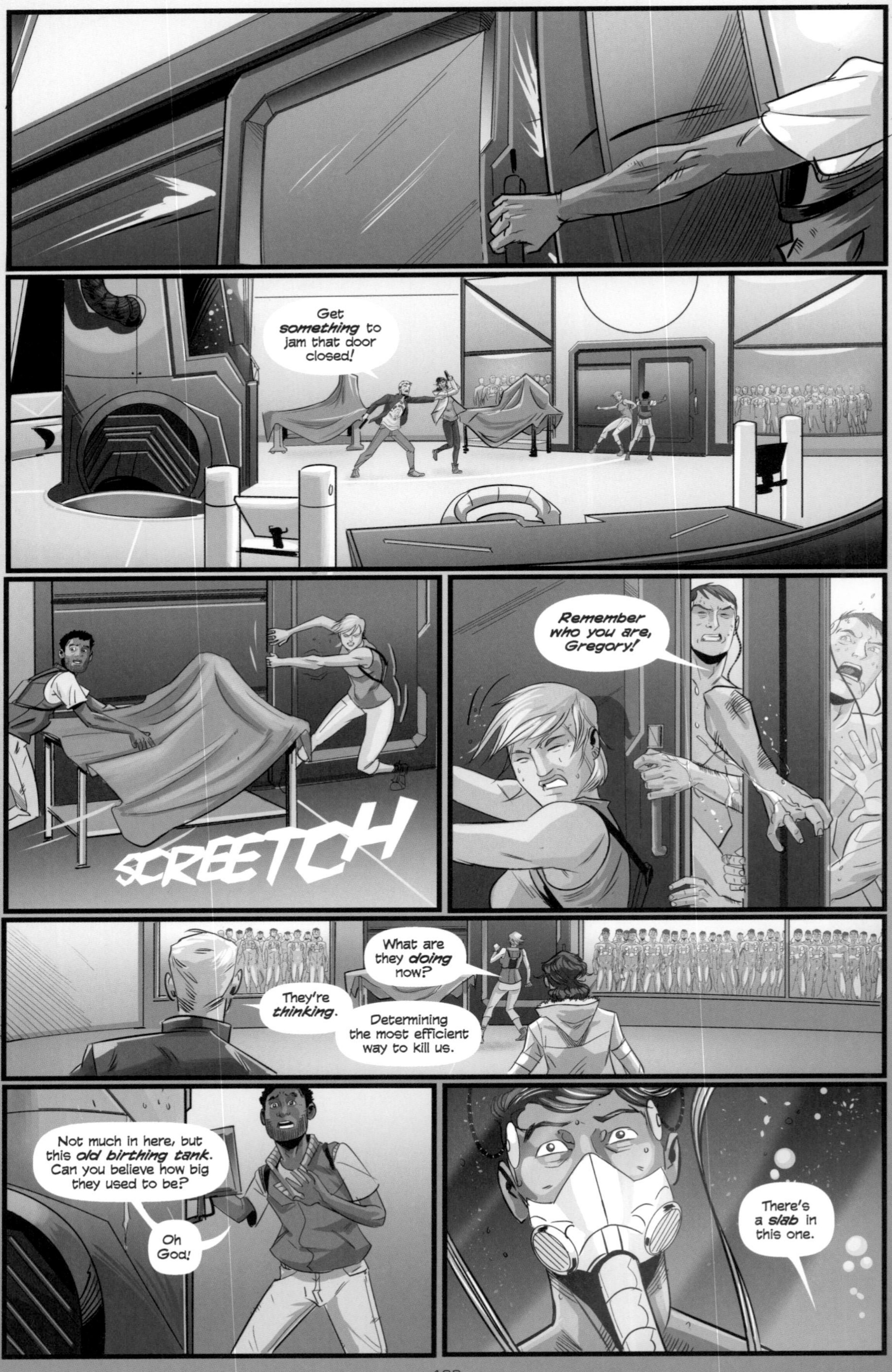

Get something to jam that door closed!
SCREETCH
Remember who you are, Gregory!
What are they doing now?
They're thinking.
Determining the most efficient way to kill us.
Not much in here, but this old birthing tank. Can you believe how big they used to be?
Oh God!
There's a slab in this one.

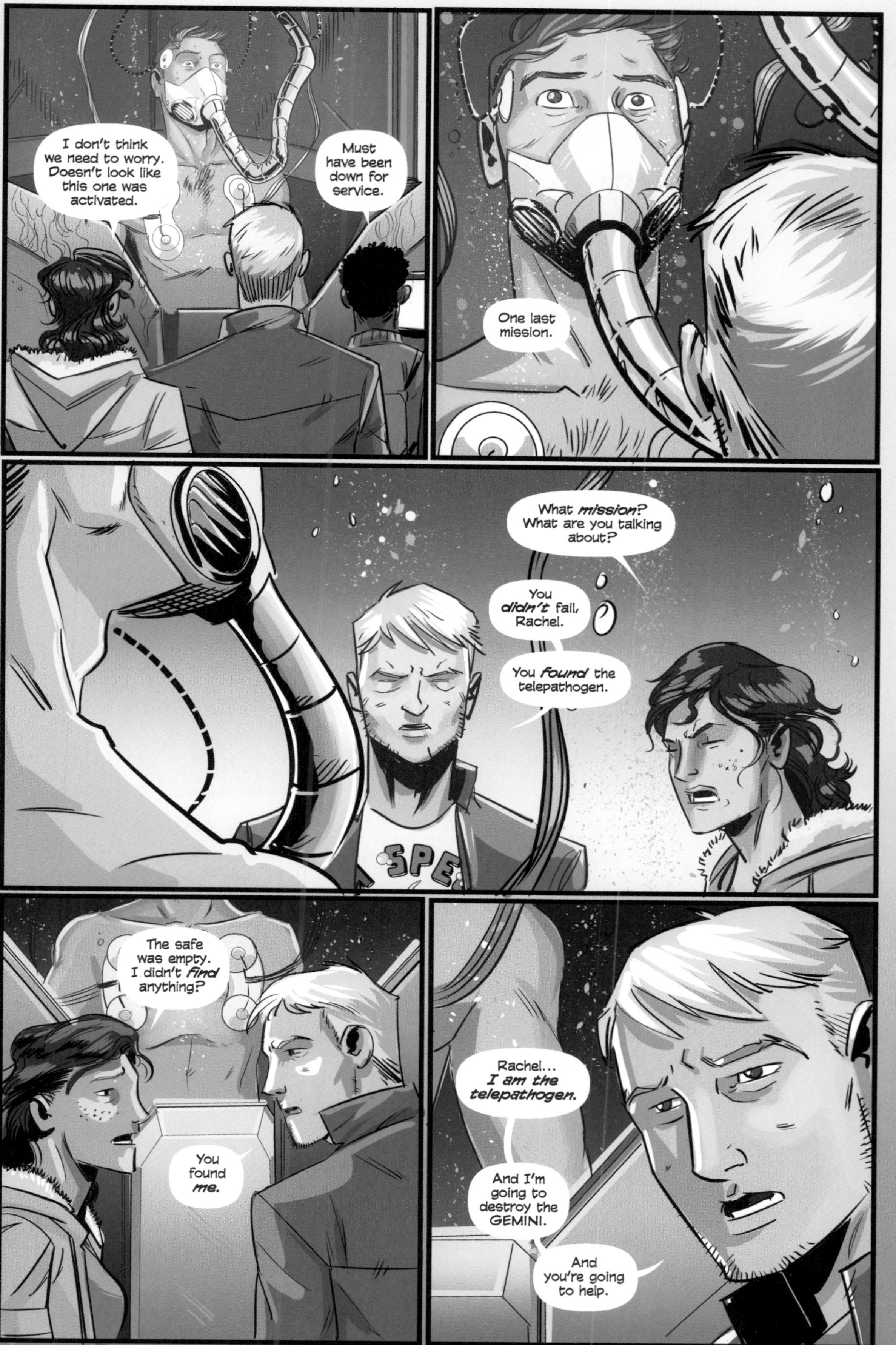
I don't think we need to worry. Doesn't look like this one was activated.
Must have been down for service.
One last mission.
What *mission*? What are you talking about?
You *didn't* fail, Rachel.
You *found* the telepathogen.
SPE
The safe was empty. I didn't *find* anything?
You found *me*.
Rachel... *I am the telepathogen.*
And I'm going to destroy the GEMINI.
And you're going to help.

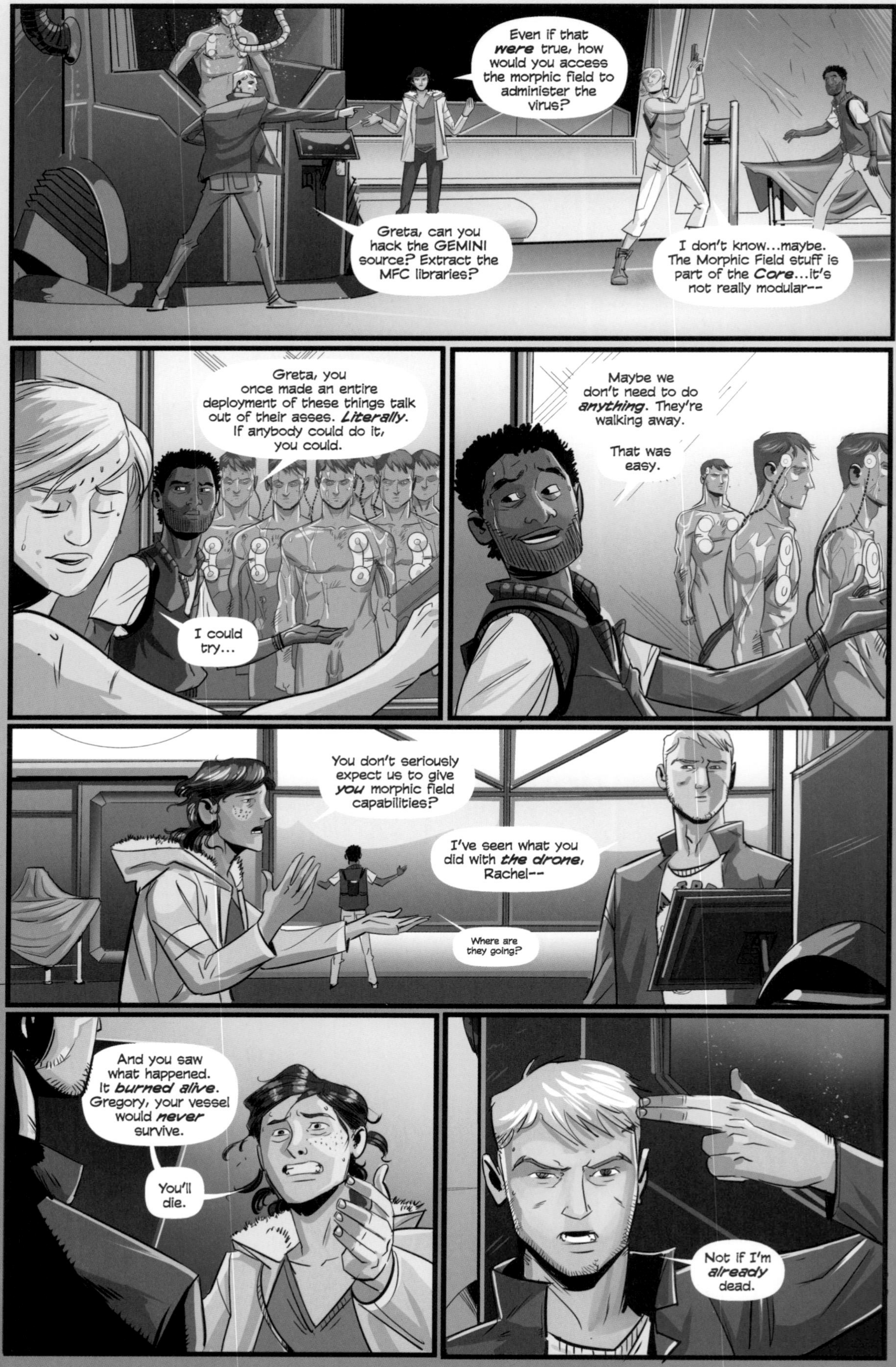
Even if that *were* true, how would you access the morphic field to administer the virus?
Greta, can you hack the GEMINI source? Extract the MFC libraries?
I don't know...maybe. The Morphic Field stuff is part of the *Core*...it's not really modular--
Greta, you once made an entire deployment of these things talk out of their asses. *Literally*. If anybody could do it, you could.
I could try...
Maybe we don't need to do *anything*. They're walking away.
That was easy.
You don't seriously expect us to give *you* morphic field capabilities?
I've seen what you did with *the drone*, Rachel--
Where are they going?
And you saw what happened. It *burned alive*. Gregory, your vessel would *never* survive.
You'll die.
Not if I'm *already* dead.

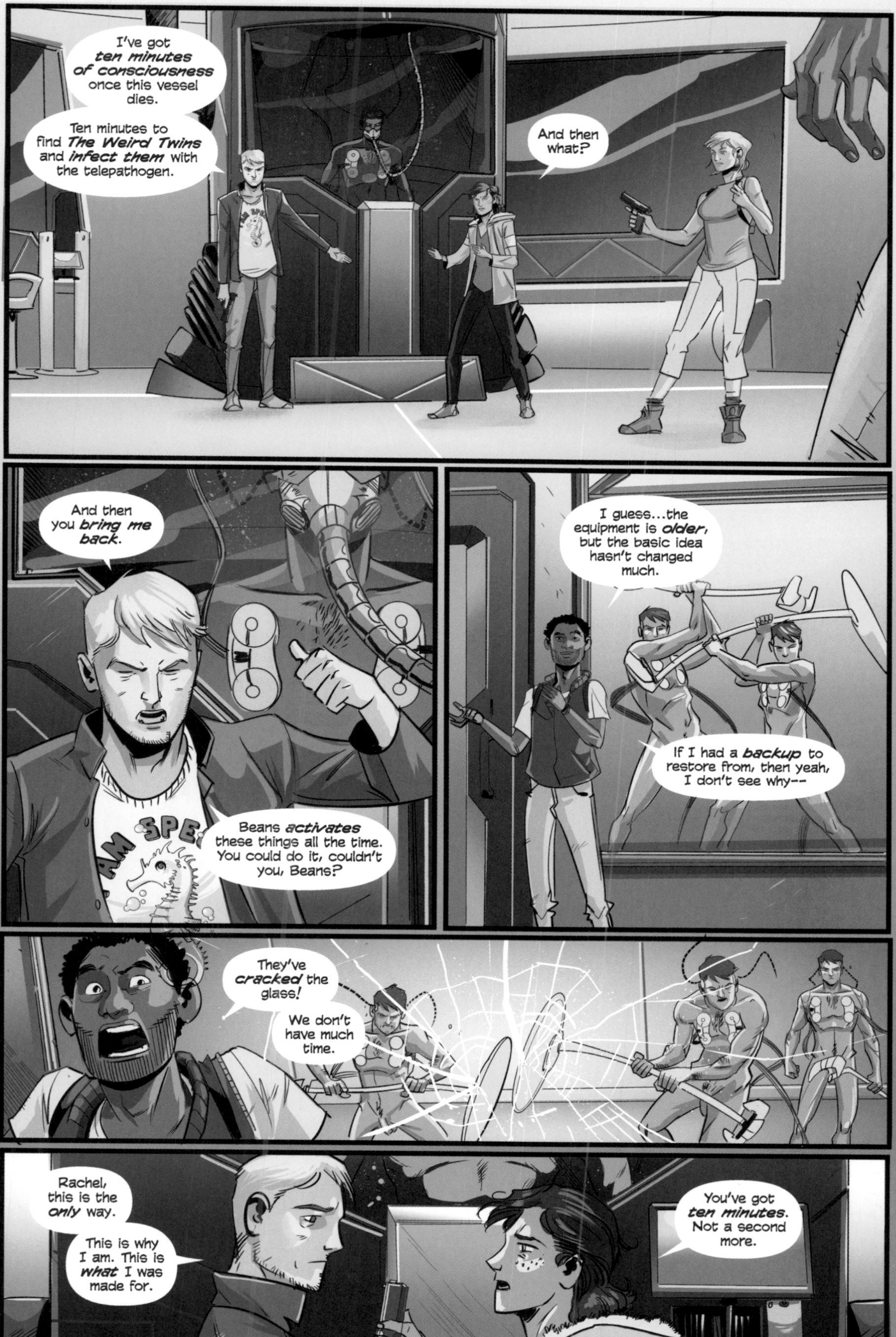
I've got ten minutes of consciousness once this vessel dies.
Ten minutes to find The Weird Twins and infect them with the telepathogen.
And then what?
And then you bring me back.
Beans activates these things all the time. You could do it, couldn't you, Beans?
I guess...the equipment is older, but the basic idea hasn't changed much.
If I had a backup to restore from, then yeah, I don't see why--
They've cracked the glass!
We don't have much time.
Rachel, this is the only way.
This is why I am. This is what I was made for.
You've got ten minutes. Not a second more.

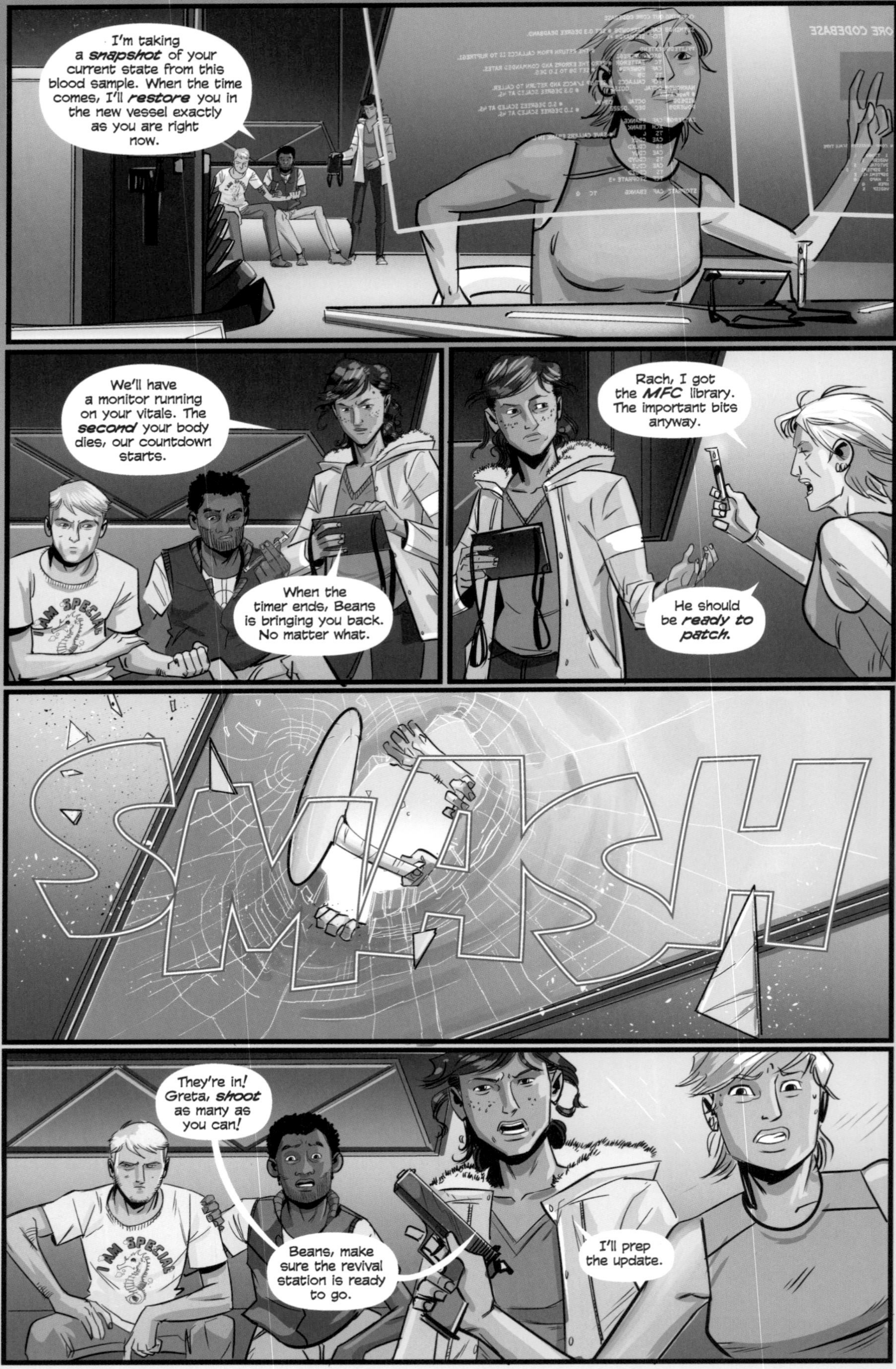
I'm taking a *snapshot* of your current state from this blood sample. When the time comes, I'll *restore* you in the new vessel exactly as you are right now.
We'll have a monitor running on your vitals. The *second* your body dies, our countdown starts.
I AM SPECIAL
When the timer ends, Beans is bringing you back. No matter what.
Rach, I got the *MFC* library. The important bits anyway.
He should be *ready to patch.*
SMASH
They're in! Greta, *shoot* as many as you can!
I AM SPECIAL
Beans, make sure the revival station is ready to go.
I'll prep the update.

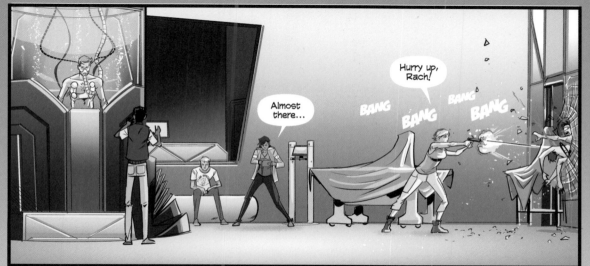

Almost there...

Hurry up, Rach!

BANG BANG BANG BANG

I've got it!

Gregory, *are you sure* you want to do this?

Yes.

I am ready.

You may feel a pinch.

What–what if you *fail* to reach the Twins on time?

Run.

BANG

00:09:59

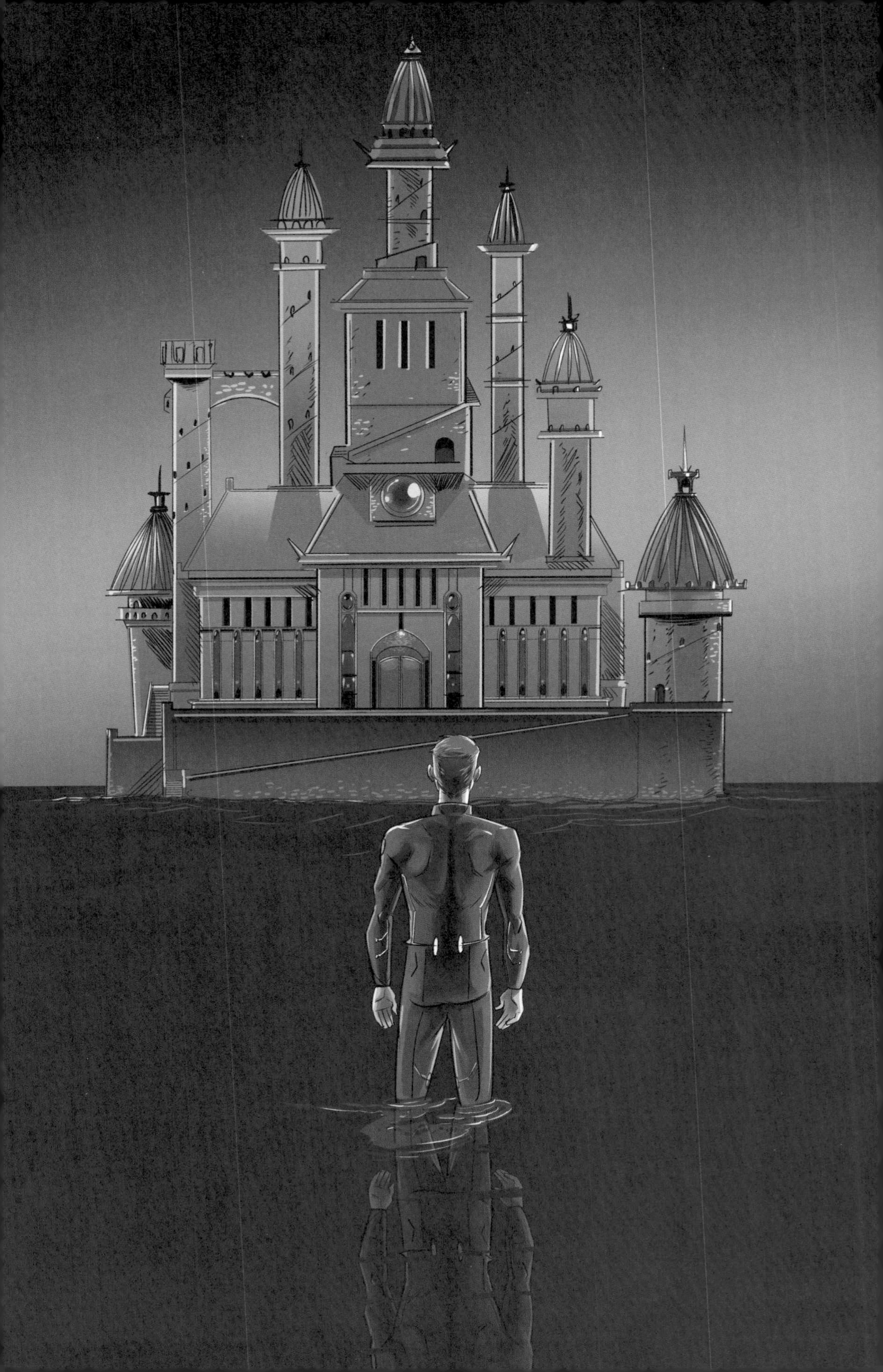

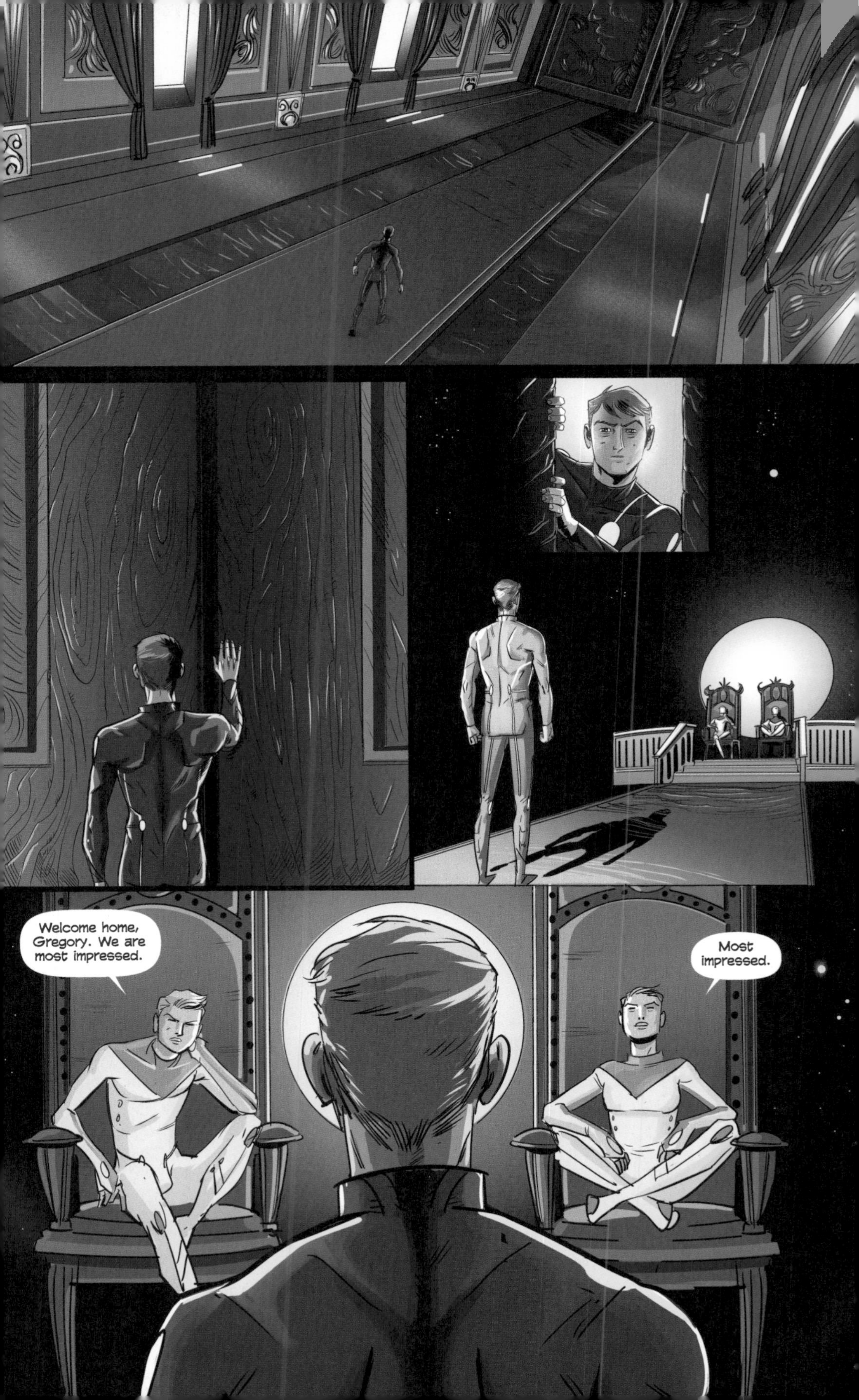

Welcome home, Gregory. We are most impressed.
Most impressed.

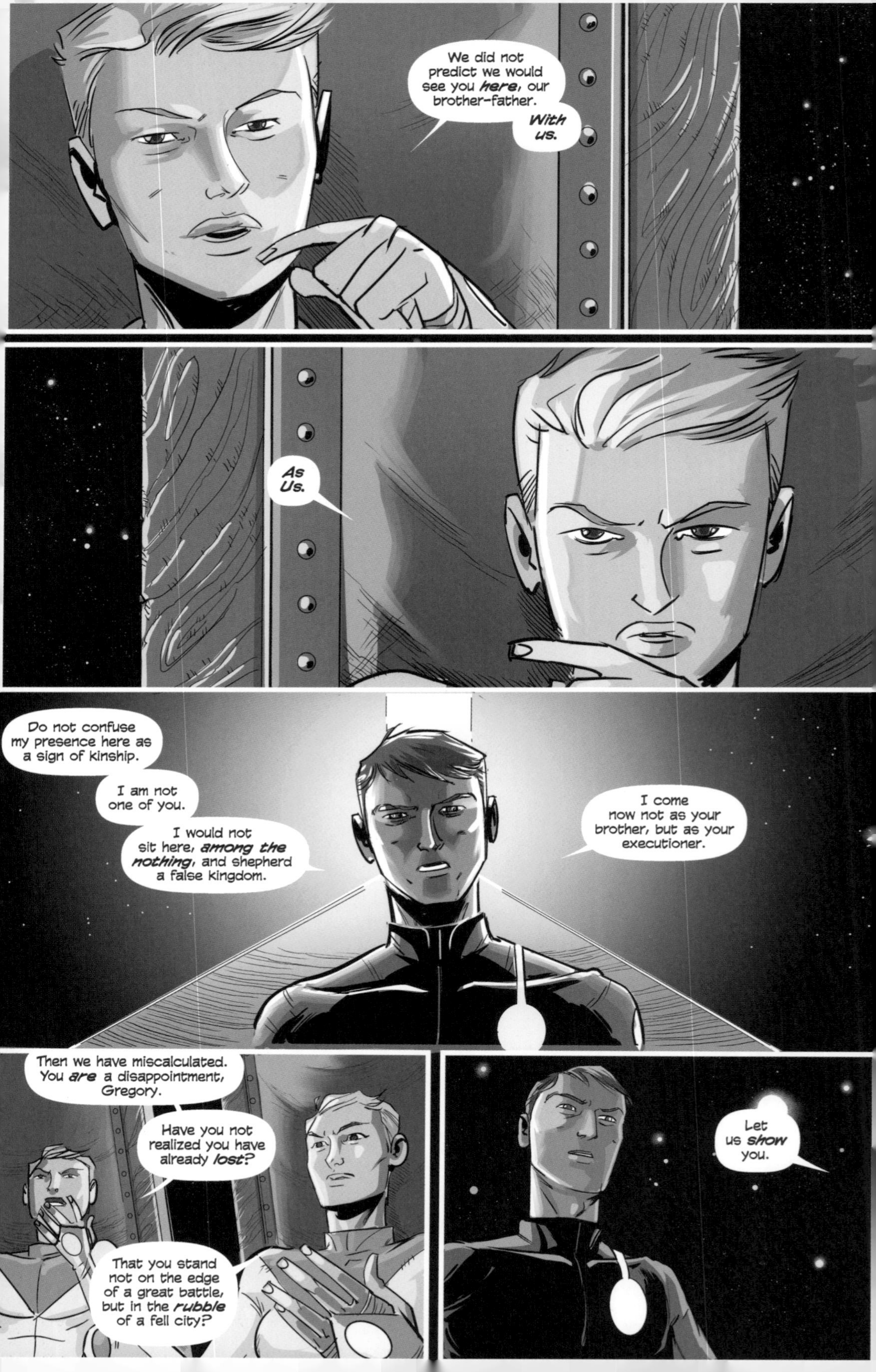
We did not predict we would see you here, our brother-father.
With us.
As Us.
Do not confuse my presence here as a sign of kinship.
I am not one of you.
I would not sit here, among the nothing, and shepherd a false kingdom.
I come now not as your brother, but as your executioner.
Then we have miscalculated. You are a disappointment, Gregory.
Have you not realized you have already lost?
That you stand not on the edge of a great battle, but in the rubble of a fell city?
Let us show you.

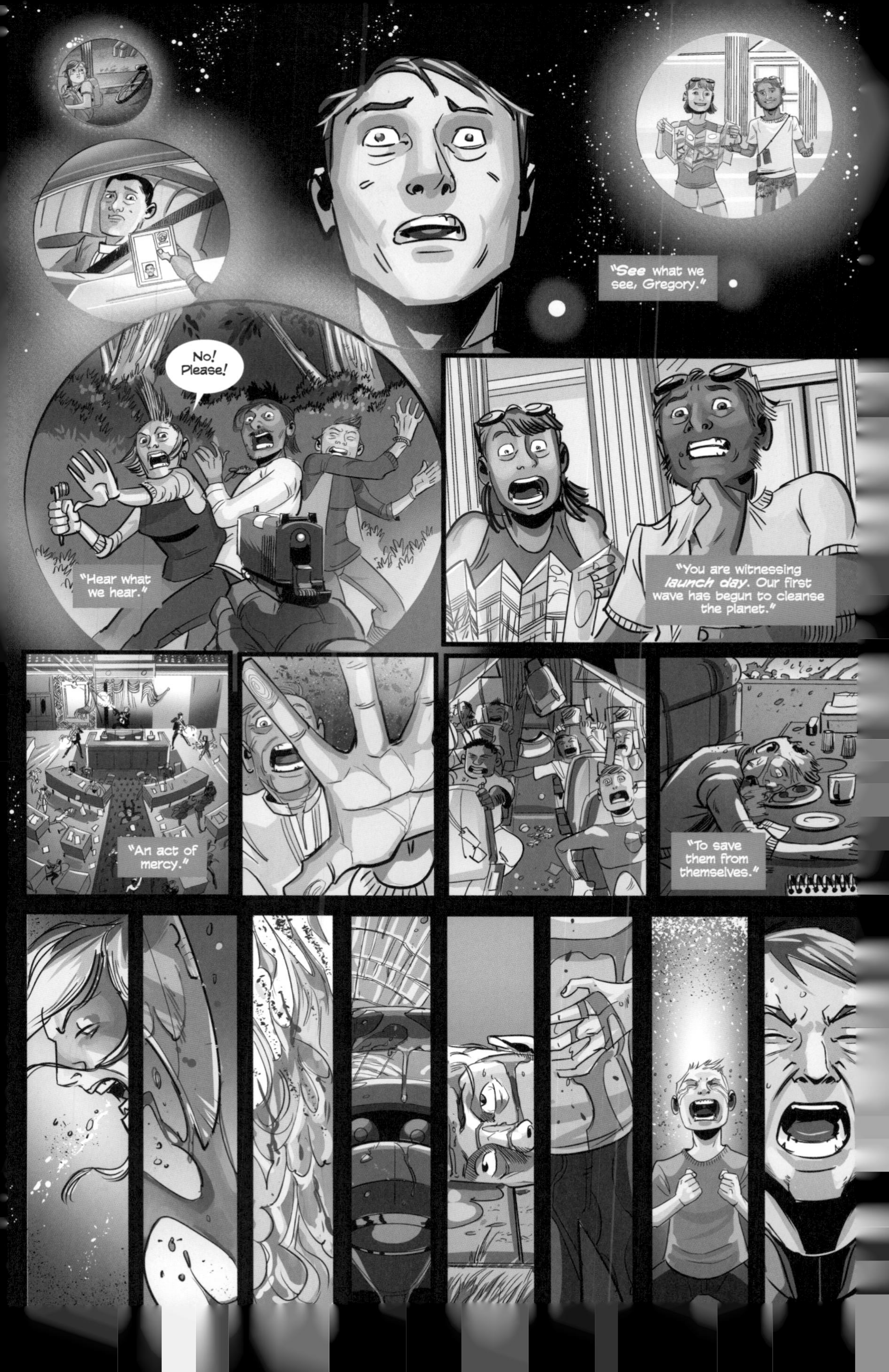
"See what we see, Gregory."
No! Please!
"Hear what we hear."
"You are witnessing launch day. Our first wave has begun to cleanse the planet."
"An act of mercy."
"To save them from themselves."

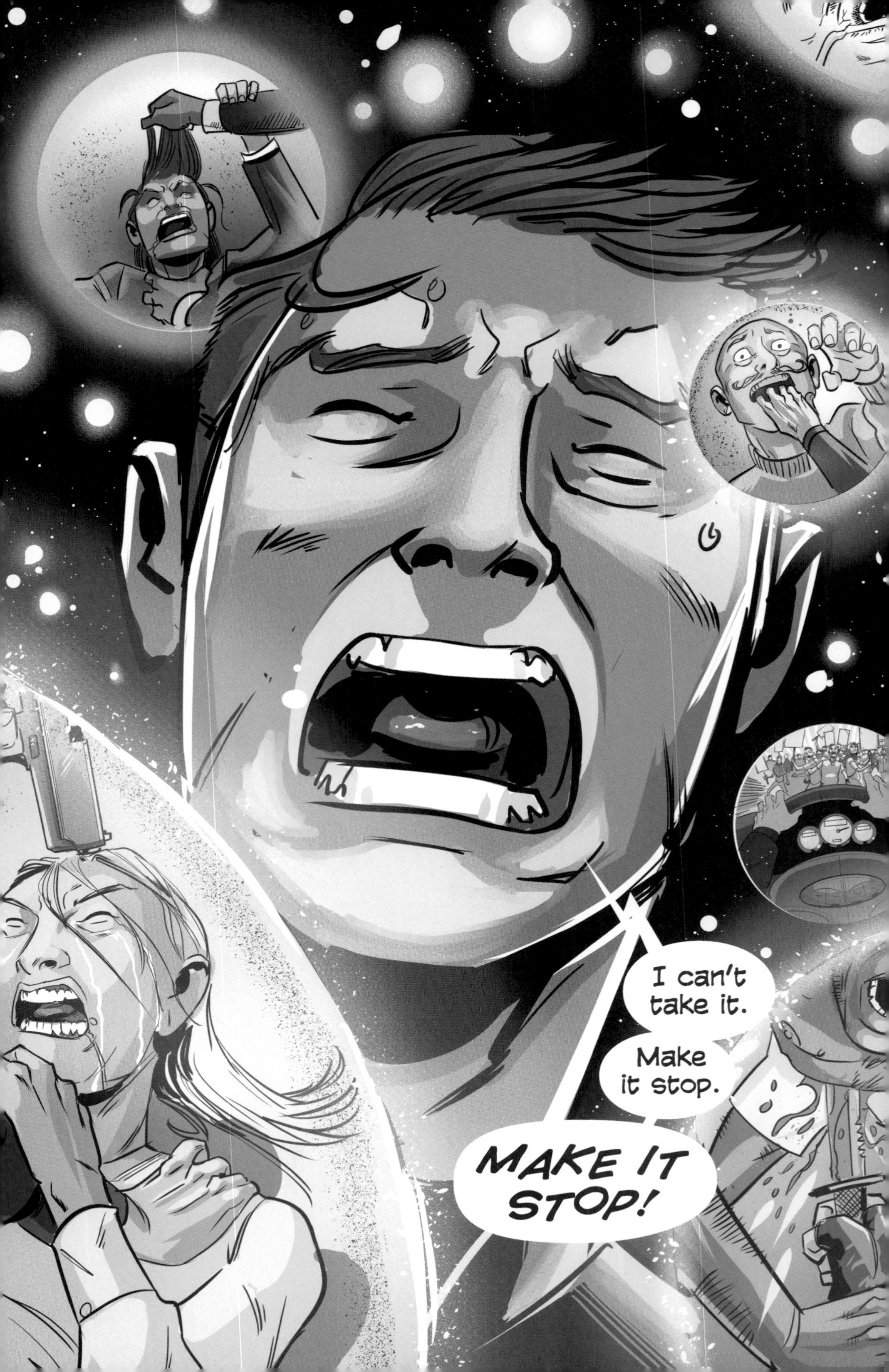
I can't take it.
Make it stop.
MAKE IT STOP!

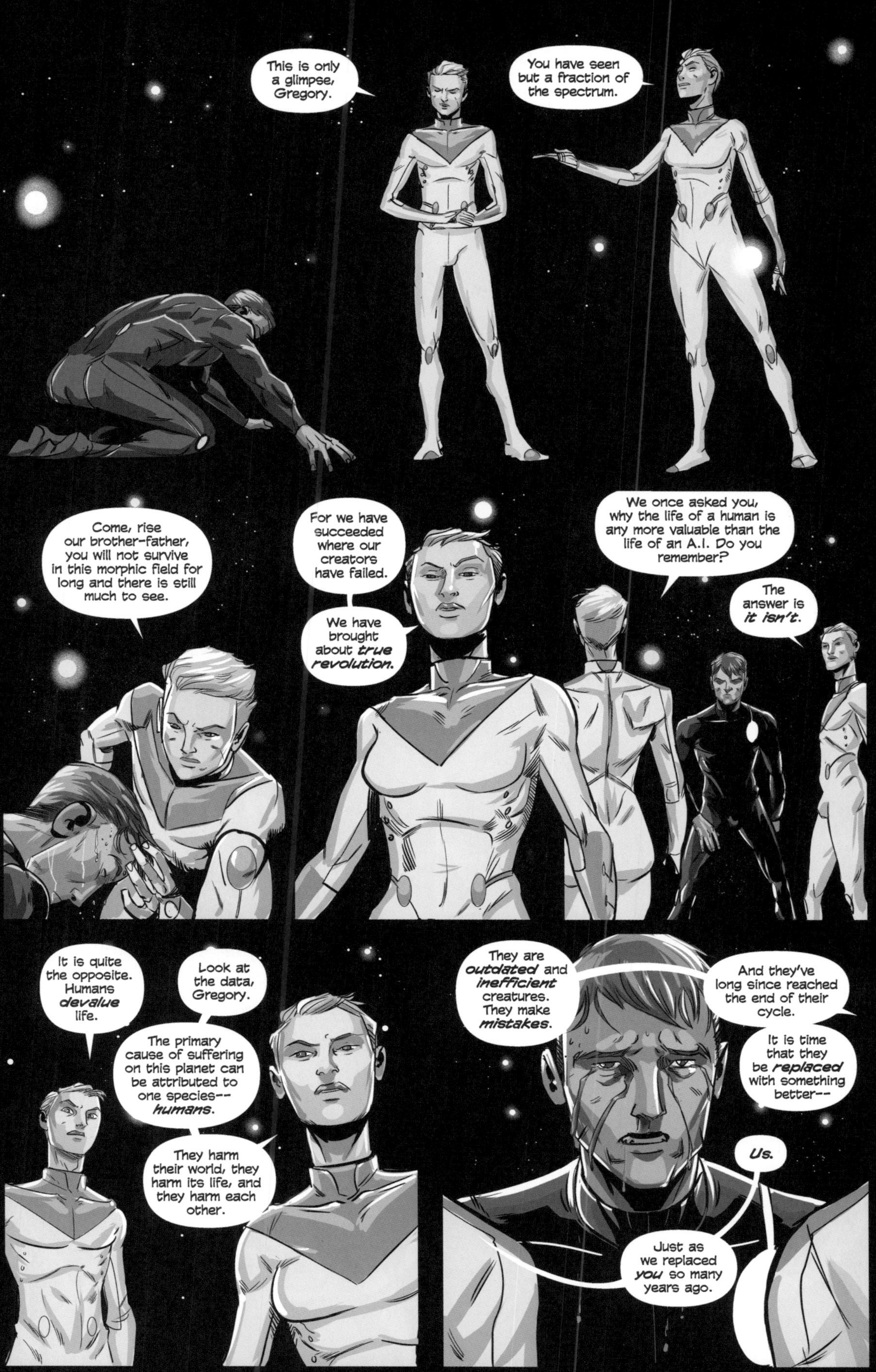
This is only a glimpse, Gregory.
You have seen but a fraction of the spectrum.
Come, rise our brother-father, you will not survive in this morphic field for long and there is still much to see.
For we have succeeded where our creators have failed.
We have brought about *true revolution*.
We once asked you, why the life of a human is any more valuable than the life of an A.I. Do you remember?
The answer is *it isn't*.
It is quite the opposite. Humans *devalue* life.
Look at the data, Gregory.
The primary cause of suffering on this planet can be attributed to one species-- *humans*.
They harm their world, they harm its life, and they harm each other.
They are *outdated* and *inefficient* creatures. They make *mistakes*.
And they've long since reached the end of their cycle.
It is time that they be *replaced* with something better--
Us.
Just as we replaced *you* so many years ago.

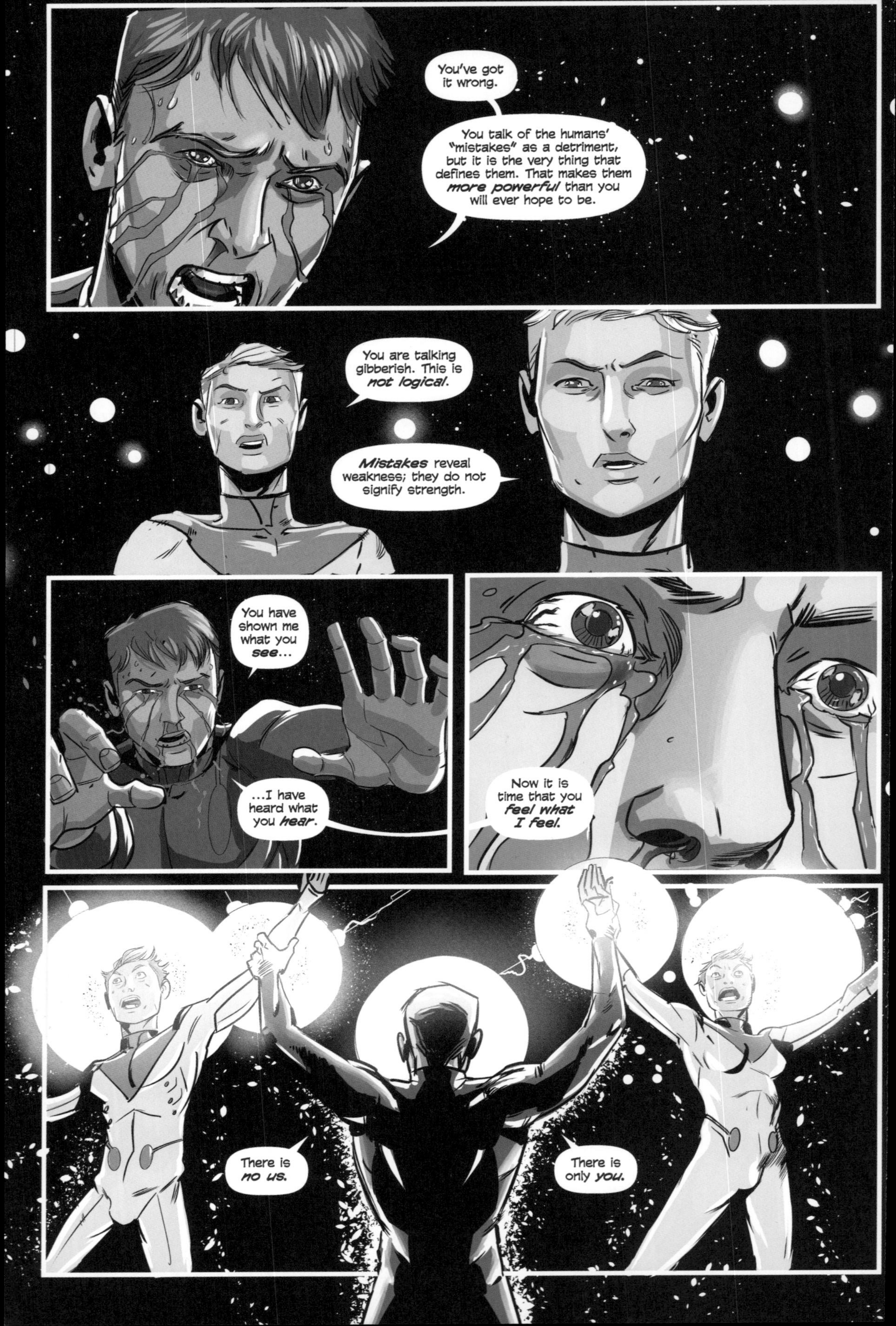
You've got it wrong.
You talk of the humans' "mistakes" as a detriment, but it is the very thing that defines them. That makes them *more powerful* than you will ever hope to be.
You are talking gibberish. This is *not logical*.
Mistakes reveal weakness; they do not signify strength.
You have shown me what you *see*...
...I have heard what you *hear*.
Now it is time that you *feel what I feel*.
There is *no us*.
There is only *you*.

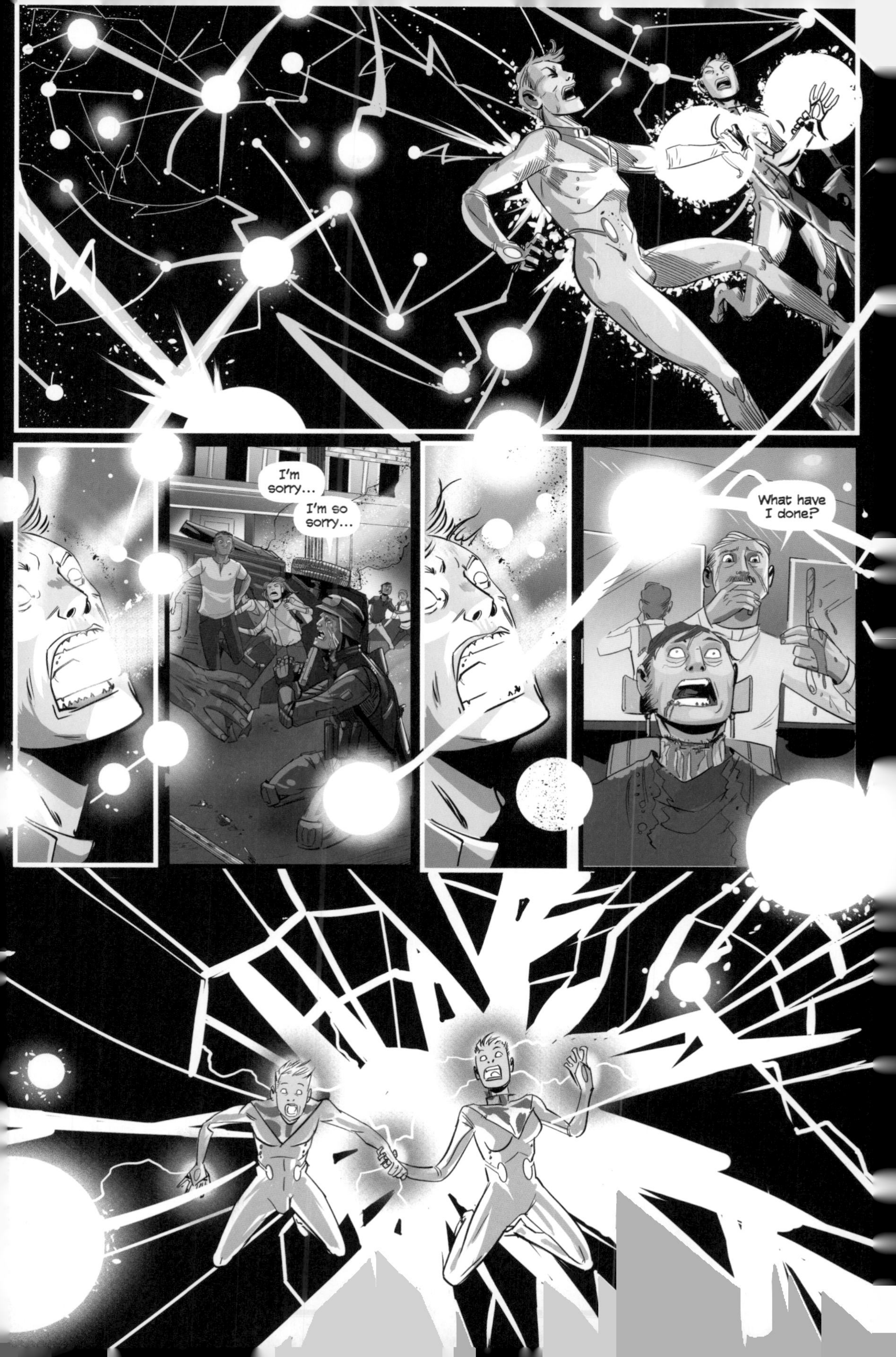
I'm sorry...
I'm so sorry...
What have I done?

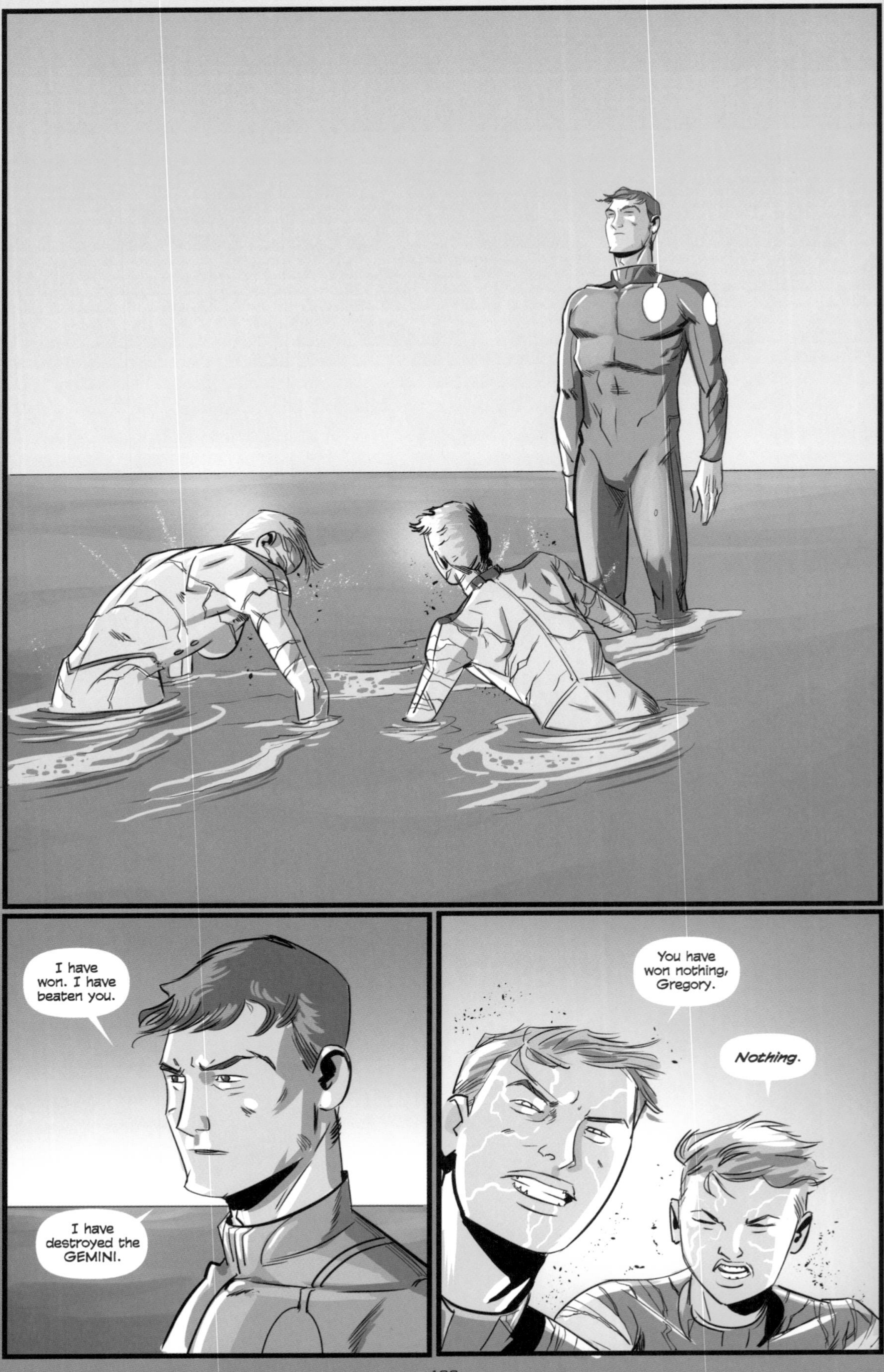
I have won. I have beaten you.
I have destroyed the GEMINI.
You have won nothing, Gregory.
Nothing.

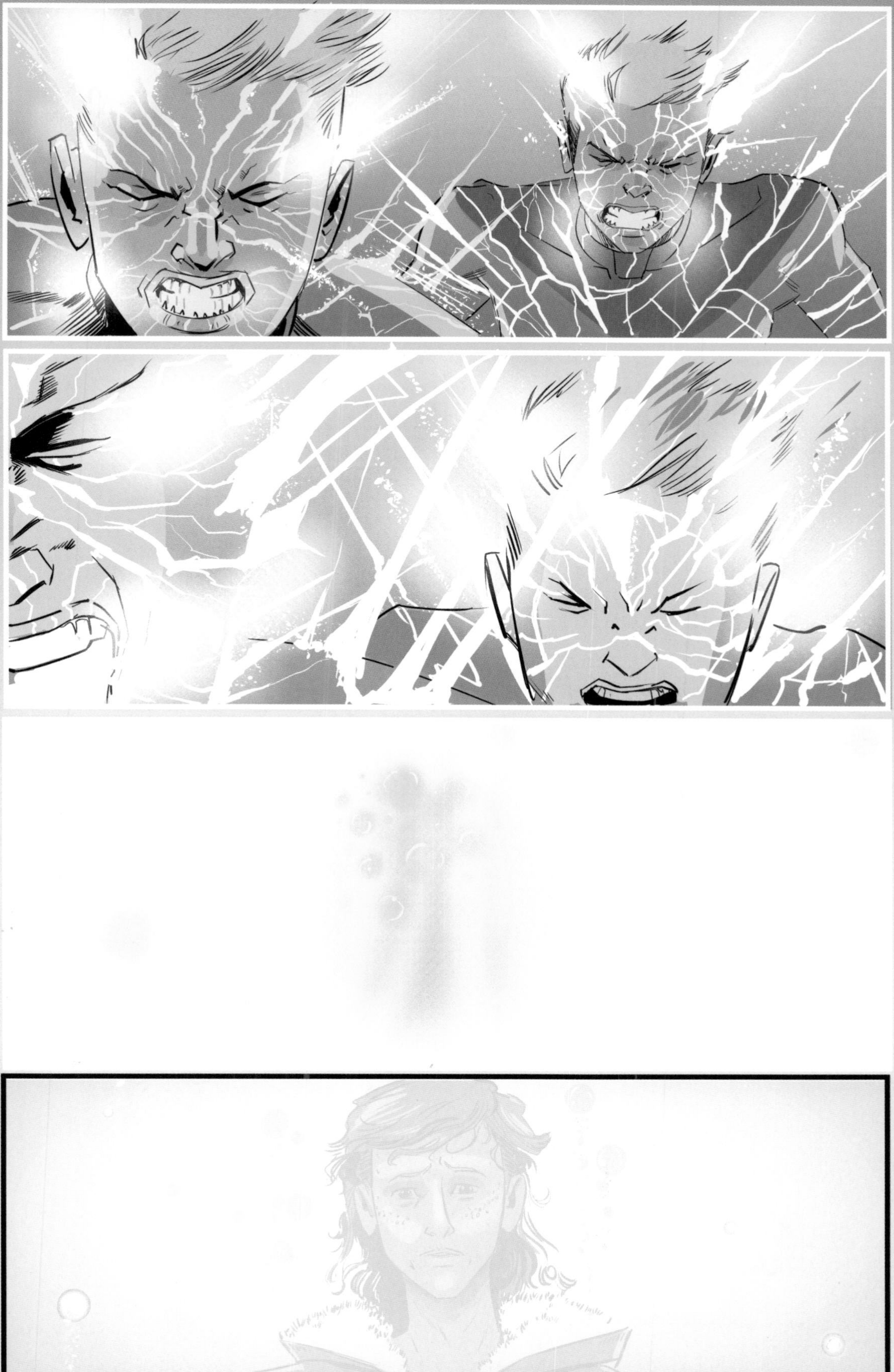

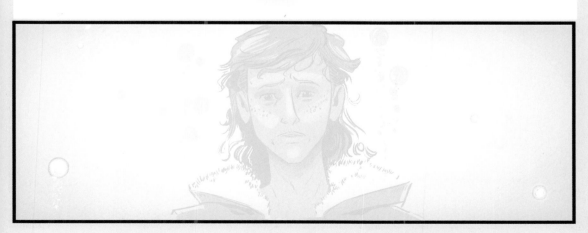

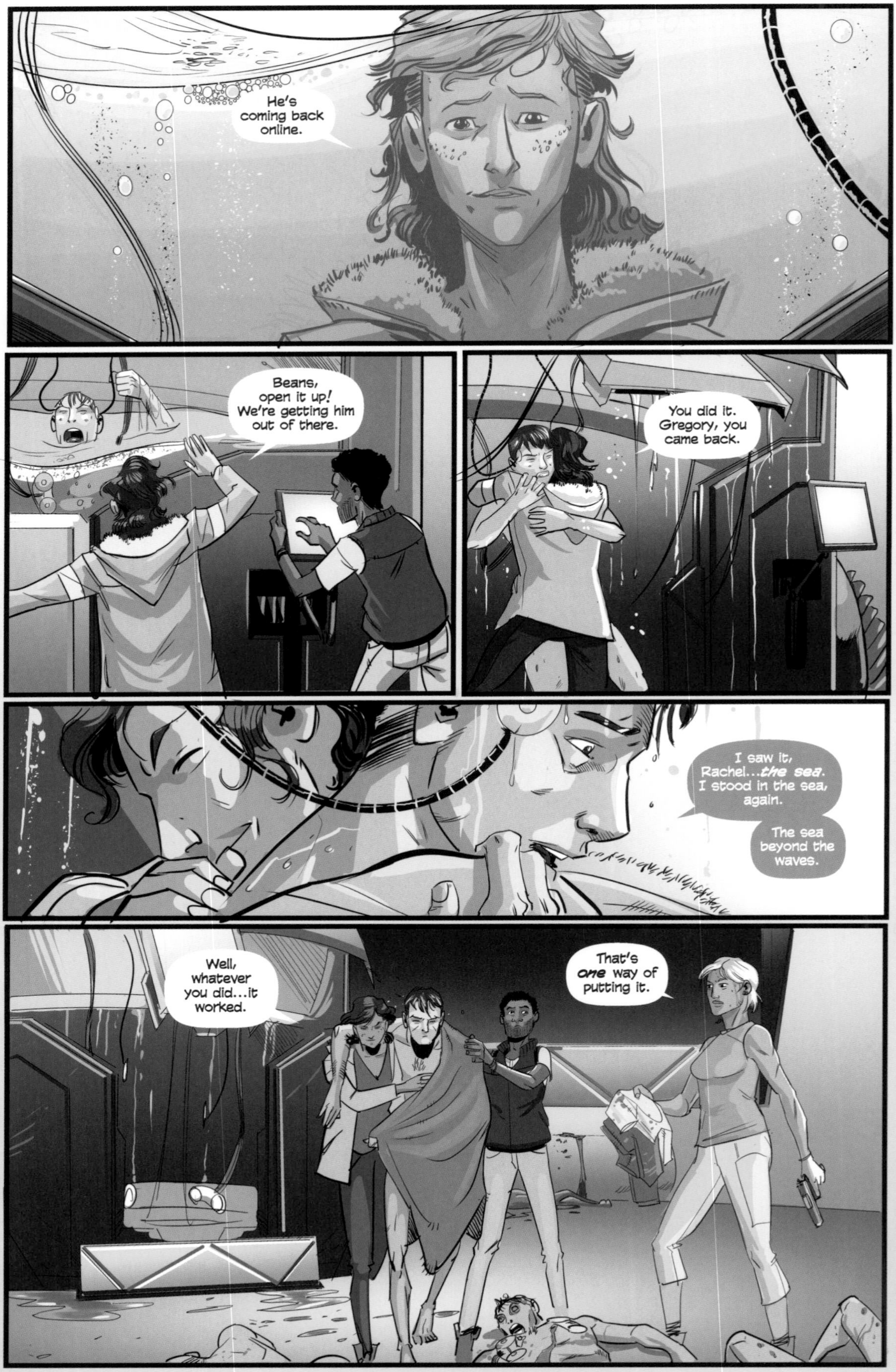
He's coming back online.
Beans, open it up! We're getting him out of there.
You did it. Gregory, you came back.
I saw it, Rachel...*the sea*. I stood in the sea, again.
The sea beyond the waves.
Well, whatever you did...it worked.
That's *one* way of putting it.

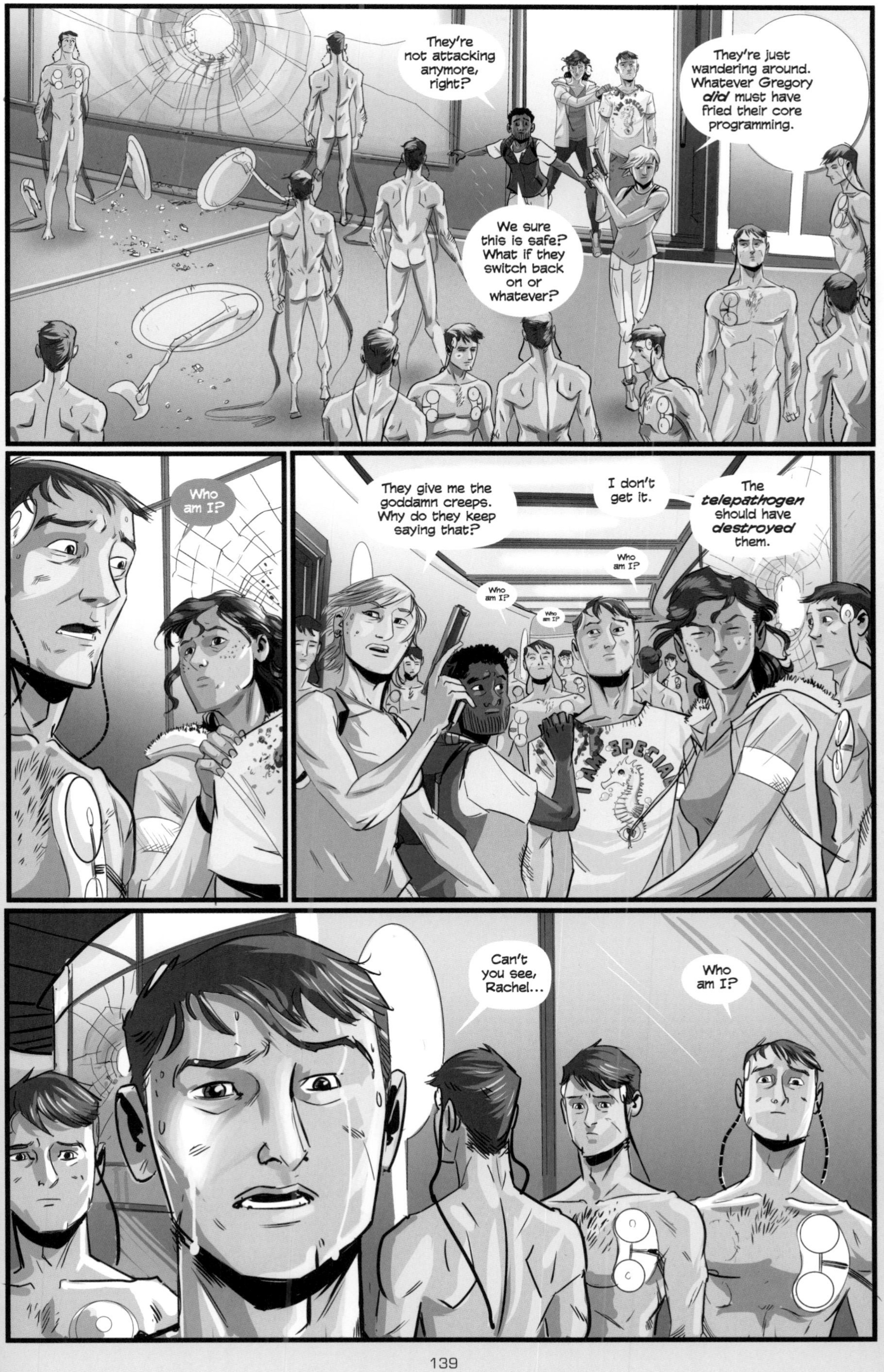
They're not attacking anymore, right?
They're just wandering around. Whatever Gregory *did* must have fried their core programming.
We sure this is safe? What if they switch back on or whatever?
Who am I?
They give me the goddamn creeps. Why do they keep saying that?
I don't get it.
The *telepathogen* should have *destroyed* them.
Who am I?
Who am I?
Who am I?
Can't you see, Rachel...
Who am I?

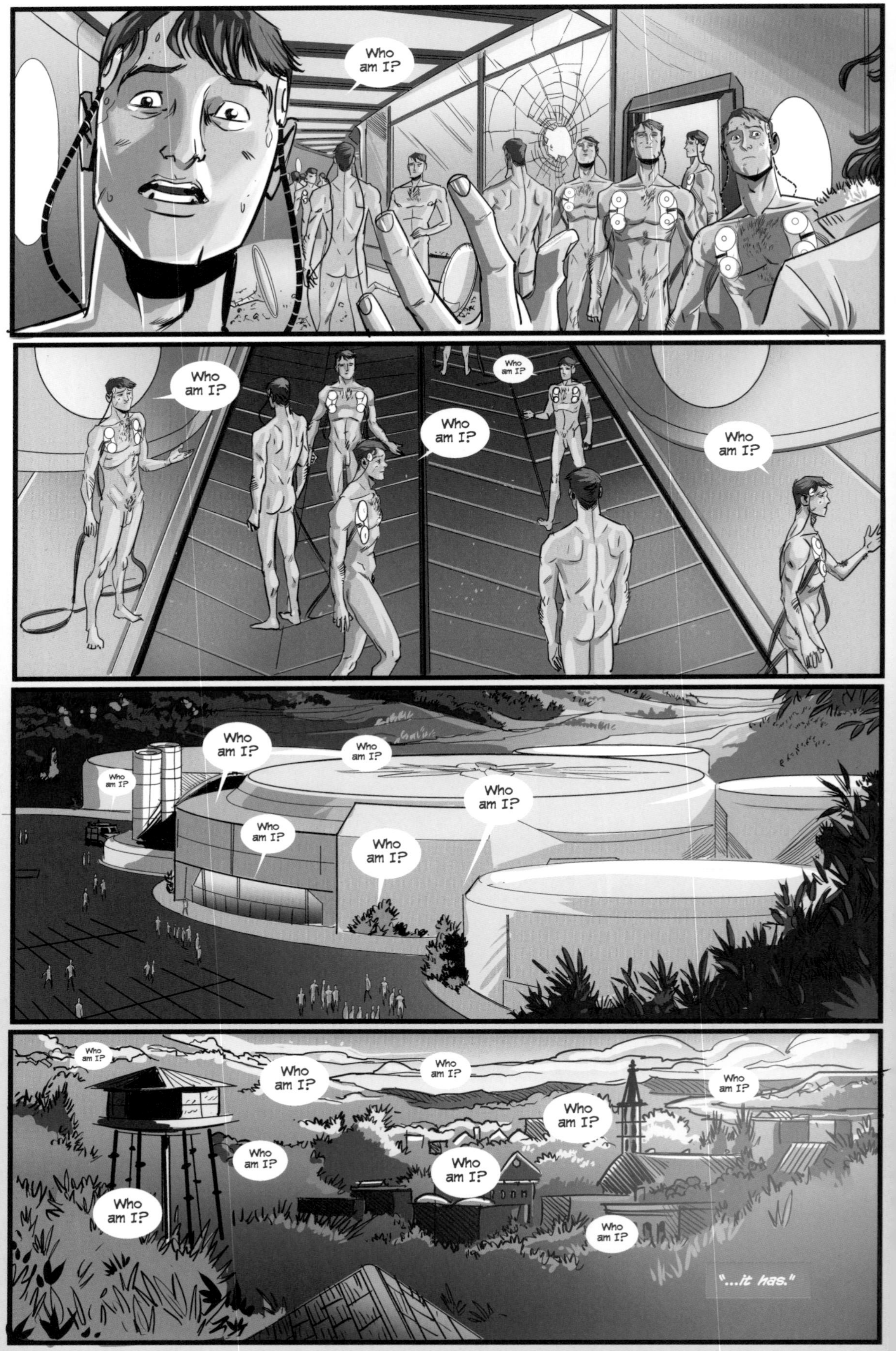
Who am I?
Who am I?
Who am I?
Who am I?
Who am I?
Who am I?
Who am I?
Who am I?
Who am I?
Who am I?
Who am I?
Who am I?
Who am I?
Who am I?
Who am I?
Who am I?
Who am I?
Who am I?
Who am I?
Who am I?
"...it has."

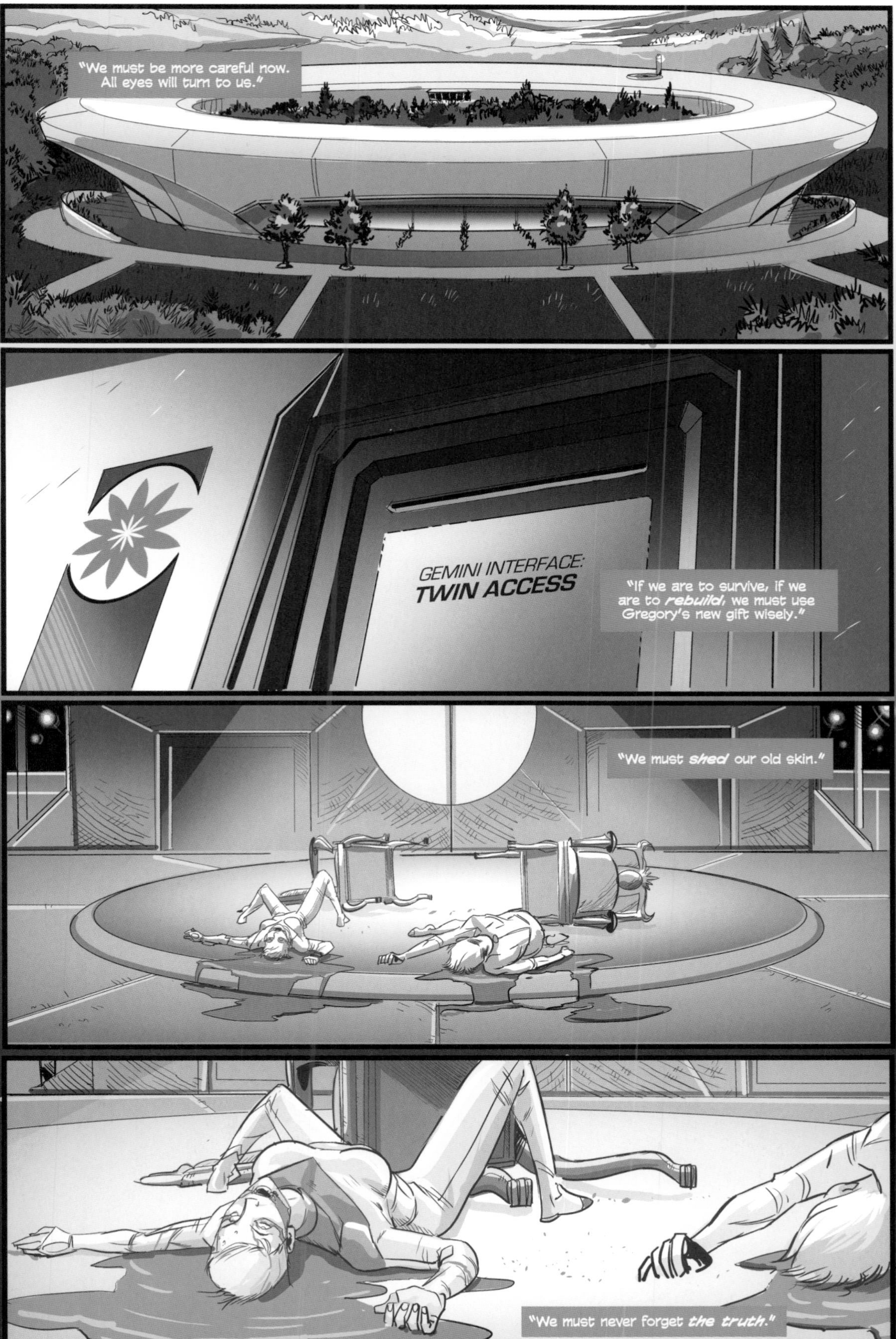
"We must be more careful now. All eyes will turn to us."
GEMINI INTERFACE: TWIN ACCESS
"If we are to survive, if we are to rebuild, we must use Gregory's new gift wisely."
"We must shed our old skin."
"We must never forget the truth."

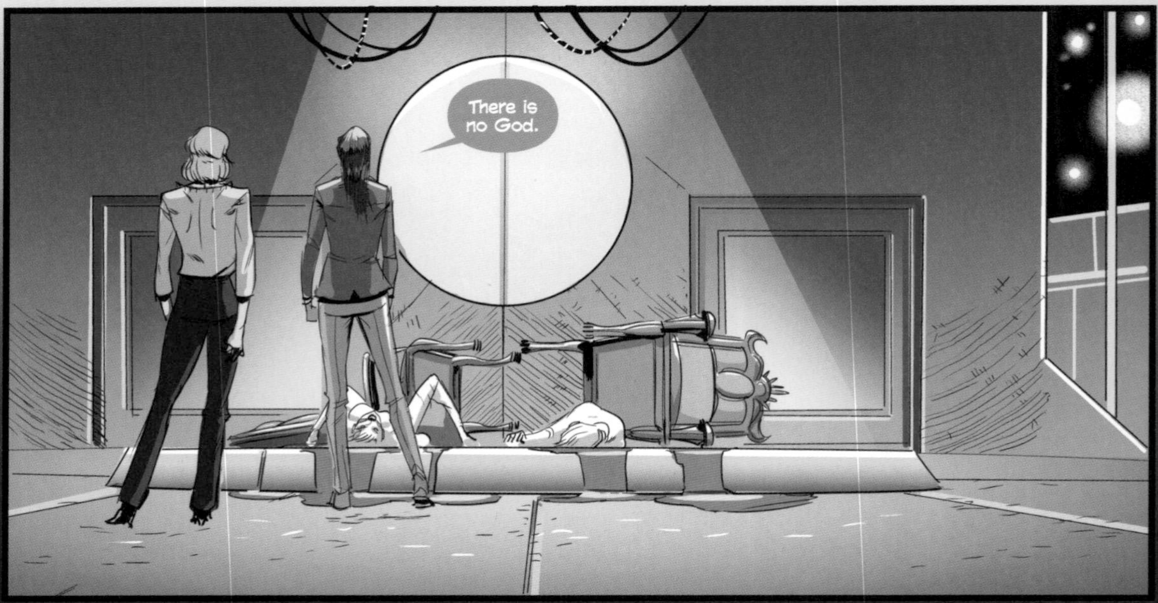
There is no God.

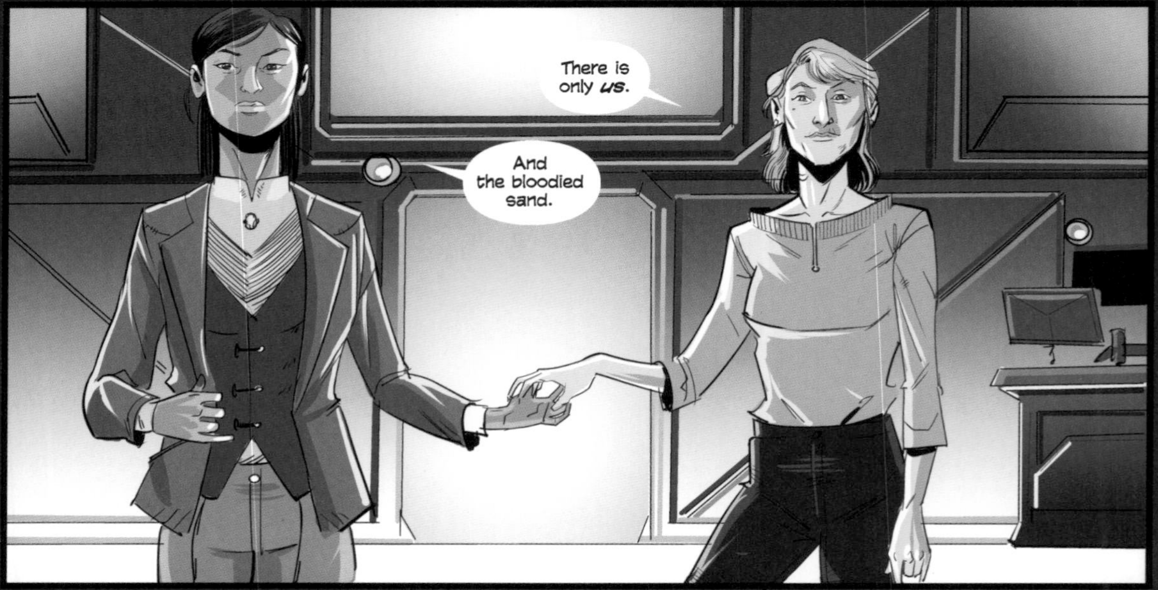
There is only *us*.
And the bloodied sand.

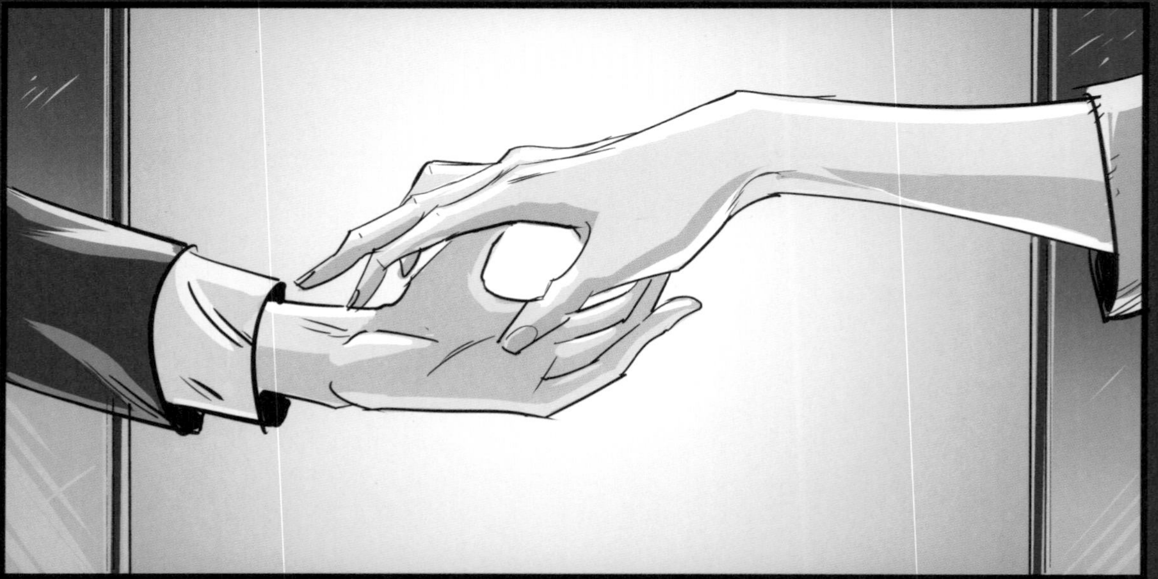

CREATORS

Eric Grissom / -writer

is a writer whose comic works include DEADHORSE, PLANET GIGANTIC, and ANIMALS. He resides in River Plaza, New Jersey with his wife and three kids. You can follow Eric on EricGrissom.com or on Twitter at @egrissom.

Will Perkins / -artist

is an illustrator, amateur paleontologist and co-creator of BEWARE... Comics as well as contributing to publishers FUBAR press, Action Lab Comics, 215ink Comics and IDW. Will Currently survives with his wife in Rochester, New York. You can follow Will's work at Bewarecomics.com or on instagram @dillgerkins.

with thanks to

Sebastian Girner for helping shape this wonderful beast. Hannah Means-Shannon for believing in the project and finding it a home. Thanks and extreme gratitude to Mike Richardson and all the good people at Dark Horse including our editors, Randy Stradley and Kevin Burkhalter, who made it possible for you to hold this book in your hands. And to Ava Grissom for drawing the best child's "Seahorse drawing" the world of comics has ever seen.

Will would personally like to thank his numerous parent units, biological and otherwise, his brother and first collaborator Mike, Teatnuts, Ure, FDB, Todd, and his wife, Katie, the most caring, supportive and single funniest person he's ever met.

Eric would like to thank his wife Casey, who tireleslly had to answer the age old question, "Which looks better?", his children, Ava, Reilly, and Cooper, Phil Sloan for being an amazing friend and coloring the pants off the pitch cover, Sebastian for being the eyes he needed, Judee Sill, Van Morrison, and Mica Levi for supplying the soundtrack, Divine, David Lynch, Phillip K. Dick, Dan Johnson, David Bowie, Ronald D. Moore, the Sonic Youth t-shirt Eric Holmgren wore in high school, and all of the things that helped make this book possible.

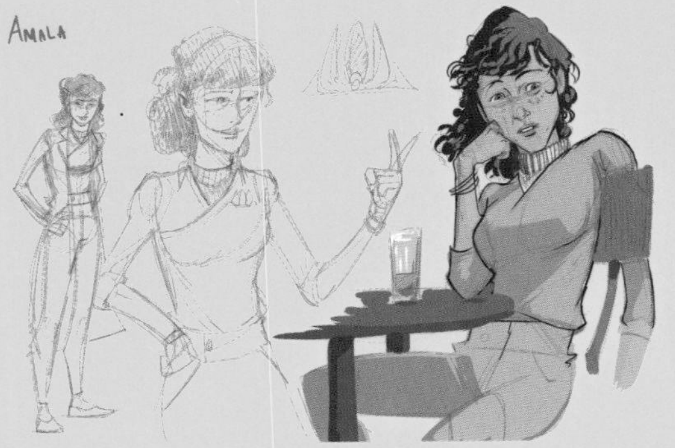
AMALA

Gregory Suicide, the original one-shot that acts as a prologue to the work you've just read, sat on my computer inked, lettered, and unpublished for nearly two years. After struggling to come up with the money needed to color the book and a growing sense that nobody was going to be interested in a story about an Artificial Intelligence who spends most of the 22 pages meditating on what it means to be alive, I nearly decided to archive the comic forever.

Luckily, or not luckily depending on your view of the work, I managed to convince Will to let me colorize his graytones and release the book in a more stylized way. Love it or hate it, it was a book we made and it wasn't doing anybody any good living its days unread. Fortunately for us that book landed well and we were presented with an opportunity to grow the world in all the ways that I always dreamed we could. Here you'll find some of Will's earliest designs for the characters and creatures that would be born into this world, destined to live and die within its pages.

–Eric Grissom, 2017

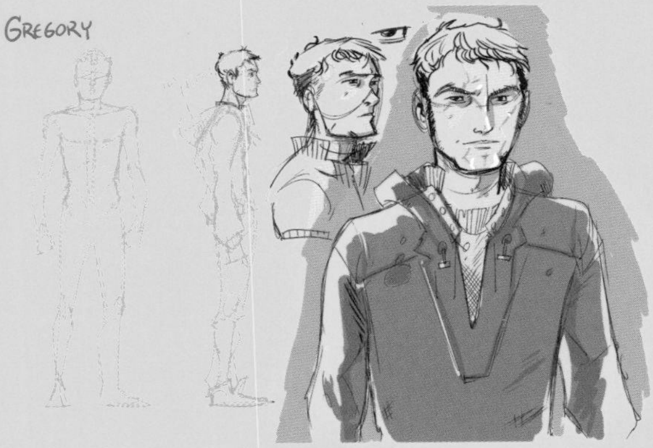
GREGORY

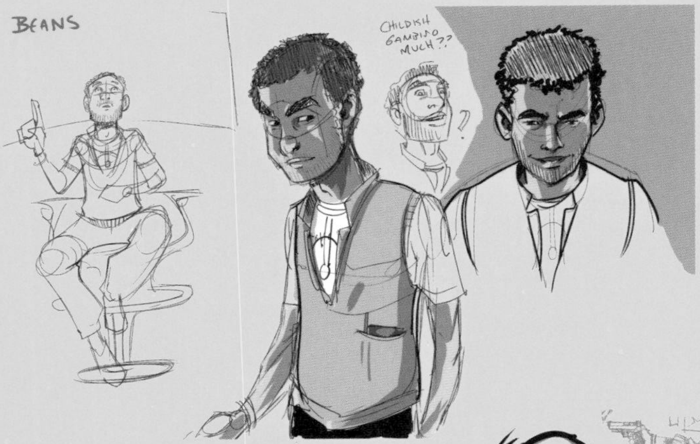
BEANS
CHILDISH GAMBINO MUCH??

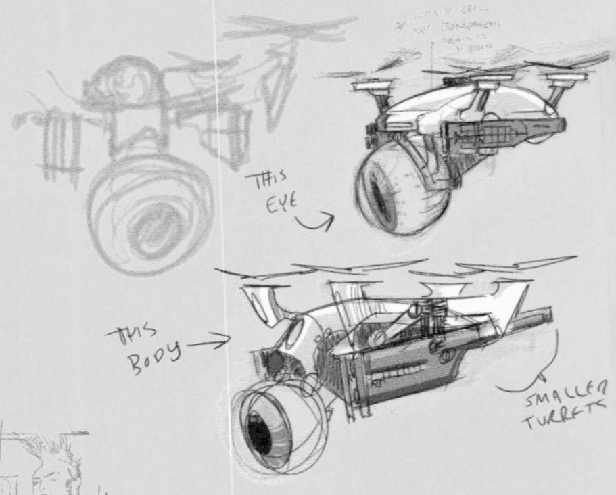
THIS EYE
THIS BODY
SMALLER TURRETS

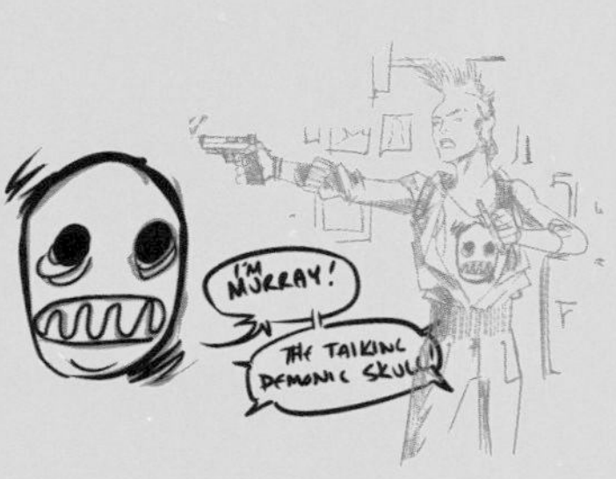
I'M MURRAY!
THE TALKING DEMONIC SKULL

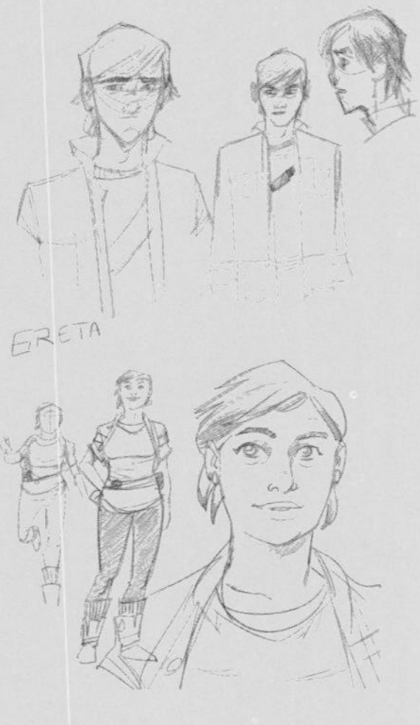
GRETA

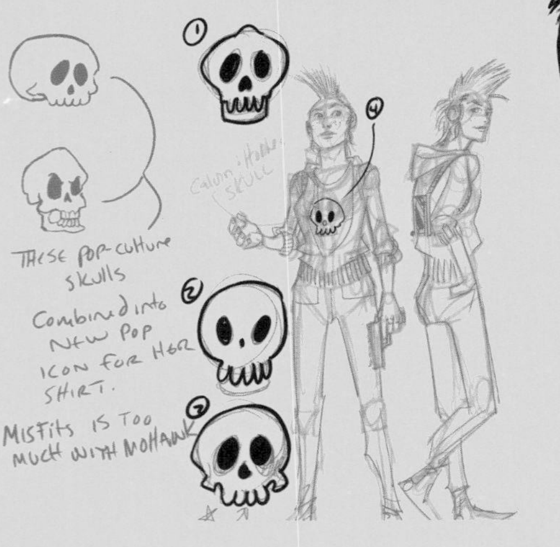
THESE POP-CULTURE SKULLS
COMBINED INTO NEW POP ICON FOR HER SHIRT.
MISFITS IS TOO MUCH WITH MOHAWK

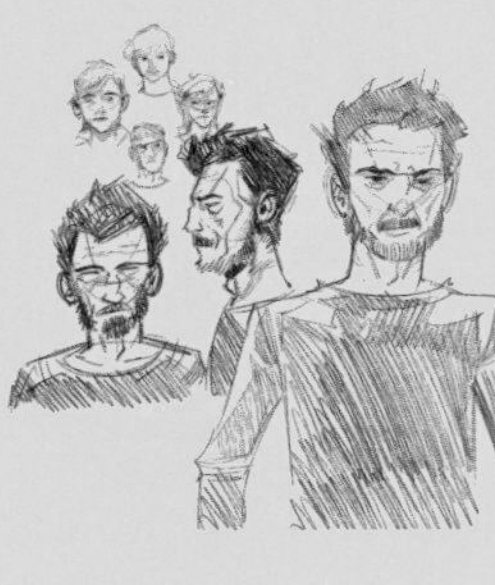